ULTIMATE CRUISE PASSENGER'S
GUIDE

THE BALTIC
Incl. St. Petersburg

©Sam Hall 2020
Published by
SamHallBooks
Dorking, Surrey, UK.
ISBN: 9781660691449:

Cover design: Arc Manor, Rockville, Maryland

To

My dearest wife, Susanna

About the Author

With nearly 50 years' experience in international journalism and travel, Sam Hall is now retired, having worked with all the major news agencies, including Reuters, for whom he was a foreign correspondent for five years and later their Chief Scandinavian correspondent. He was also an on-screen reporter covering the top international stories of the day for ITN's prestigious flagship programme, *News at Ten*.

Travelling to more than 100 countries around the world, he has covered various wars, riots and disturbances including the Nigerian-Biafran civil war, the Turkish invasion of Cyprus, the Siege of Beirut and the Falklands War.

A compulsive traveller, he walked as a young man from Barcelona to Copenhagen and as a middle-aged one nearly 400 miles across the French-Italian Alps in the footsteps of Hannibal, not to mention another 328 miles from his home in Surrey to Lands' End – an epic journey he describes in his book *'Blisters'*.

He is a widely acclaimed enrichment lecturer with 22 years' experience and has travelled the world with all the major cruise lines. He also sailed across the North Sea in an open Viking boat and travelled thousands of miles in the

High Arctic. His book *'The Fourth World: The Heritage and Destruction of the Arctic'* is considered a definitive work on the Arctic for which he was likened in his writing to that of Wilfred Thessiger.

Hall is also a filmmaker who, in conjunction with the Norwegian TV and film production companies, Bergefilm and Videomaker Nord, has won several international awards. Many of these films have been shown in more than 60 countries worldwide and ultimately earned him a Lifetime Achievement Award by the British company, CS Media.

Sam is also an accomplished lecturer, presenter and conference host, and an acclaimed hyper-realistic artist. He lives in Surrey, England with his wife, Susanna.

* * *

Other Books by the Author

The Fourth World – Life on the Ice

The Fourth World – The Marauders

The Fourth World – Expanding Horizons

The Silver Fjord

The Whaling Conspiracy

Blisters

The Really Easy Student's Guide to Making Money

The Ultimate Cruise Passenger's Guide to the Fjord People of Norway

The Ultimate Cruise Passenger's Guide – Norway

The Ultimate Cruise Passenger's Guide – Sweden

The Ultimate Cruise Passenger's Guide - Denmark, Iceland & Greenland

Table of Contents

Please note that Sweden is now almost a 100% cashless society. Most shops and attractions will no longer accept cash. This may cause some concern for cruise passengers as most public toilets will not accept cash payments either. Credit cards are accepted everywhere, even for very small amounts

The Swedish section of this book was previously published as The Ultimate Cruise Guide - Sweden.

All currency conversions are approximate and may differ throughout the book due to daily rate changes.

***

SWEDEN

An Affinity with Nature

What rarely fails to impress about Sweden is the affinity that the Swedes and the peoples of other Nordic countries have with what they call Naturen – 'The Nature'.

Note the definite article there because the Swedes, Finns and Norwegians always use it. There's an amusing ditty, which I think epitomizes what the Swedish people particularly, are all about:

> I'm glad the sky is painted blue
> And the earth is painted green.
> And that such a lot of nice fresh air
> Is sandwiched in between.

Those few lines seem to underline the importance Scandinavians attach to Nature in almost every aspect of their lives

Aldous Huxley observed that their enthusiasm for country life and their love of natural scenery are 'strongest when the climate is worst and the picturesque involves the greatest discomfort'.

Certainly, in summer, Swedes will frolic in the cool, if not downright cold waters of the Baltic even if it's raining.

In winter, their idea of a wonderful weekend is to ski perhaps 30 miles (48 kilometres) or more a day. In temperatures of as little as minus 30 degrees centigrade, which is minus 22 Fahrenheit.

Perhaps not surprisingly, Sweden is host to the world's biggest ski race.

No matter how cold it is, each year 12,000 competitors and far more applicants ski 60 miles in a single day. It's quite insane'.

The race covers the same route taken by King Gustav Vasa during his flight from the Danes in 1521. Today, people regard it more as a test of physical fitness.

Ice hockey, skiing and ski-jumping are the main winter sports – that is, if you can call ice hockey a sport at all. Not infrequently it descends into vicious fighting, as in this brutal Swedish defeat by Russia.

A more peaceful occupation is the pre-Christmas Santa Lucia festival, which is held each year on December the 13th. In the old almanac, that was the longest and darkest night of the year. On this day, young girls throughout Sweden are nominated as Lucia candidates and crowned with candles to lighten the dark winter nights. The tradition is said to date back to St Lucia of Syracuse, a martyr who died in 304 AD, although the first recorded appearance of a white-clad Lucia in Sweden was not until 1764 – and the custom did not become universally popular until the 1900s.

A pre-requisite for Lucia candidates used to be that they were blonde and virgins, but Sweden in the sixties put an end to that.

On Lucia day, the winning candidate is driven around town, usually in horse drawn vehicle, to spread light in shops, old peoples' homes and medical centres . In Stockholm, a national Lucia is proclaimed in the city hall.

In winter, snow often falls constantly between November and May. Consequently, the Swedes have had to learn to clear deep snow overnight to keep transport moving and to build icebreakers to keep the shipping lanes open in the Gulf of Bothnia.

In this part of the world, winter temperatures drop to between minus 10 to minus 53 degrees Centigrade in the far north. That's 14 degrees to minus 63 degrees Fahrenheit.

Sweden is almost exactly 1,000 miles long. It's the fourth largest country in Europe after Russia, France and Spain. In area, it's roughly the same size as California.

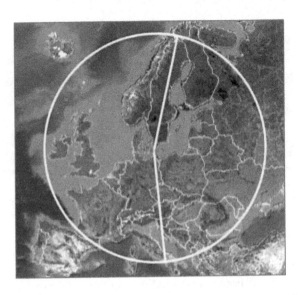

If you were to place a pin on the southernmost tip of Sweden, cut the country out of the map and swivel it round, its northernmost point would reach as far south as Rome.

Forests and lakes account for 65% of Sweden's land area. There are no fewer than 95,700 lakes in Sweden, so in summer, city residents retreat to their summer cottages where they live a basic rural life, back to the simplicity and beauty of 'The Nature'.

When you consider that the average population density in Sweden is just 30 people per square mile and no more than 2.2 people per square mile in the north, then you begin to appreciate why the countryside and 'The Nature' have had such an enormous impact on the people and their character.

Even the capital, Stockholm is part of an extensive

archipelago and built on 14 islands. There are parks everywhere, so you can be in countryside within 10 to 15 minutes even if you live in the centre of Stockholm, home to nearly two million of the country's 10 million population. This is a modern, bustling city encircling the old, picturesque medieval town known as 'Gamla Stan'.

So, while you may think that located up at the top right-hand corner of Europe, Swedes are isolated and insular, they

are in fact world leaders in many fields of industry. They are also renowned for showing concern for the world's disadvantaged and leading the way in terms of equality, social justice and women's rights.

The Swedes pay high taxes. A single person may end up paying

as much as 60% of their salary to the tax authorities and may wonder whether they are working for themselves or the State.

In return, they receive five weeks paid holiday from the day they are employed. For every child that is born, the parents are entitled to 16 months of paid parental leave, which they can split between them in any way they choose.

Everybody, regardless of their income or standing, receives quality healthcare, dentistry and education. What's more, those who live in Stockholm, often called the Venice of the North, can say that they live in arguably one of the most beautiful cities in the world.

In Stockholm's medieval Old Town, every building has its own history and one of the most important events was with the Reformation in 1527, when the King made Sweden a protestant state. It meant that church services no longer had to be held in Latin, but in the language of the people, regardless of their nationality. That in turn meant that each nationality needed its own church, not least the German church, a reminder of the importance and influence of the Hanseatic trading block from the 14th to the 17th centuries.

Storkyrkan, (The Great Church), is the oldest in Stockholm. The first Swedish king was crowned there in the 14th century and it has hosted royal occasions ever since. Originally Catholic, it also became Sweden's first Lutheran church after the Reformation.

It has been Lutheran for five centuries now and 95 per cent of all Swedes adhere to this religion, although most only attend church services for births, weddings, and funerals, and sometimes Midsummer's Eve, Christmas Eve and New Year's Eve.

Just across the water, the City Hall reflects the more humanist aspect of the Swedish character. Built in 1923 with eight million red bricks, it's all about people working together for their community.

In the Council chamber, carpenters fashioned the ceiling to look like that of a Viking long house.

The walls of the Golden Hall, where Stockholm City Council meets to discuss issues of the day, comprise about 19 million pieces of mosaic, each one created with real gold.

On the far wall 'The Queen of the Lake', the symbol of Stockholm, stands at the centre of the world. On her left side is the western world with the Eiffel Tower and Statue of Liberty and on the right side the Orient with Indian elephants and a Turkish flag. On her sides are signs of the zodiac symbolizing the universe.

Thus, Sweden, symbolized by the Queen of the Lake, stands at the centre of the Universe. Well, it's a point of view!

The founders of Stockholm built the city on 14 islands that were subsequently linked together with more than 50 bridges.

From the tower, you can see the islands clearly, as well as the Old Town (*Gamla Stan, pronounced Gamla Stahn)* and the Royal Palace, where the changing of the guard reminds us that Sweden once was a great power.

King Gustavus Adolfus, who ruled in the 1600s, extended

the nation's influence around the Baltic and as far as south as Poland.

Today, Sweden is passively neutral, modern and understanding – its soldiers, for instance, permitted to wear hairnets to prevent their rifles from snarling their long hair.

Nowadays, Sweden has a constitutional monarchy and the royals, whose blue-blooded cousins range from Catherine the Great in Russia to Louis the 16th in France, no longer live in the Royal Palace. They prefer a quieter life at Drottningholm's Palace on the outskirts of town where they reside in beautiful surroundings close to 'The Nature', despite the Palace being open to the public.

From the earliest Viking times, Sweden had either waged war or been forced to defend herself. Indeed, the Swedes were at war almost constantly from the early 14th century until the mid-19th century.

In the 14th Century, German Hanseatic merchants gained almost total control of Sweden's foreign trade, as well as its domestic economy and its politics. The Danes conquered the southern counties of Sweden but ended up fighting wars for decades until the Swedes won them back. There were several Danish-Swedish wars, not least the Northern Seven Year's war with the Swedes battling against the union of Denmark and Norway, which was allied with Lubeck and Poland.

Then came the Second Northern War, the Scanian War, the Great Northern War and the Russo-Swedish war, not to mention parts of the Napoleonic Wars. For the militarily ambitious Swedes, things were not going too well, not least financially. Wars cost money and lots of it!

Still, they had made conquests in Russia, in the Baltic States and in Finland, which would remain a part of Sweden for some 800 years. As a result, Finland today is bi-lingual, with all its attendant problems, such as dual language road signs and government documents.

By the mid-17th century, Sweden had nonetheless become a great power, with territory encircling the Gulf of Bothnia and the Baltic Sea. Indeed, people called the Baltic 'The Swedish Lake'.

The man who made all this possible was King Gustav II Adolf, otherwise known as Gustavus Adolphus the Great, the 'Lion of the North', the founder of modern warfare and of Sweden as a Great Power.

In order to strengthen his navy, King Gustav ordered a series of ships to be built, each with two full gun decks.

The first ship of these vessels would be his flagship. When she was completed, she was one of the most powerful vessels in the world at that time.

She was armed with 64 cannon that could fire 250 kilos. That is equivalent to 550 pounds of ammunition in a single broadside. When the heavy iron shot left the muzzles, it travelled almost at the speed of sound, twice as much and twice as fast as the largest warships of other European navies.

The ship was christened 'Vasa', after the elite Vasa dynasty from which the King was descended. She was magnificent, a war machine the like of which had never been seen before. This was a ship that symbolized Sweden's naval power.

The stern was decorated richly with sculptures based on

Roman and Greek antiquity and the Old Testament. There were fantastic and frightening creatures, including wild men, sea monsters and tritons, too, all painted in bright colours, emphasized with gold leaf to tremendous effect.

The ship was a statement intended to glorify the authority, the wisdom and the military prowess of the King himself.

On the 10th of August 1628, as the ship prepared to slip her moorings, crowds gathered on the quayside outside the Royal Palace. Among them were ambassadors and diplomats from all over Europe.

As this was Vasa's maiden voyage, the captain allowed the crew's girlfriends, wives and families on board. The plan was for them to sail a short distance and leave the ship a little way outside the harbour.

There was very little wind and despite having ten sails set, Vasa drifted for a while on the current, but as she entered less sheltered waters, she suddenly heeled to port. Then another, stronger gust billowed the sails and Vasa listed so far that water began to pour through the open gun ports.

Panic ensued. The crew tried to move the cannons to starboard, but to no avail. Slowly, to the horror and distress of the watching guests, Vasa slipped beneath the surface. Crew and guests dived overboard. Some managed to swim ashore. Small boats picked up the others, but 30 of those on board drowned.

Within hours, people were asking why. Vasa, the Swedish Navy's mightiest ship had sailed only about 800 yards before sinking in full view of everybody ashore.

The answer was that the gun decks, heavy cannon and ornate stern were far too high and too heavy for the small hull, so the centre of gravity was also too high above the surface of the water.

Meanwhile, the hunt was on for someone to blame. Just one day after the Vasa sank, the Council of State set up an enquiry into the fiasco. Their immediate problem was that the King himself had approved the design, so the tribunal could hardly embarrass him.

What did they do? They took the easy way out and instead blamed the original designer, who had conveniently died before the ship was launched and could hardly defend himself from the grave.

Then, 331 years later, an engineer and amateur archaeologist, Anders Franzén, began a systematic search for the Vasa wreck. For months, all he found were rusty iron stoves and bicycles and much else about which to keep silent. Using a grapnel and coring device, he eventually found some old black oak, later confirmed to be from the wreck.

Franzén and the navy's most experienced salvage diver, Per Edvin Fälting, managed to persuade influential Swedes and institutions that the ship should be raised and preserved. This proved to be a colossal task. Between 1957 and 1959, navy divers burrowed through the mud and dug six tunnels underneath the ship, an incredibly dangerous operation.

Next, they pulled massive steel cables through the tunnels and in an operation that took months, finally managed to attach them to two floating pontoons. By pumping the pontoons almost full of water, then tightening the cables and pumping the water out again, Vasa eventually broke free of the mud.

On the 20th August 1959, the media scrum and the crowds watched as if transfixed as the first spars of Vasa broke the surface. It was an extraordinary and emotional moment.

Moments later, the outline of the whole ship emerged.

Back from the dead, 331 years after sinking.

Much remained to be done, of course. They had to pump out thousands of tons of mud and water from the hull.

Only then, could the ship be moved into dry dock, preserved and finally moved into the museum that is now considered one of the ten best in the world. For years, experts sprayed the ship with water mixed with special preservatives so that the timbers would not shrink and crack.

Divers spent another five years retrieving thousands of artefacts, jewellery, clothing, tools, coins and, almost unbelievably, even food and drink. Altogether, they provided an extraordinary insight into early 17th century shipbuilding and everyday Swedish life.

The story of Vasa is of a fiasco, the greatest scandal in Swedish naval history, but two men and an army of divers, workers, administrators, financiers and volunteers managed to transform the disaster into a triumph.

The Vasa sinking crushed the confidence of the Swedish military. Worse, wars and military adventures had cost the nation a fortune and the ordinary citizens had to pay for it. As a result, there were inevitably popular uprisings, as well as general unrest and eventually civil war.

As Sweden's power gradually dissipated and its wealth diminished, draining the state coffers was no longer an option. With too many people and not enough jobs, there was not enough food. The very word 'agriculture' was synonymous with poverty and even starvation for large numbers of people who earned their living from the land.

One of the areas worst hit by the depression was the southernmost county of Skåne, the hub of the nation's agriculture. People had farmed the land there since 3000 BC and had always had a close relationship with Denmark just across the water.

Indeed, as we've seen, much of southern Sweden was part of Denmark until the Swedes established sovereignty over it in 1658.

At the time, Sweden's old enemy, Denmark dominated the sound between the two countries. In order to circumvent this, King Gustav Vasa ordered engineers to construct a canal that would link the rivers and the largest of Sweden's lakes between Stockholm and the west coast. It was a huge undertaking. In fact, it would be another 250 years, long after

Gustav Vasa's time, before the Göta Canal, as people subsequently named it, was completed. The route from the west coast to the Baltic is 382 miles long and consists of two canals with 64 locks rising to a height of 300 feet above sea level.

Fortunately, engineers needed to excavate only 60 miles of the route. Even so, it took 58.000 soldiers armed only with wooden spades some 22 years to build it.

Today, the canal is one of the main tourist attractions in Sweden, billed by tour companies as the perfect way to relax and appreciate 'The Nature'.

Beneath all that pretty countryside, Sweden is rich in resources. Much of the country is densely wooded and the forests here provided the vast supplies of timber that were needed to keep the furnaces going at the glassworks which have made Sweden famous the world over.

Legend has it that in the 16th century, King Gustav Vasa's courtiers would round off an evening's feasting by smashing as many expensive Venetian glasses as they could lay their hands on. The King, not surprisingly, became fed up

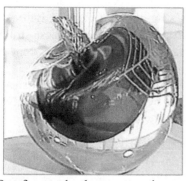

with this. So, he invited Venetian glassblowers to his court, on the basis that it would be cheaper to break glassware made in Sweden, rather than the imported variety.

Today, many glassblowers are directly descended from those first immigrants. Kosta, Orrefors and other companies are now world leaders, their designers clearly inspired by 'The Nature.'

Unfortunately, by the early 1900s, Sweden was one of the poorest nations in Europe. Unemployment, poverty and constant hunger prevailed.

Encouraged by the United States Homestead Act of 1862, which promised and almost free to settlers who travelled west, hundreds of thousands of people had little to lose by leaving their homes for a new life on the other side of the Atlantic. Most entered America through Ellis Island. By 1910, no fewer than one million Swedes, one-fifth of the population, were living in America.

Today, Americans with Swedish roots can trace their ancestors at the Emigrant Institute at Växsjö, a small town in Småland. A library of 25,000 books and 2,000 Swedish-American church and club records on microfilm make it relatively easy for people to trace their family histories.

Oddly enough, the exodus coincided with the country's Industrial Revolution, which provided jobs and attracted agricultural workers to the towns and cities. In time, their success would finance one of the world's most advanced welfare states. Financed by a highly developed export-oriented economy and high taxes, this ensures that the nation's income is distributed across the entire society.

The logo 'Made in Sweden' is the umbrella under which companies like Volvo, Saab, Scania, SKF, Ericsson, Alfa Laval and Hasselblad became world renowned.

Sweden also supports its own aerospace industry. This has become even more important recently given the more aggressive tactics of Russia's fighter aircraft in the Baltic.

Scania and Volvo are two of the largest truck manufacturers in the world, exporting some 95 per cent of heavy vehicles.

Volvo recently took a bold decision to power all its cars with hybrid or electric engines by 2019 – potentially spelling the end for petrol engines worldwide.

The country's paper and pulp industry provides newsprint for newspapers and magazines the world over. The Swedish sawmill industry is still the largest in Europe and accounts for about 10% of the world's exports. SKF is the world's largest ball bearings company.

Robotics, IT and telecommunications, are all major industries – and Sweden produces more robots than any other country in the world.

Despite Japan's dominance of the digital camera market, Hasselblad is Europe's only remaining camera manufacturer.

For exporters, the importance of Sweden's second city, Gothenburg, and its port is immeasurable.

Gothenburg is Sweden's largest seaport, with 14 miles of harbour and a million square feet of warehouse space. More than 14,000 ships and some 25 million tons of goods, 30% of the country's exports, pass through the port every year. Meanwhile, port workers load and unload more than 800,000 containers every year.

Gothenburg is also a fun and very beautiful city which, with more than 20 parks and a glorious coastline on its outskirts, is known as the Garden City.

It also has the largest amusement park, Liseberg, a kind of Danish Tivoli with a huge funfair, stomach churning rides, 13 restaurants and nightclubs, and four theatres.

The advantage of Gothenburg is that it's within easy distance of the west coast archipelago, a holiday playground known as the Golden Coast, which comprises some 250 miles (402 kms) of smooth granite coastline. The city arguably has more boats per capital than any other city in Europe.

Much of the wealth to finance Swedish industry – not to mention the centuries of war, came from the province of Dalarna in north central Sweden and especially from the copper mines at Falun.

In centuries past, 900 men toiled underground by torchlight here. In the boom times in the 1650s, about 70% of the world's copper, including the copper roofs that cover the Palace of Versailles near Paris, all came from this mine.

Today, it's a modern industrial site belonging to the Stora Company, which dates to Viking times and is the oldest incorporated company in the world.

Legend has it that an American company that wanted to do business with Stora asked if Stora could verify how long they had been trading. Stora Kopparberg's management responded by sending them a copy of the oldest preserved share in the company. It granted the Bishop of Västerås 12.5% ownership and was issued in 1288!

Stora Kopparberg has been producing the base for deep red paint that you see coating summer houses throughout Scandinavia ever since.

Another mining operation, in northern Sweden, has had enjoyed similar success, but with a disastrous effect. LKAB is the world's largest underground iron ore mine, with approximately 250 miles (402 kms) of roads under the surface. The mine is located between the towns of Kiruna and Malmberget.in the far north of Sweden. There is enough high-grade ore there to last for decades to come. The problem is that some of the richest deposits lie directly beneath the two towns.

The iron ore 3,280 feet (1,000 metres) underground forms in horizontal seams, one on top of the other, so the miners use explosives to break them up in order to extract the ore.

Without realizing it, as the miners removed each layer, they left a cavernous void. The strata of the original, supporting deposits began to crack and, in the 1970s, one section of the wall collapsed, creating a giant sinkhole on the outskirts of Malmberget.

Over the years, this sinkhole grew alarmingly bigger. Worse, several other holes also began to appear. As a result, the mining company had no option but to move both the entire town and its 15,000 residents.

Moving houses, however, is not as simple as it seems. Given that the houses were ten metres wide and the trailers carrying them were only three metres wide, it was a huge challenge. Adding to the problem, the route was treacherous. There were many sharp bends, so driving round too quickly meant that the house could easily slide off. To prevent this, the engineers used chains to secure the homes to the trailer, under which they installed anti-tilting bars.

They still needed to be extremely careful. The roads in the area were uneven and if they drove into a depression, they could easily become stuck. Getting the house and trailer out again could also be very expensive.

When, the team put all this to the test, they realized that the roads in town were rather narrower than they thought, which called for strong nerves and precision driving.

One office worker decided to have a look, opened his upstairs window, but seeing an entire house approaching with fewer than 18 inches clearance, quickly thought better of it!

There was a bridge to cross, too, but the railings were eight inches higher than the anti-tilting bars, so the only way to cross safely was to raise the bars to a precarious level.

If the house wobbled even marginally while crossing the bridge, there was a real danger that it would slide off and the whole operation could end up in the river below.

In fact, they made it with just a few centimetres to spare. One resident watched as her house inched across the bridge.

"It feels so unreal,' she said. "The same house but being taken to a different place. If I hadn't seen it with my own eyes, I would never have believed it.'

The operation progressed painfully slowly. It took five weeks to move just one house. By the time the team had moved the first street of houses, winter was upon them. Snow, icy roads, darkness and temperatures of minus 15 degrees Centigrade were now additional hazards.

Despite all the odds, the new town was finally re-located. he residents still call the new location Malmberget, which means ore mountain, but the houses are all re-numbered now and have another address. That hardly seems to matter. The people of Malmberget were saved from being swallowed up by the sinkholes. The residents even wrote a song about it.

On the other side of the ore mountain, the city of Kiruna faces similar problems. The iron ore here provides 90 per cent of all the iron in Europe, enough to build six Eiffel towers every day.

Such is the global demand for iron ore, that by 2033, engineers will have moved the whole of Kiruna two miles to the east.

That said, much of the 'new town' will comprise new apartment blocks and attractive squares. There will be a new town centre and High Street, fire station, library and swimming baths. The current Town Hall and Church will be moved from their current locations. Again, it is a colossal challenge, but it is an opportunity for the town to re-invent itself.

The cost is estimated at some £350 million pounds ($459.3 million, €412.1m), a sum that will surely rise with time.

Swedish ingenuity is unbounded. Even on a small scale.

A typical example is that with so much forest and timber available, woodcrafts abound. For centuries, farmers and villagers in the county of Dalarcarlia carved the *Dalarhäst*, or Dalar horse, as toys for their children.

Then, during the 19th century, people began painting them with bright designs, and ultimately, they became a symbol of Sweden itself.

The Swedes are devoted to the countryside and its traditions. Dancing round the Maypole or just dancing round a sunshade on Midsummer's Eve, the most important festival after Christmas, is a favourite pastime.

On Midsummer's Eve, Swedish children pick seven different wildflowers, dream of a future husband, wife or partner, and play happily until well after midnight.

In the far north of Sweden is the territory that we call Lapland, which extends from northern Norway to the Kola

Peninsula in Russia. Swedish Lapland is home to some 250,000 reindeer and 20,000 Sami people.

Not all of them herd reindeer. For those that do, their lives are dictated by the annual life cycle of their animals; calving, migrating to the mountains, rutting, rounding up and slaughtering. It is an extremely hard life, fraught with challenges. These are discussed in detail in *The Ultimate Cruise Passenger's Guide – Norway*.

* * *

Gothenburg (Göteborg)

The Main Attractions

Gothenburg is Sweden's second largest city with a population of nearly 600,000 in the city centre and roughly a million in the greater city area.

A university city, it is vibrant, trendy and bristling with attractions for all tastes, whether just rattling along in one of the city's blue and white trams for a cheap tour of the city or visiting some of the many excellent museums.

Perhaps Gothenburg's greatest advantage is that almost all the attractions are within walking distance. Stroll along the 17th century canals, wander along the waterfront with its aquariums and nautical inspired museums. Spend some time in fabulous and vast shopping centres, relax in the King's Park (Kungsparken) or go window shopping along the fashionable main avenue, (Kungsportsavenyn), lined with boutiques, bars and elegant shops.

Whatever you do in Gothenburg, you will soon realise why some residents believe the city should be Sweden's capital rather than Stockholm. It will never happen, of course, but it does go to underline the importance of the city and the pride its population has in it.

Stora Teatern and Kungsportsavenyn

The Port of Gothenburg – at first an exceedingly dreary looking place – is the largest port in the Nordic countries. Between 650,000 and 750,000 containers, 40 million tons of goods, nearly 600,000 Ro-Ro units and some 300,000 cars pass through it each year.

The port employs around 22,000 people and attracts 40-45 cruise ships and 1,733.000 passengers a year.

Gothenburg has always been a centre for trading, industry,

shipping and shipbuilding. In the 18th century, the Swedish east India Company set up its headquarters here.

The city itself dates to 1621, when King Gustavus Adolphus bestowed upon it a royal charter as a trading colony. With extensive fortifications, it was mostly populated by Dutch, German and Scottish traders and engineers attracted by charitable tax incentives.

At the time, there were no towns on Sweden's west coast, so in return for the tax favours, the Dutch, German and Scottish engineers first drained the marshlands and then built the town for the King.

It was a fair trade because although the Dutch eventually took over the town politically, introducing the Dutch language and laws. In 1652, the Swedes eventually gained control of it and under their rule, the town prospered and, in the 19th century, evolved into the progressive manufacturing and industrial city it is today.

Visitors can acquire a 'feel' for those early days in the **Haga district,** which is the oldest part of Gothenburg and dates to 1648. The cobbled pedestrian street, *Haga Nygata,* is lined with vintage, three story timber houses originally built as housing for workers between 1870 and 1940.

In the 1960s and 1970s, Haga became a major hippy community, a few of whom remain even to this day.

The old working-class district, once a down-at-heel suburb renowned for noisy bars and poor-quality housing, has always attracted artists and artisans. Unique local shops sell everything from toys, tea and spices to antiques, olive

oil, handmade soaps , marzipan and chocolate. Today, it is one of the prettiest areas in Gothenburg.

After wandering about for a while, the practice in Sweden is to have a break and '*fika*' – have a cup of coffee.

As the Swedes ideally like to do this a couple of times a day, there is also an abundance of pavement cafés and

konditoria, small coffee and cake shops, the most notable of which, in Haga, is **Café Husaren.**

Here, you can gorge on homemade cakes and *smörgås,* the traditional Swedish open-top sandwiches piled high with shrimps, roast beef, egg and cod roe, or a score of other

combinations as you sip your cup of filter coffee, which is usually taken black.

If one cup of coffee is not enough, refills are free so you can get as high on

caffeine as you like. If you are not a coffee person, try a hot chocolate with a freshly baked cinnamon bun the size of a dinner plate.

Arguably the largest buns of their type in the world, these have become so appealing to tourists that both they and Café

Husaren have become one of Gothenburg's top ten attractions.

Of course, you can find much cheaper and equally tasty cinnamon buns *(kanelbullar, pronounced kaneel-bullar)* in countless other cafés.

What's more, you won't feel that you have just eaten a slab of concrete. That said, whilst the enormous versions are a relatively expensive tourist gimmick, they are fun to eat.

If you happen to be in Gothenburg during a weekend, Haga is a hive of activity as store owners set up their stalls along the pedestrian street, Haga Nygata, transforming it into a huge market.

Happily, Haga is within walking distance of the city centre. However, you can also get there by taking a tram to either Hagakyrkan (Haga Church) or Järntorget. Tram 1, 2, 3, 5, 6, 9, 10, 11 and 13 call at both stops.

Real foodies can find coffee, cheese, spices, Swedish meat balls, elk and reindeer meat and all kinds of other goodies from all over the world in the *Market Hall (Stora Saluhallen).*

This is Gothenburg's largest marketplace and has been since the 1850s, when stall holders set up shop in a semi-circle around the side of Kungstorget (King's Square).

The current building dates to 1889, when it replaced the previous stalls. Today, there are about 40 different stalls and restaurants in

this vast food haven and the choice is mouth-watering.

Another fascinating venue, especially for seafood lovers, is **Feskekôrka (The Fish Church),** an iconic indoor fish and shellfish market built in 1874 and so named because the architect, Victor von Gegerfelt, was inspired by Norway's wooden stave churches and wanted a space with no supporting pillars.

Inside, fishmongers display everything from pickled

herring, crayfish and huge hunks of tuna to cod, shellfish of all kinds and fresh fish landed in the morning, as well as smoked fish, frozen fish, fish patties, fish cakes and so on.

Walk up to the mezzanine level and you can feast on fresh fish sandwiches, oysters and wash them down with the local Ocean beer. Just follow your nose to Rosenlundsgatan, a short distance from Kungsparken (The King's Park).

Wherever you go in Gothenburg, the shopping is terrific. The streets around the Kongstorget and the Cathedral are partially pedestrianized and a delight, and if it is raining, there are huge, modern shopping centres with numerous restaurants, boutique shops and chain stores to visit.

Gothenburg is often called 'The Garden City' because of its numerous parks. A block away from the Fish Church Market, *Kungsparken (The King's Park)* is a popular picnic spot. Modelled on English parks, its greatest assets are the magnificent trees, especially when in their full autumn bloom.

The park, which was completed in the mid-1850s, extends in a south-westerly direction from the Stora Teater and Kungsportsavenyen along Nya Allén almost to Järntorget.

Adjacent to Kungsparken and running in a north-easterly direction the *Horticultural Society park (Trädgårdsföreningen) i*s also bordered on one side also by Nya Allén and, on the other by the canal.

Laid out in 1842, this lush patch of greenery is dotted with flower beds and tiny cafes and is a popular place for office workers to sit quietly eating their lunch on a sunny day. It is also home to Europe's largest rosarium, which boasts some 2,500 varieties.

In the centre of the park, the 19th century **Palm House** (Palmhuset) is an impressive building of glass and cast iron and redolent of London's Crystal Palace.

It contains five sections: the Palm Hall, the Mediterranean Hall, the Camel Hall, the Tropical Hall and the Water Hall, each heated to different temperatures to create the best environment for the plants, which include a fabulous collection of camellias and tropical lily pads six feet across.

Similarly, the ***Botanical Garden (Botaniska Trädgården) on*** Carl Skottbergs Gata, just south of the city centre, was inaugurated in 1923 and offers around 16,000 species of plants in nearly 100 acres of gardens and greenhouses.

Here, there is a herb garden, a rock garden with a spectacular waterfall and more than 6,000 different plants. It also has one of the largest collections of tropical orchids in the country, as well as a selection of carnivorous plants and a rare Easter Island tree that is now extinct in its natural environment.

The garden, established by the eminent Swedish botanist Carl Skottsberg, also has a restaurant selling snacks, sandwiches and hot meals.

Entrance to the Botanical Garden is free, but entry to the greenhouses attracts a reasonable fee of SEK 20 (£1.65, $2.15, €1.90). Tram numbers 1,2,5,6,7,8,10,11 and 13 all call at the Botanical Garden.

Close by is the ***Änggården Nature Reserve,*** which comprises an arboretum with thousands of shrubs and trees and seems quite wild after the well-ordered gardens.

From the Botanical garden, you can cross the main road over the footbridge into Gothenburg's largest park, ***Slottskogen.*** This leafy 130-acre expanse of greenery is laced with paths winding through a landscape that is part formal park and part natural forest of beech, linden, maple and oak trees.

More exotic trees include Dawn Redwood and Serbian spruce, which combined with the azaleas make it a fabulous attraction, especially in Spring and Autumn.

Slottskogen is a great place to go jogging or to play

miniature golf or volleyball on designated courts. There is outdoor gym equipment should you feel like a little exercise and, if you don't, there is also a mini zoo where you can see Gotland ponies, elk, sheep and even seals and penguins.

In the northern part of the park, closest to the city centre, you can find *Slottsskogen Observatory (Slottsskogsobservatoriet)* on the top of the hill. It is well worth a visit if are interested in stars and planets.

For passengers who just want to get away from it all and spend a day in the 'country', Slottsskogen is the perfect place to relax and have a picnic (weather permitting!). Alternatively, you can have lunch in one of several cafés serving sandwiches, light meals, cakes and pastries – or at the Villa Belparc restaurant for something more substantial.

The park and the zoo are open year-round, and the admission is free. Take the same trams as listed for the Botanical Garden.

Another relaxing way to see Gothenburg is to take a canal tour. Cruise shuttle buses usually stop by the Stora Teatern (Grand Theatre) or at Gustav Adolf's Square nearby.

If you walk to the bridge over the canal, you can buy tickets there for the *Paddan Tour,* a classic guided boat tour which takes you under 20 bridges and out to the harbour. The tour takes 50 minutes and costs SEK 190 (£15.50, $20.50, €18.00).

Another way to see the city, of course, is to leap on and off the 'Hop on, Hop off buses, which cost approximately the same amount.

Parks, of course, are for good weather. Museums are for rainy days and Gothenburg has no shortage of fascinating museums to visit.

The *Museum of Art (Konstmuseum),* in Götaplatsen at the southern end of the main street, Avenyn, is arguably Gothenburg's most important art museum with works by Rubens, Rembrandt, Van Gogh, the Impressionists, and Picasso.

The museum claims always to have been contemporary, in the sense that it has always acquired contemporary art, even in the past.

It is also heavily biased towards Nordic art with works by such artists as Norway's Edvard Munch, Anders Zorn, a fabulous portrait artist whose pencil sketches are sublime, and Carl Larsson, whose naïf and nostalgic paintings of Stockholm and the Stockholm archipelago made him one of Sweden's most popular artists.

There is also a magnificent sculpture hall and, in the Hasselblad Centre, regular photographic exhibitions are held featuring both Nordic and global artists.

Immediately in front of the museum, the statue of Poseidon, by the Swedish sculptor Carl Milles, caused quite a stir when it was inaugurated in 1931.

Prudish citizens were horrified to see that the 22-foot (seven metre) high figure was not only naked but, in their view, somewhat overly endowed.

Such was the storm of protests that the authorities were required to execute surgery and poor Poseidon today is a much lesser God for it.

One of the most fascinating museums is the *Universum* on Södrävägen, next to the Liseberg amusement park (about which more later). For anyone interested in rain forests, animals, birds, chemistry, technology, this is a 'must see' venue. Here you can experience the humidity of a rain forest, complete with butterflies, marmosets, toucans, red ibis and other tropical birds running and flying free.

The Ocean Zone, a series of aquariums, some of them the largest in the world containing more than 660,000 gallons (three million litres) of water and hundreds of fish species, including sharks.

The West Coast aquarium is noteworthy because of its panoramic viewing window, which measures 16 x 4 s52 x 13 ft). This is made with scratch-proof acrylic rather than glass and is 10½ inches (27 centimetres) thick in order to withstand the pressure from 238 gallons (900,000 litres) of water. It is truly spectacular.

There is also a reptilarium and, as Universum is primarily a science centre, there are plenty of hands-on scientific exhibits with lots of buttons to press.

Universum is open 365 days a year from 10am until 6pm. From 6th July-11th August it remains open until 8pm. Tickets cost SEK 190 (£15.50, $20.50, €18.00) for adults with a concession price of SEK 155 (£12.65, $16.70, €14.70) for seniors.

The Gothenburg City Museum (Göteborgsmuseum) is located in an old East India shipping warehouse on Norra Hamngatan and covers the birth of the city at a time of childhood diseases, high death rates, war and conflict to its ultimate destiny as a multicultural metropolis. This is a journey through history with 17th century-style social media and exhibits that enable visitors to listen to the pop music of the time.

The tour begins with recent excavations that shed new light on the 1500s and 1600s with the help of real-life stories, unique artefacts and archaeological finds. Visual and interactive scenes depict a sumptuous baroque salon of the privileged classes and, conversely, visit the former city slums, showing how the city developed from a fortified town to the present day.

Permanent exhibitions include stories of the Viking Gods and how a farmer discovered a unique Viking ship – the remains of which are on display.

There is also a Children's museum in which children can crawl through tunnels and generally enjoy themselves while their parents take some time off.

The museum is open Tuesdays-Sundays from 10am until 5pm, and until 8pm on Wednesdays, except for national holidays. It is closed on Mondays. The entry fee for adults is SEK 60 (£4.90, $6.45, €5.70).

Gothenburg is also home to Scandinavia's largest amusement park, *Liseberg,* which is intended for everyone, most especially young people. It comprises beautiful gardens, outdoor shows and good food.

That said, it is not necessarily a good idea to eat if you intend to go on any of the rides. This is a park for adrenalin junkies with a revered wooden roller coaster called Balder, a speedy spinning 'wheel' that soars 138 feet (42 metres) into the air and Europe's longest dive roller coaster with a nerve-racking vertical drop of 164 feet (50 metres). Not for nothing is it nicknamed Valkyria. As if that was not enough to bring on a nervous breakdown, there is also the suitably named Atmos Fear, Europe's tallest (414 feet,116m) free-fall tower.

No doubt a doctor would recommend the less stressful options of which there are many, including carousels, fairy-tale castles, an outdoor dance floor, adventure playgrounds, and shows and concerts.

Most cruise passengers who prize sense above insanity would probably enjoy the landscaped gardens dotted with impressive sculptures rather more than the white-knuckle rides.

Should you suddenly be possessed with a desire to keep your stomach intact, Liseberg also offers extremely high-quality vegetarian buffet lunches at the Green Room for SEK 165 (£13.50, $17.80, €15.65)

Opening times are varied from month to month and sometimes day to day, but overall during the months of June, July, and August, they are likely to be between 11am and 11pm. Ticket prices are SEK 110 ($8.99, $11.85, €10.45) with free admission, unusually, for guests who are under 110 cm tall. Whether that includes people of a greater age is well worth testing.

This ticket price does not include any rides. Entry plus as many rides as you like costs SEK 485 (£39.60, $52.32-0, €46.00), a fee that may also make your stomach churn over.

* * *

Malmö

Turning Torso, Malmö

The Main Attractions

Malmö is Sweden's third largest city after Stockholm and Gothenburg, but it is not a major cruise port, nor is it a Gothenburg. In fact, at the time of writing only two cruise lines call here, each with three visits in the year.

One reason for this is that Malmö is a jumping off point for Copenhagen across the Öresund Strait and as there are any number of cruises to Copenhagen, they clearly obviate the need to go to Malmö.

Nonetheless, Malmö is not without its attractions. Like Gothenburg, it is a city of parks and it has the highest concentration of restaurants in Sweden per capita. The city is also renowned for its food (possibly because of its Danish connections?)

Perhaps the most stunning attraction in the city is the **Turning Torso** office and apartment building, the first twisted skyscraper in the world. This is the highest building in the Nordic countries and the second highest in Europe rising 57 stories and 623 feet (190 metres) high.

Santiago Calatrava, a Spanish architect, sculptor and engineer, designed the building, having previously created a white marble sculpture called *Twisting Torso,* which represented a twisting human being.

The new futurist design comprises nine five-storey pentagons that corkscrew clockwise so that the uppermost segment is positioned at exactly 90° in relation to the ground floor. The first three segments contain offices and the rest of the building contains 147 luxury apartments.

Not only is Turning Torso a remarkable building in terms of design, it is also pioneering because 100% of the energy consumed within it emanates from such renewable sources as solar, wind and geothermal power. Moreover, each apartment has an organic waste disposal unit that converts all waste material into energy.

Unfortunately, the skyscraper turned out to be something of a white elephant; there was little interest in buying the apartments so the owners, HSB, (a cooperative organization operating in property development and management), were forced to let them instead.

Since the building was inaugurated in 2005, four years after construction began, HSB has tried to sell the building, because it ultimately cost almost twice as much as originally estimated.

From around 1000 AD to 1300, Malmö was a Viking settlement and did not receive its city arms until 1437. Back then, the city and the southern county of Skåne, in which it is located, were a part of Denmark. They did not become a part of Sweden until 1658.

From 1710-14, the plague wiped out a large proportion of the populations of southern Sweden and the epidemic was especially virulent in Malmö, where from June until December 1712, at least 2,000 of the 2,700 population succumbed, as did half the regiment based in the city.

Like most towns and cities along the west coasts of Sweden and Norway at that time, the principal occupations were within the salt and herring industries.

Today, Malmö's economy is based on the heavy construction and transport industries, postal services and, to some extent, the production of furniture.

The city has experienced difficult times on several occasions, especially between 1970 and 1995, when it ran up debts of more than one billion Swedish kroner (£80,685 million, $105,777 million, €95,130 million) and companies made some 27,000 people redundant.

Conditions began to improve in 2000, partly due to an economic integration with Denmark and partly as a result of the new, five-mile (7.8-kilometre) long *Öresund Road and Rail Bridge*, which opened in July 2000, thus for the first time making it possible to drive from Gibraltar to the North Cape in Norway.

It was a magnificent achievement. Before it was built, the Öresund Strait was an impediment to transport and trade. Not surprisingly, the idea of a bridge was a dream throughout the 20th century. Engineers and others put forward all kinds of proposals but without the money to build them or, for that matter the political will, none of these ideas survived.

Originally, the thought was to link Elsinore in Denmark to Helsingborg in Sweden, because that is the narrowest part of the strait. However, political and economic reasoning underlined the advantages of the Copenhagen-Malmö link, not least the proximity to Copenhagen and the possibility of creating a more vibrant economic region with a population of nearly four million inhabitants.

The result is that workers can now commute from one side of the sound to the other, thus creating jobs and links between Danish and Swedish companies and institutions.

The 9.94-mile (16 kilometre) link comprises three sections – the cable-stayed bridge, which accounts for about half the distance, an artificial island and a tunnel.

On the bridge, the railway travels on a deck beneath the motorway, but when they reach the islands of Peberholm, they run parallel to each other.

The island, built with material dredged from the seabed, is 2.48 miles ((four kilometres) long, more or less the same distance as the tunnel, which as constructed with concrete sections cast on land and then towed to the site, where they were lowered in a trench in the seabed.

Happily, the artificial island has become a mini-Nature park because the flora and fauna have been left to develop naturally and without interference. Since its creation, botanists have identified more than 500 plant and tree species, although the trees are stunted due to high winds. The island has also become home to a variety of beetles, rare spiders, butterflies, a rare green toad and a breeding ground for birds.

Crossing the bridge by car is no more than a ten-minute journey and this has been of special benefit to Malmö's economy. The city does have its challenges, though. Generous immigration quotas in Sweden mean that Malmö now numbers among its population 174 different nationalities, speaking 150 languages. The total population of the city is nearly 342,000, of whom more than 135,000 have a foreign background and approximately 100,000 were born outside Sweden. In fact, 54% of the population have at least one parent who was born abroad, with most coming from the Iraq, Iran, Syria, Africa, the Balkans and Denmark.

Not surprisingly, this had led to tensions within the community and particularly in the Rosengård district, where gang warfare and gun crimes are high enough to cause the Swedish Post Office to cancel package deliveries there.

As one resident noted, however, Malmö remains a safe city and the levels of crime and gang warfare is nowhere near as high as in the United States. "The gangs don't go after civilians and the only times civilians get hurt is by accident, so basically if you don't bother them, they won't bother you', he said.

All the areas cruise passengers are likely to visit are safe. Indeed, more than one million people visit Malmö each year so there is absolutely no need for concern.

Sensibly, passengers will take the usual precautions applicable to all cruise destinations; don't flaunt jewellery, don't take large amounts of cash with you and keep handbags and wallets safely tucked close to your body. Then you can go out and enjoy the sights.

The 15th century *Malmöhus Castle* on Malmöhusvägen is the oldest Renaissance castle in Scandinavia. Built in 1434,

it replaced an earlier fortress built by the King of Denmark, Eric of Pomerania, in the days when Sweden, Denmark and Norway were part of a united kingdom that also incorporated northern Poland.

Over the years, the castle has been used as a fort and a prison in which prisoners deserving of the ultimate punishment (or not) were beheaded.

In the 16th century, King Christian III of Denmark ordered a major reconstruction, demanding that it should not only be a fortress to protect the city but also to keep an eye on shipping in the Öresund Strait, and serve as a county governor's residence, as well.

During the Middle Ages, the fort also served as a mint producing Danish coinage and in the 16th century was the scene of 'wild parties' held by Crown Prince Frederick.

During the war, it was also a relocation centre for survivors of the Nazi concentration camps.

Today, the castle is the largest museum in southern Sweden and part of the Malmö Museums organization. It holds both temporary and permanent exhibitions and includes an aquarium with fish, reptiles, spiders and other cold-blooded animals, vintage vehicles and a submarine.

Just across the road, *The Science and Maritime House (Teknikens och Sjöfartens Hus)* is home to several exhibitions covering the maritime history of Scania. *The City of All Times* describes Malmö's development from the 1850s until the present day.

Impressions – Linnaeus, Science and the Printed Word focusses on Nature and how people in the 18th century were thirsty for knowledge.

Vehicles of the Future begins in the 1900s and takes visitors into the future, while *Muscles and Motors* explains how steam engines, electricity, gas, oil and petrol changed the world.

Smart is an exhibition highlighting how people from the county of Skåne invented a plethora of utensils from toothpicks to pacemakers and nanotechnology.

Here, you can also see displays of shipping, aviation and engineering. There is an interactive 'knowledge park' for those who love to press buttons and make machines work – and even a Robot Jazz Band. This is a life-size sextet with a conductor that played to shoppers in a local department store in the early 1900s. Now, it gives a 'live' concert on Saturdays between 1pm – 2.30pm. The museum is open every day from 10am-7 pm except on public holidays.

The castle complex also incorporates the *Malmö Art Museum*, founded in 1841 and now one of the leading art museums in Scandinavia. It is home to some 40,000 paintings, sculptures and applied arts dating from the early 1500s until the present day. It focusses on Nordic modern and contemporary art and boasts a unique collection of fin-de-siècle paintings brought from Russia and acquired in 1914 at the Baltic Exhibition in Malmö.

The museum is open from 10am until 5pm every day except public holidays. Incidentally, all state museums in Sweden are now free of charge.

Within walking distance of the Old Town is the *Modern Art Museum*, situated in the turbine room of a converted power station built with brick in 1901. This is a branch of the Stockholm Modern Art Museum and can be found in *Ola Billgrens plats*

Specializing in 20th and 21st century Scandinavian and international art, it claims to have the only significant collection of 20th century art in Scandinavia and includes works by Kandinsky, Matisse, Picasso and Dali.

Just to add to the potential confusion is the *Malmö Konsthall (Malmö Art Hall)* on *St. Johannesgatan*. Opened in 1975, this is one of the largest spaces for contemporary art in northern Europe. It is light and spacious thanks to a roof comprising 550 light domes and a sloping skylight.

A popular venue that attracts some 200,000 visitors each year, its focus is to show national and international art from the classics of modernism to current experimentation.

Rotating exhibitions are frequent and in the hopes of erasing the boundaries between different art forms, there are numerous specialist exhibitions with the accent on theatre, film, poetry, video, multimedia, music, and so on.

The bookshop offers a wide selection of art literature from around the world as well as posters, postcards and catalogues.

An unusual museum is the *Cog Museum* on Skeppsbron, a short walk from the central railway station. This fascinating establishment focusses on 14th century oak trading ships called cogs, which were clinker built with planks, had a

broad beam and one mast and a square-rigged single sail similar to those used on Viking ships.

The museum has two reconstructed medieval ships, the largest of which is 29 metres (95 feet) long and is a copy of the largest known cog in the world. Visitors can experience life on board during boat trips at mid-day and 2pm.

One of the oldest buildings in Malmö is *St. Petri kyrka (St. Petri church)*, sometimes described as St. Petri Cathedral. Founded in the early 1300s, it was modelled on the church of St. Mary in Lübeck, Germany and is built in the 'Baltic Brick Gothic' style.

Just off the main entrance, there is a chapel known as the 'Merchant's Chapel', so called because local merchants used it as a meeting room. The chapel in those days was sealed off from the main church by a wall.

During the Reformation, the ceiling murals were painted over with white paint and remained in this state until the early 1900s, when the paint was removed to reveal them once again. Today, they are considered the best-preserved ceiling murals of the late Middle Ages.

After the Reformation, the chapel – dedicated to Mary – was no longer used for church services and became a storeroom. Later, it became a fire station.

The church is fascinating because of the stone epitaphs dating back to the 17th century (the wooden epitaphs having been burned during the Reformation). At one stage, the entire floor of the church was covered with grave slabs from the Middle Ages, testament to the wealth of the city and its commerce.

As mentioned earlier, Malmö, like Gothenburg, is a City of Parks.

Slottsparken (The Castle Park) is one of the most extensive parks in the city with 52 acres (21 hectares) of open grassland, artificial hills, extensive views, a rock garden and large areas of woodland.

Once a training ground for the Malmö Household Regiment (the Malmö Hussars) based at the Malmöhus fortress, the area was later the venue for an industrial and trade fair in 1886.

When the exhibition closed, the city fathers decided to create a park and hired the Danish landscape architect Edvard Glaesel to design it.

In 1900, The park opened as intended for people of all ages (hence the number of park benches). The main theme, however, is water. A large lake, two ponds, a swamp area and a fountain all designed in the style of a Japanese garden give the park a sense of serenity.

Glaesel also created a large festival area that is today extremely popular and used regularly for a variety of events.

In 1980, officials decided to link the park to *Kungsparken (The King's Park)* with a bridge over the canal and a smaller bridge to the castle garden.

Centuries ago, it was a graveyard, but in 1869, the Danish landscape designer, Hoegh Hansen, transformed it into a romantic park inspired by English landscape gardens.

Hoegh Hansen also wanted to simulate a botanical garden and to that end, gardeners planted numerous exotic trees which distinguish this park from others in the city.

The largest park in Malmö is *Pildammsparken*, a 45-acre (111-hectare) classic park created around several 17th century ponds, once, which once served as the city's water supply. Each year, gardeners plant more than 10.000 flowers in what is known as 'Flower Alley'. The park is also home to a variety of bird species.

It is also a great place for joggers with a paved path round the great pond. For passengers, and especially crew, *Ribersborg Beach* is likely to be a popular place to spend a few hours on a summer's day. This is a narrow man-made beach, southwest of the harbour and this is where you will also find the *Ribersborgs Kallbadhus (Cold Swimming Baths)*, opened in the 1890s. The baths comprise two large outdoor sea pools and five saunas at the end of a long boardwalk and, in the words of its website, offers a 'sauna with

fantastic views of the sea, ice-cold sea bathes in the winter, refreshing baths in the summer, wood-fired hot tubs, massages etc.' Visitors also bathe here naked.

There is a restaurant that serves a wide range of hot dishes, salads, sandwiches and cakes etc.

The baths are open from 9am to 9pm from May until the end of August. The entrance fee is SEK 70 (£5.70, $7.51, €6.65) for a one-time visit.

* * *

Rønne, Bornholm

The Main Attractions

A graceful lighthouse and the unusual, if not idiosyncratic, 'witch's hat' tower of St. Nicholai Church dominate the Danish port of Rønne and what at first appears to be a potentially boring little town. How wrong that assumption would be!

For hidden among the red roofed buildings of Rønne, there are old-world streets, attractive gardens and cobbled courtyards lined with low-timbered houses, many of them once the homes and shops of Hanseatic merchants and Danish aristocrats.

What Rønne lacks in major attractions it gains from its rich and often unhappy history, its charm and hidden gems. Despite a fluctuating population of only about 13,500, it is the largest town on the Danish island of Bornholm and its largest port. Once focused entirely on herring fishery, it is today crisscrossed busily by fishing boats, ferries, pleasure boats, cargo and cruise ships.

Most visitors to Bornholm tend to come from Denmark, the United Kingdom, Sweden, Germany and Poland. Passengers from cruise ships are given a warm welcome and shuttled to the town centre about a mile (1.5 kilometres) away in coaches painted brightly and, in the eyes of some perhaps gaudily, by enthusiasts of graffiti.

Indeed, the few examples of graffiti in the town centre come almost as a welcome break from an inevitable immersion into the past. (I did say 'almost'!).

Sitting more or less equidistantly from Denmark to the west, Sweden to the North, Germany to the southwest and Poland to the south, the island of Bornholm inevitably became of strategic military value and interest – especially to Denmark, Sweden and Lübeck (Germany.)

In a sense, this was a pity because their interest immersed a peaceful island of rocky outcrops, pine forests, farmland and sandy beaches in several wars.

The origins of Rønne are unknown, but probably Viking era fishermen settled on the westernmost point of the island at the turn of the first millennium.

Presumably they thrived because in the last quarter of the 13th century their descendants built a small church there and dedicated it to Saint Nicolas, an early Christian Bishop.

Christian believers considered him to be a bringer of gifts and as a patron Saint of just about everybody from sailors and merchants to brewers, children and students, remorseful criminals and even usurers.

As the settlement expanded into a market and trading town during the 14th century, it became of greater interest to foreign influences, notably the Danes, the Archbishop in southern Sweden and German princes.

The Germans were particularly interested in Bornholm because of its strategic military value and as a gateway to the Baltic Sea, and especially the island of Gotland, off the Swedish east coast.

By the early 1400s, Rønne was being ruled by the Danes and had evolved into a thriving trading port. The town's success, however, resulted in the Lübeck princes and merchants sacking the town on several occasions, eventually taking control of it in 1525.

Greed, however, proved to be their downfall. Demanding higher and higher taxes from the people of Rønne merely fanned the flames of rebellion and in the mid-1500s, the citizens drove the Lübeckers out of town and, once again, the Danes took control of the town.

By the end of the 16th century, the herring fishery had diminished considerably and in the early 17th century, Rønne again fell victim to the plague that had already ravaged southern Sweden and twice decimated the town's population, in 1619 and again in 1655.

Three years later, during the second Northern War, the Swedes inflicted a devastating defeat on the Danish-Norwegian Union, which was obliged to cede Bornholm to them.

In 1660, however, a local uprising forced the Swedes to flee and the island – and Rønne – returned to Danish control.

Following the decline of the herring fishery, which never really recovered, the population of Bornholm turned instead to ceramics, an industry that has continued to the present day with scores of ceramic shops in Rønne alone.

Apart from ceramics, glassmaking and other arts and crafts, Rønne's economy today relies on fishing, farming and most particularly tourism.

The town's ill fortune did not end with the end of  the herring fishery, however. During the Second World War, a single German battalion occupied Bornholm, which subsequently acted as a listening station for German troops until the end of the war.

The Russians subsequently demanded that the Germans surrender the island, a 'request' the German commander of Bornholm declined. As a result, Russian aircraft bombed the island on the 7th and 8th of May 1945. More than 200 homes were flattened during the raid, although only ten people were killed.

On the following day, May 9th, Russian troops invaded and occupied the island, claiming that they were 'liberating' it from the Germans, whom they sent packing back to Germany.

The Danes, not surprisingly, did not concur with this view and always regarded the Russian presence as an occupation, especially as they remained on the island for almost a year. In any event, the Soviets finally agreed to vacate the island and in April 1946, finally withdrew their troops. Bornholm was once again Danish.

Rebuilding Rønne and other towns took several more years, however. Most of the houses in the town had been destroyed and the city fathers were keen to restore it to its full former glory. Sweden and the Danish Faroe Islands contributed housing and finance and eventually the town was restored to its current state.

Happily, not all the old houses were destroyed and two streets, Laksegade and Storegade, are still lined with original homes once owned by medieval merchants.

Arguably the best way to appreciate the rich history of Rønne is to visit *The Bornholm Museum,* located at Skt. Mortensgade No. 29, which traces the evolution of the town from the pre-historic age.

It is a fascinating museum that is well presented and with Bronze and Iron Age exhibits as well as Roman coins, pottery, paintings and gold artefacts, through to early 20th century shops, workshops and a schoolroom.

There is also the intriguing story of the Bornholm Long Case Grandfather clocks. In 1744 a Dutch ship went aground on the rocks near Rønne. Onboard, local fishermen found five English grandfather clocks of considerable value.

These ended up with a local turner, Poul Arboe, who together with some other craftsmen, had never previously seen such clocks, so they spent months studying the mechanisms and gradually repairing them.

After that, it was only a matter of time before Arboe decided to create one himself – and thus was born a new industry in Rønne. More turners learned the techniques and continued making Bornholm long case clocks until 1900.

The Bornholm Museum is open from 10am-5pm. Admission is free.

The Defence Museum (Førsvarsmuseet) is housed in an old round tower with walls 11 feet (3.35 metres) thick at Arsenalvej No 8. Soldiers built the tower in 1744, but in fact it has never been used for military defence purposes. The museum describes the defense of Bornholm through some 500 years and not least the invasion and occupation by both the Germans and Russians during the Second World War.

Among the cannons, weapons, vehicles, uniforms and other exhibits is an original German Enigma code machine, which local people found in a ditch at the end of the war. There is also a Second World War tank and the remains of a V1 flying bomb which landed on the island by mistake during testing procedures. Fortunately, it carried only concrete rather than explosives.

The museum is open from 10am-4pm Admission is DKK 65 (£7.65, $9.70, €8.70) and DKK 50 (£5.85, $ 7.45, €6.70) for seniors.

On a more peaceful note, ***St Nicolas's Church, (Skt. Nicolai Kirke)*** – the one with the distinctive tower and witches' hat spire – replaced the original, smaller church which dated to 1275.

That church, however, was almost doubled in size and completely refurbished in 1918, although some remnants of the original church are still visible in the Nave.

A wooden altar replaced the original during the 1915-1918 reconstruction and a variety of carved crosses were

installed at the end of the pews. The pulpit, likewise, also bears a carving of a cross representing the Tree of Life. All these works were by executed by the Bornhom carver, Christian Koefoed, who died in 1958.

A large chandelier created in Lübek in 1620 recalls a less happy time in the island's history while the model of the 72-gun Danish frigate 'Dannebrog' hanging from the ceiling dates to 1873.

Originally a sailing ship, she was clad in iron in the mid-19th century and became a steam ship with a less than illustrious career: she ultimately became a target ship and 1897 was dispatched to the knacker's yard. Quite why a model of her is hanging as a votive offering in the church is not explained.

Continuing to focus on history, **Hjorths Ceramic Factory (Hjorths fabrik),** located at Krystalgade No.5, has a 150-year history of creating terracotta and ceramics according to the original methods.

Immediately you enter the workshop, you are transported back to the 1860s, when Lauritz Hjorth began making terracotta from local clays. His family owned a sizeable area of woodland, which provided timber for the original kilns that were used until the mid-1960s, when gas and electric fired kilns were introduced.

The ceramics produced here, mostly jars and containers designed for pharmacies, were exported to such major European capitals as Berlin St. Petersburg, London, Paris and Vienna.

During the high season from July 1-August 9, there are guided tours (included in the price) at 10am and 2pm. These take you through the entire process from the arrival of the clay to the workshops, ceramists at work, glazing etc.

The museum also offers touchpads with text and videos showing the various processes in English, Danish and German. As with most good museums, there is also a shop!

The factory, which still produces ceramics for export abroad, notably to Japan, is open from March 1st-May 12th and from October 21st-November 30th, Monday-Friday 1pm-5pm and 10am-1pm on Saturday. It is closed on Sundays and public holidays. From May 13th-October 20th, opening hours are Monday-Saturday 10am-5pm.

The entrance fee is DKK 70 (£8.20, $10.45, €9.35), which is a good deal given the fascinating experience in an historic environment that is still producing superb works of art for export.

Along with St. Nicolai Church the **Rønne Lighthouse**, is the most imposing building in the town. Topped with an octagonal cast iron tower, it was built in 1880 and decommissioned 109 years later. It stands 59 feet (18-metres) high but is dwarfed by the Dueodde Lighthouse, a little inland from the southernmost point of the island.

This much more modern structure was completed in 1962 is the tallest lighthouse in Denmark at 154 feet (47-metres) above sea level. Marking the southern entrance to the Baltic Sea, it is considered one of the most important lighthouses in the region.

Whereas the north and east coasts of Bornholm are rocky, the west and southern coast is bordered with a narrow strand of white sandy beaches, and at Rønne, **Antoinette Beach i**s one of the most popular with those who want to get away from it all for a while.

The beach, just to the north of the town is approximately four miles long and backed by woodland and a walking and cycle path, so there are plenty of secluded, sheltered and quietly beautiful spots from which to choose.

Bornholm's Birds of Prey Show (Bornholms Rovfugleshow) located at Lundsgardsvej No.4, Nyker, Rønne may not be everybody's cup of tea but it does offer the chance to see eagles, hawks, owls and parrots close up.

The aim of the daily shows is educational but unfortunately the presentations are in German and Danish, but not English. Still, it is a good opportunity to see these wonderful creatures flying freely in an attractive setting surrounded by lakes, cliffs and a great view. There is a small café selling coffee, cake, ice-cream and snacks, too.

There is a show every day from 11am-1200. The site opens one hour earlier. Tickets cost DKK 120 ($14.10, $17.90, €16.05) with a DKK 20 (£2.35, $3.00, €2.70) discount for seniors. Payment is in cash at the gate.

What makes this a good day out is the wide variety of birds; the Griffon vulture or Goose Beak, larger than most eagles … the Red Macaw, which is also partly green and blue, and one of the largest parrot species … Silky Fowls with an extra rear toe and plumage that is easily confused with fur … and the Laughter Bird – the Kookaburra – which isn't laughing at all, but warning others of its species of danger.

That said, they do tend to make *us* laugh!

* * *

Karlskrona

The Main Attractions

Karlskrona, a baroque, nautical city scattered across 30 islands in Sweden's southern archipelago, is not surprisingly a major naval base. Indeed, it is Sweden's only remaining naval base. It is also Sweden's only baroque city.

With some 36,000 inhabitants, it is the headquarters of the Swedish coast guard, whose job it is to keep an eye on the 1,650 islands in the archipelago and the myriad of small boats plying back and forth.

People living on the larger islands tend to devote themselves to agriculture and fishing. The smaller islands are populated mostly by holidaymakers in their summer cottages and by people who crave privacy with superb views and wide horizons.

Ferries to the different islands abound, leaving Fisketorget (Fish Square) and Handelshamn (Trade Harbour) and often calling at several islands on one trip. It makes for a beautiful day out, especially for passengers who want to escape the city bustle, breathe the air and soak in the atmosphere of a Swedish summer among the islands.

(Note to crew members: if you opt to spend a few hours in the archipelago, do take a bike. It's a great way to see the islands).

Larger ferries connect Karlskrona with Gdynia in Poland. There are two return trips a day and more than half a million people use the service annually.

When the King decided to move Sweden's main naval base and shipyard from Stockholm to the southern archipelago in 1680, he did so for two reasons; firstly, to ensure a more or less ice-free base year-round and, secondly, to keep the fleet closer to the Danes who had occupied southern Sweden until 1660.

Fifty years later, more than 1,000 people were working at the shipyard, much of which is still in use today, as are many of the baroque buildings from that era.

The Old Shipyard (*Gamle Skeppsvarvet)* now listed as a UNESCO World Heritage site, is one of Karlskrona's main attractions. Here you will find buildings and technology covering more than 300 years of shipbuilding.

These include the **Polhems** *Dock (Polhemsdockan)*, which is still in use and the longest wooden building in the country, *Repslagarbanan (Rope Making Hall)*, where you can see how ropes of different sizes and types were made.

The hall is 364 yards (1,092 ft or 333 metres) long, which enabled rope makers to create coarse hawsers a cable long – a cable being the equivalent of a ship's anchor chain, which is to say 600 feet, 100 fathoms or 182 metres.

Inside the rope making hall, 364 yards (333 metres) long.

There is also a guided tour to Lindholmen, which shows Karlskrona from the sea perspective and takes you out to the former naval yard. You can only visit Lindholmen with a guided tour. During the summer there are regular tours and you can buy tickets at the Tourist Office *(Karlskrona Turistbyrå,* located in the main square *(Stortorget No 2).*

The Swedish coast has always been subjected to Russian submarine intrusions and Karlskrona naval base was no exception. Since the 1960s, there have been 20 such incidents. The Swedish Navy dropped depth charges on several occasions, although no submarines are known to have been sunk.

In 1981, a Soviet Whisky class submarine ran aground about 18.6 miles (30 kilometres) from Karlskrona. The Swedish and international media showed an intense interest because Swedish officials believed the Soviets would try to rescue the vessel.

With the Swedish navy and other armed forces on high alert, the government decided to release the submarine and its crew in order to avoid worsening their relations with the Soviet Union.

A year later, another foreign submarine, later deemed to have been from the Soviet Union, entered Swedish coastal waters. This time the Swedes dropped 44 depth charges and detonated four mines.

Perhaps fortunately, the submarine's crew managed to slip through the net and although tensions with Moscow were heightened, the situation was nowhere near as critical as it would have been had the Swedes sunk the submarine and killed its crew.

Nor did this incident stop the Soviets intruding into Swedish waters and spying. As recently as 2014, the Swedes recorded encrypted messages on an emergency frequency used by the Russians, but once again no submarine was found.

Probably the best way to experience the nautical history of Karlskrona is to visit the 'must see' *National Naval Museum.*

Figureheads from ancient ships in Galleon Hall (Galjonshallen).

Situated on the tiny island of Stumholmen and reached across a small bridge from the eastern end of the city centre, this is a treasure house of all things relating to the history of the Swedish Navy.

Here you can see reconstructions of a battle deck in wartime, any number of model boats, and arguably the world's finest collection of figureheads that once graced the bows of ancient Swedish navy warships.

In the submarine hall, there are three submarines; the high-tech *Neptun,* her predecessor and Sweden's first submarine, the *Shark* from 1904.

On the quayside outside the main building, you can see Sweden's royal sloop and the minesweeper, HMS *Västervik,* on which officers and officials from Stockholm interviewed Russian officers and diplomats after the grounding of the Russian whisky class submarine outside Karlskrona in 1981.

It's a great way to capture the smells and sounds of life on board a navy vessel and experience everyday routines and navigational challenges.

The museum curators are also involved in research and are charged with the preservation of an archive of naval drawings, a photographic archive and a library.

King Carl XVI Gustaf, the present king, opened the present museum and today it is one of the most popular tourist destinations in southern Sweden with nearly 200,000 visitors a year, about 30 per cent of them from abroad.

There is a restaurant servicing hot meals, salads, coffee, pastries and cakes.

Admission to the museum is free and the museum is open daily, except for public holidays, from 10am to 4pm or until 6pm in June and August except for Wednesdays when it stays open until 7pm during those months. It is closed on Mondays from January until April.

You can also delve into the past at *Drottningskärs kastell (castle),* a 17th century fortress on the island of Aspö, a 25-minute ferry ride from Handelshamnen (The Trading Port). The ferries leave approximately every hour (twice hourly in July and August).

Horatio Nelson described the fortified tower on the island of Aspö as 'impregnable', although in its 300-year history there has never been a shot fired in anger from it. Built at the same time as the naval base in 1680, the castle's four bastions are named after the Swedish queens, Maria, Hedvig, Ulrica and Christina.

Opening times for Drottningskärs Kastell are June-August: 12 noon- 8pm on Mondays, 10am-8pm on Tuesdays – Saturdays and 12-5pm on Sundays. At other times of year, the fortification is open only on Saturdays between 12 noon and 4pm.

The castle is one of two fortresses to be built on islands at either side of the inlet to the naval base. The other fortress is **Kungsholms Fort**, which unusually can be accessed from

the sea through a gap in the fortress walls into a remarkable circular harbour.

The museum focusses on the story of the fort and coastal

artillery. A small but beautiful garden inside the walls contains numerous exotic plants collected by officers on navy ships sailing to foreign parts.

You can only visit the fortress, now some 330 years old, by taking a guided two-hour boat trip from Fisktorget and you have first to buy the tickets from the Karlskrona Tourist Office in Stortorget or from the Naval Museum.

Tickets cost SEK 340 (£27.70, $36.00, €32.10) with no concessions. Adults must carry proof of identity, which for cruise passengers could mean a photo document other than your passport, which may be held by the ship.

This is because the Swedish Navy still uses the fort as part of the national defence.

Back in the centre of town on Borgmästaregatan 21, is the *Blekinge Museum,* an evocative museum that focusses on fishing and boat building. This may not sound especially enticing, but it also includes an impressive stone house called *Grevagården*, once the private palace of Count Hans Wachtmeister, an admiral in the Swedish  navy in the late 18th and early 19th century.

One of the few homes to escape the devastating fire in 1790, it was recently renovated and converted to World Heritage site status.

At one stage it contained thousands of odd artefacts, ranging from wax models of the faces of people suffering from syphilis to fans and fashions. For obvious reasons, some of these were cleared during the conversion. There is also a small baroque garden and a café.

Opening times are 11am-5pm Tuesday to Friday, 11am - 4pm at weekends. Closed on Mondays. Admission is SEK 80 (£6.50, $8.50, €7.55).

Another fascinating small museum for anyone interested in historic cars is the *Classic Car Museum (Bilmuseum)* at Östrahamngatan 7D.

Here you can see the famous Volvo Amazon, described in 1986 as Sweden's most beautiful car, the murdered Prime Minister Olof Palme's last car and other Swedish classics., mostly from the 1950s.

The museum is in the same premises as the *Karlskrona Porcelain Museum*, located in the factory that once produced the exhibits.

The two museums are open only from the 18th June until the 3rd August, between 11am and 4pm, unless you pre-book a guided tour by calling 0455-361223.

Meanwhile, there are three important churches worth seeing. The first is the twin-towered *FredriksKyrkan (Fredriks Church)* in the main square, Stortorget which, incidentally, is said to be the largest square in Scandinavia.

Nicodemus Tessin the Younger designed this Lutheran church, influenced by Italian architecture and is baroque in style. Construction began 1720, replacing the city's wooden church. It was consecrated 23 years later in 1744 and named after King Frederick I. The neoclassic pulpit was installed 110 years after that, in 1854. With room for 350 chairs, the church has undergone many renovations and updates over the centuries, most recently in 2018, not always with everyone's approval.

The old font designed by ship builder Gilbert Sheldon has gone, replaced by an ultramodern oval font of marble filled to the brim with water and reminiscent of an infinity pool.

The altar is also now of an extremely modern design. The effect is to have taken away the warmth and charm of the church in favour of a colder, more clinical look.

Although rich in history, the church today shows little signs of it. Instead, it has become a church of the future which, in the words of the Bishop, "is poised for a new era that calls for new thinking'.

In one of the towers, there are 35 carillon bells, which ring three times a day. Some may think in sorrow, perhaps?

Nixcodemus Tessin also designed ***The Church of the Holy Trinity (Trefaldighetskyrkan),*** sometimes also called ***The German Church*** because in the mid-19th century, it was the church used by the German congregation in the city.

The original church was consecrated in June 1709, but it was destroyed 81 years later when fire ravaged the city. Only the damaged outer walls remained. Citizens were able to save only two brass chandeliers from 1722 and a tablet of the church in relief from 1789. These still hang in the church today.

Construction of a new church began a year later and was finally re-opened in 1802. It was originally named after Frederiica Dorothea Wilhelmina, the Queen of King Gustav IV Adolf. When he was deposed and ultimately banished, the church assumed its current name.

A neoclassical domed roof such as this is extremely rare in Sweden. Inside, the roof painting deceives the eye into thinking that the dome is higher than it is.

The third of the 'important' churches is ***Karlskrona Admiralty Church (Amiralitetskyrkan,*** built in 1685 with wood and painted in the famous 'Falu' red paint made with ore from the copper mines in Falun, central Sweden. This is one of the largest wooden churches in Sweden.

By the steps leading to the church entrance, there is a wooden carving of a mid-18th century beggar holding a placard that reads:

I beg of you, humbly
Even though my voice may be weak,
Come, put a penny in
But first lift my hat.
Blessed are those who care for the poor.

The beggar is known as Gubben Rosenbom (Old Man Rosenbom), who became famous primarily because of Selma Lagerlöf's book *Nils Holgersson's wonderful travels through Sweden*, in which he is said to be the captain of the

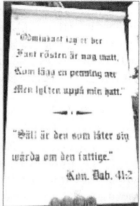

ship *Dristighet (The Drifter)*.

Rosenbom is also believed to have been a famous beggar who froze to death outside the Admiralty Church on New Year's Eve, 1717, exactly where he stands today. He is thought to have been Mats Hindriksson Rosenbom, who lived at Björkholmen in Karlskrona in the late 17th century.

The real Rosenbom was apparently a junior naval officer not a captain and was never on the ship *Dristighet*. It seems he owned a cottage, Chapmansgatan No 7, in Karlskrona, where he lived with his wife and children.

It is known that he did not die in Karlskrona – and therefore not in front of the Admiralty Church. Nor did he die between 1705 and 1717, although his widow applied for a 'mercy grant', possibly to pay for a funeral.

This could have been for the funeral of one of the children rather than Rosenbom himself as there is no record of him being buried in Karlskrona. One possibility is that he died during the 1705-1706 war in Poland or shortly afterwards.

Still, the wood carving outside the church shows him wearing the clothes of a boatman and it may well be that there were two Rosenboms. Who knows?

In any event, the statue outside the church is a replica. The original was taken inside the church better to preserve it. Meanwhile, the money collected by lifting the replica's hat is donated to the Rosenbom Foundation and passed on to local organizations in Karlskrona.

As for the church itself, it was consecrated in 1685 and originally able to seat about 4,000 people, making it the largest wooden church in Sweden. It is also known as Ulrica Pia Church, after Queen Ulrike Eleonora of Denmark. Pia, incidentally, is the feminine form of the Latin 'Pius', which, of course, means 'Pious'.

To begin with, the wooden church was meant to be only temporary, but fortunately the community never managed to acquire enough money to demolish it, so the stone version was never built.

The church is still used and is also a popular concert venue. The altar painting, incidentally, is a replica of Rubens' *The Coup de Lance* which hangs in Antwerp cathedral.

The **Admiralty Clock Tower (Admiraltyklockstapeln)**, erected in 1699, was built so that dock workers in the naval base would know the time, but after 1909, people used it as a bell tower for the Admiralty Church. It stands at the centre of a park about three blocks from the church.

Finally, **Wämöparken** on **Hastovagen**, about 3 kms (2 miles) north of the town, comprises old cottages that have been transported from different areas of Blekinge county, lots of forest walking tracks and excellent picnic spots. There is a mini-zoo with goats, chickens, pigs, ducks, rabbits, hens and other farmyard creatures and a small but inexpensive café.

It is a very pleasant way of spending the day if you don't feel like wandering around the town or going to museums. The atmosphere in the park is great, the natural environment is attractive and from time to time, flea markets are held there.

Wämöparken has grown in popularity in recent years. Many come here to grill, walk the dog, look at the animals or the beautifully preserved cultural-historical buildings.

These can be visited from mid-May and as long as the season allows, usually until Halloween, every day between 10-15 am.

Opposite the coffee house you can take the opportunity to play a game of chess. There is also a maze.

The hiking trail is suitable for wheelchairs and is well signposted.

* * *

Kalmar

The Main Attractions

Kalmar Castle
Old Town (Gamla Stan)
City Park (Stadsparken)
Krusenstiernsk Garden
Kalmar Cathedral
Kalmar Art Museum
Kalmara County Museum
The Warship *Kronan*
Maritime Museum

This is a charming city with cobblestone streets, historic buildings, parks, art galleries and gorgeous gardens. It is a town to wander in and soak up its character. It is also a thriving little town with a population of about 36,500 people, 9,000 of whom are students at the local university.

Surrounded by water, the city centre is located on the island of Kvarnholmen, so the air is always fresh. Several multinational companies are established here and there is a plethora of pubs, restaurants, shops and galleries.

The good news is also that Kalmar is an environmentally friendly place. There are bicycle lanes everywhere, garages have biogas pumps. Cars are increasingly hybrid, fuel-efficient or electrically driven. Street lights use low energy bulbs, and all new buildings must be insulated thermally with weatherproof windows.

Kalmar has experienced many difficult times over the ages, from sieges and wars to the plague and, more recently, economic challenges. The city has always attracted industry and Kalmar Verkstad used to make steam engines, trains and large machinery here. Unfortunately, the factory closed in 2005.

Similarly, the Kalmar Shipyard, founded in 1679, closed in 1981. A Volvo factory turned out cars of several models from 1974 until it closed in 1994.

All told, thanks to relocations and closures in the 1990s and in the first decade of the 21st century, some 2,000 people in industry lost their jobs – a considerable blow in a city of only 36,500 people.

Today, the city relies heavily on paper and sawmills, steel mills, aluminium plants, the building material industry, car manufacturing and shipyards.

The greater Kalmar area has been settled since the stone age and there is evidence of a town here from around 1050 AD during the Viking age. In the 12th century, defenders of the town built a round lookout tower as protection.

This was subsequently expanded and would later become the scene of many bloody sieges, not least because of its strategical location, with the Swedish-Danish border only a short distance to the south.

Kalmar's oldest city seal dates to the mid-13th century and it is thus the oldest known city seal in Scandinavia. It was here, on the 13th July, 1397 that the Swedish and

Norwegian heads of state signed the treaty that established the Kalmar Union, an arrangement that lasted 126 years until 1523.

The city's proximity to Denmark, the borders of which contained the provinces of Blekinge, Halland and Scania, led to several conflicts.

In 1505, King John of Denmark ordered the execution of the Mayor of Kalmar, its city councilors and several leading burghers who had been instrumental in helping the Swedes wrest the city from Denmark in 1503.

Later, in 1599, following the Battle of Stångebro, the Swedish regent Duke Charles deposed his nephew, the Polish-Swedish king, Sigismund III Vasa, as King of Sweden.

Duke Charles captured the city, seized *Kalmar Castle* and then ordered 22 of King Sigismund III Vasa's loyalists

to be beheaded or hanged, according to their status.

The victims that were beheaded included three Swedish noblemen, a priest, a chaplain and various governors. Such lesser mortals as custodians, mercenaries and secretaries were hanged.

Needless to say, there was no trial and as a demonstration of his power, Duke Charles ordered the heads of the beheaded to be placed on poles at the city gate. He eventually became King Charles IX of Sweden. Later, Kalmar residents would refer to these two incidents as the 'Kalmar Bloodbath'.

In the mid-16th century, King Gustav Vasa and his sons Erik XIV and John III of Sweden ordered Kalmar Castle to be extended and re-fortified, and it has not changed since that work was completed.

The castle was built not only as a fortification, but as a Renaissance palace, furnished and decorated in the continental fashion.

It also took centre stage in the bloody Kalmar War of 1611-1613, when the Danes besieged it. That was the first of many sieges during the Scanian War some 60 years later. All told, the castle was blockaded 22 times.

Kalmar's strategic importance later declined and when the King moved his naval base to Karlskrona, Kalmar ceased to be a major military centre.

The castle is open throughout the week. Opening times vary but are usually between 10am and 4pm and, from May until October until 6pm or 8pm. Tickets cost SEK 110 (£9.00, $11.80, €10.45) or SEK 95 (£7.75, $10.20, €9.00) for seniors.

In the immediate vicinity of the castle, the ***Old Town of Kalmar (Gamla Stan)*** (*pronounced Gamla Stahn*) is a great place for an afternoon stroll. Beautifully preserved 17th and

18th century wooden buildings, many painted in the famous deep red paint, *Falu Red,* in central Sweden, line the winding, cobbled streets.

As happened so often in medieval towns, in 1647, fire ripped through the Old Town, so the city council decided that the town should be moved in its entirety to the middle of Kvarnholmen Island.

The citizens were not particularly happy about it, but the councillors gradually pressured them into moving. Ironically, after the move, wealthier elements of the society moved back to the old site, where they built the summer houses that you see today.

Another pleasant way to spend time in Kalmar is to wander around the *City Park (Stadsparken),* established in 1880 and inspired by the romanticism of English parks.

Just a short distance from the castle, the park has many ancient and exotic trees and shrubs, including walnut and Caucasian wing nut trees, bamboos, and a temple tree.

From the City Park, at the junction of Kungsgatan and Stensövägen on is another delightful spot, *Krusenstiernska Garden.* This is a small garden filled with old fruit and

walnut trees, fruit shrubs, flowers, herbs and medicinal plants.

The main building, now a small museum, is a perfect example of how the lower aristocracy lived in the 19th century and is filled with artefacts from both Sweden and abroad.

These all belonged to the von Krusenstierna family who lived here from 1874 until the mid-20th century, when they bequeathed it to Kalmar County's memorial association and Kalmar City.

There is a small café selling freshly baked cakes and juices made from the berries and fruits in the garden. It is an ideal way to spend half an hour or so writing postcards home, especially in early summer when the apple blossom is in full bloom, its sweet scent wafting over the entire garden.

Additionally, the garden has some 200 walnut, cherry and plum trees. The garden is one of Sweden's 14 clone archives and is responsible for preserving the mandates (i.e. varieties of trees that have been named and spread locally) of apple, pear, gooseberry, white currant and other species.

The clone archives are part of the National Swedish Gene Bank.

In the event of inclement weather, the obvious places to visit are the Cathedral and museums.

Kalmar Cathedral (Kalmar Domkyrka) is located in the main square (*Stortorget)* and is one of the few buildings still in its original state from Sweden's period as a great power.

This is reflected in such interior furnishings and fixtures such as gravestones, epitaphs and the baroque altar, designed by Nikodemus Tessin the Younger in 1704.

Work on the Cathedral began in 1600 but progress was slow, thanks to the four-year Scanian war between 1675 and 1679. The Cathedral was eventually completed in 1703.

Kalmar Art Museum (Kalmar konstmuseum) located in the City Park (Slottsvägen) focuses on regional contemporary art 'related to people's future and the challenges of the region', according to its website. It adds that the museums goal 'is to be a meeting place for reflection, discussion and new impressions, to act as a voice in the public debate and to constitute a cultural engine in the Kalmar region.'

That may sound like gobbledygook, but it is a philosophy that has paid off. The museum's international profile has attracted considerable attention and the museum certainly counts as an interesting Swedish art institution.

Kalmar Art Museum sponsors lectures, talks about artists and talks by artists, as well as seminars related to exhibitions and projects.

A central part of the programme is educational and designed for children, young people and adults in a bid to further convey art and design to a wide audience.

The museum is closed on Mondays, open between 12am and 5pm on Tuesdays, Thursdays and Fridays, from 12-8pm on Wednesdays and 11am to 4pm at weekends. It costs SEK 50 (£4.05, $5.30, €4.72) for adults and SEK 40 (£3.25, $4.25, €3.78) for seniors. There is no charge on Fridays.

Kalmar county museum (Kalmar läns museum), housed in a former steam mill on Skeppsbrogatan, chronicles the history of Kalmar County and offers a variety of temporary and permanent exhibitions throughout the year, ranging from archaeology to the 'Cold War and Warm Everyday Life in Kalmar County 1946-1991'.

By far the most important exhibit, though, is the Swedish warship ***Kronan (The Crown)***, which sank off the south coast of the island of Öland in 1676.

Similar to the *Vasa* ship in Stockholm but twice as large, the wreck of the treasure ship, *Kronan* was discovered and salvaged in 1980 together with more than 30,000 artefacts and Sweden's largest ever trove of gold coins, some of them on display.

The exhibitions explain how, at noon on June 1, 1676, was hit by cannon shot during a battle between the Swedish and United Danish-Dutch fleet. The ship literally exploded and sank four miles (six kilometres) and in a depth of 88 feet (27 metres) off the village of Hulterstad on Öland's southeastern coast. It was one of the largest ship disasters in Swedish history with only 40 of the 850-crew surviving.

The sinking of Vasa in Stockholm harbour, however, was more embarrassing, given that the King signed off the design and that it was Vasa's maiden voyage, watched by ambassadors from all over Europe and most of the Swedish dignitaries of the time.

Some of *Kronan's* cannon are placed in the museum entrance, but on Level 3, there is a more detailed look at both cannon and some or the more exciting artefacts. Here you can also try to load one of the cannons – no easy task!

The gold treasure, part of the battery deck and a model of the wreckage give a clear indication of the ship's power and its tragic fate.

The museum cinema regularly shows film of the salvage work as it progressed. There is also a gift shop and a fourth-floor café selling good value meals, including a Swedish smorgasbord, with views of the harbour.

If it is raining outside, why not start lunch on the fourth floor and worked your way down from there? There are certainly worse ways to spend an afternoon!

The museum is open every day of the week between 10am and 4pm. From 25th June to 19th August, it remains open until 8pm on Wednesdays.

Another fascinating museum, especially for the nautically minded, is ***Kalmar Maritime Museum (Kalmar***

Sjöfartsmuseum), located next door to an old hot-bath house on Södra Långgatan. This somewhat quirky little gem contains approximately 3,000 nautical objects, from ship models to authentic exhibits of all kinds.

Shipping companies and individuals donate more artefacts every year.

The non-profit museum documents the entire 20th century shipyard history in Kalmar and it is now regarded as one of the most interesting of the country's smaller museums. It even smells of tar. Kalmar Maritime Museum opens at 11am until 4pm (12-4pm on Sundays and is well worth the extremely reasonable entrance fee of SEK 50 (£4.05, $5.30, €4.72), SEK 30 (£2.40, $3.20, €2.85) for seniors.

Finally, if you have been to Kalmar previously, you may want to rent a car and drive to the island of Öland across the four mile (six kilometre) long bridge.

Inaugurated in 1897, it was at one time the longest bridge in Europe, but now counts as the third largest following completion in 1998 of the Vasco da Gama bridge across the River Tagus in Lisbon and the bridge across the Öresund between Malmö and Copenhagen.

The Öland bridge, however, is still the longest bridge entirely within Swedish territory. It rests on 156 concrete pillars and took four and a half years to build. Construction workers used 100,000 cubic metres of concrete to do so.

And that takes us neatly to our next port of call, Borgholm, on the island of Öland!

* * *

Borgholm, Öland

The Main Attractions

Borgholm Castle	**90**
Solliden Palace	**91**
Borgholm Church	**92**
Vida Museum	**93**
Ölands Museum	**94**
Ismantorps Fortress	**94**

Covering an area of 520 miles (1,350 square kilometres) over a length of 85 miles (137 kilometres), Öland is mostly farm and agricultural land with long, white sandy beaches aplenty. It is not surprising then that the island is Sweden's most popular holiday resort.

Borgholm has only recently emerged onto the cruise ports of call, so very few ships have visited this historical 'city'. Technically, it is not a city because in Sweden, a town must have 10,000 citizens to reach that status.

However, it received its city charter in 1816, so even though it has only 3,100 inhabitants, officials still like to call it a city. That said, the Official Statistics Office in Stockholm continues to regard it a town.

In fact, it is not much more than a seaside holiday venue, highly popular with the Swedes who rent cottages or stay at one of the 25 extremely well organized campsites or holiday villages on the island during the summer months.

Lying 12 miles (20 kilometres) north of the Öland bridge, the town has a pleasant yacht harbour a cannon shot from the ruined **Borgholm Castle (Borgholm Slott)**, which succumbed to a fire in 1806. Fortunately, there is enough of it still standing to have become one of the island's main attractions.

This was one of the mightiest fortresses in Sweden and stands as a reminder that the island was on the frontline during the Swedish-Danish wars.

Dubiously described as 'the most beautiful castle ruins of Scandinavia', the size of the fortress is almost overwhelming. Built by King Karl X Gustav in the mid-17th century, it was home to many people over the centuries, but Karl X Gustav was the only Swedish king to live in it for any length of time.

He had a strong passion for food, women and war and it is said that his waist measured more than six feet (two metres)), which seems to prove the point about his eating habits but perhaps not so much about his women.

The people of Öland were not happy bunnies when he arrived with an entourage of about 500 hangers-on, not least because the people were required (forced is perhaps a better word) to serve them and provide them with supplies, which in the case of the King meant huge amounts of produce.

Today, the bare limestone walls are all that is left to remind us that centuries ago, it bristled with kings and their families, architects, bailiffs and watchmen, prisoners and guards, and craftsmen and women.

During the construction period, it was alive with masons, lime burners and mortar makers, carpenters, smiths and stone masons not to mention scaffolders, glaziers and painters. In its heyday, it would have been a magnificent symbol of Swedish military might. It also housed farmers, prisoners and soldiers, many of whom were not Swedish. Indeed, back then, there was more Danish and German spoken than Swedish. Today, Borgholm Castle is not only a tourist attraction, it is also a venue for concerts and major events throughout the year.

As Sweden's smallest city, Borgholm is considered to be the 'capital' of Öland, which is Sweden's second largest island after Gotland to the northeast. It is also a holiday home for the Swedish Royal Family, who come to the island each summer. They stay in their official summer residence, **Solliden Palace, (Sollidenslott),** an extensive Italian-style country house one-and-a-quarter miles (two kms) outside Borgholm.

Visitors to the palace's website are greeted with this message from the present King, Carl XIV Gustav:

"Welcome to the beautiful park of Solliden with its luxuriant trees, shrubs and flowers. Solliden is a part of our cultural heritage, which is of special concern to me. It was built by my great-grandmother, Queen Victoria, and was completed in 1906. When my great-grandfather, Gustav V, died in 1950, I inherited the palace. It is my intention to preserve Solliden, so that future generations will be able to enjoy its unique and glorious gardens.' Carl Gustav.

Carl Gustav is Sweden's 74th king and, all being well, he will be succeeded by Crown Princess Victoria, whose birthday is celebrated each year at Borgholm's Sports Ground and at Solliden.

In the early 1900s, Sweden's then future Queen Victoria suffered from poor health and desperately needed to get away from city life in Stockholm. She found that the climate on Öland provided not only peace of mind but that the climate alleviated her sickness. As Crown Princess, she had been active throughout the construction of the palace and was inspired by the Villa San Michele in Capri. She chose the location and the Swedish architects and building contractors.

When Victoria died in 1930, she bequeathed Solliden to her husband, King Gustav V and it was from him that it passed on to Carl Gustav. He and his family made the palace their private summer home and developed the public parts of the castle gardens. The present Queen Sylvia has also taken an interest in the gardens and has added new plants each year.

In the gardens, there is a pavilion, as well as Italian, English and Dutch gardens. There are open between 10th May to 31st August between 11am and 6pm. On Midsummer's Eve (21st June), the park closes at 2pm. In September, the park closes at 4pm with the last entry an hour earlier.

The entrance fee is SEK 120 (£9.80, $12.75, €11.35) or SEK 100 (£8.15, $10.60, €9.45) for seniors. Cash is no longer accepted.

Back in town, **_Borgholm Church_** in Östra Kyrkogata is worth a quick visit. It was consecrated in 1879, seven years after construction began.

The exterior, with its yellow walls and white buttresses, looks more like a mini town hall than a church, with a spire in the centre, the aisle in the east wing and the west wing having once been a school.

The parish built the west wing first, in 1872, and it was completed a year later. A lack of money meant that the parish had to wait another six years before the church was completed.

The exterior has not undergone any major changes since then. The original, neoclassical interior, however, was renovated in 1835 and re-decorated again in 1960-61.

Just outside Borgholm, the *Vida museum* is located at Halltorp, 7.5 miles (11 kilometres) south of Borgholm. The No 101 bus from Borgholm bus station to Kalmar stops at Halltorps Gård and leaves every half hour. The journey takes about 35 minutes.

Founded and designed by Barbro and Borge Kamras, who owned the museum from 2001 until 2015, it has a sizeable collection of contemporary art, comprising paintings, glass and sculptures as well as fashion, design, books, jewellery, posters, ceramics and graphics. Some say the glass collection is the best in Sweden.

The entire museum is curated with taste and attention to detail and the staff are friendly beyond measure. In 2015, the original owners handed over the museum to Hampus Vallien and Emilia Thor, who now curate it on a day to day basis.

The museum, which is also a venue for concerts, special events and weddings., is open from 10am until 3pm. Entry costs SEK 80 (£6.50, $8.50, €7.60).

Rather more difficult to get to is Halltorp, the location of *Öland's Museum*, located at Himmelsberga Bygata No.1, about 12 miles (20 kilometres) from Borgholm on Route 136. This is another pleasant open-air museum comprising a 'village' of carefully preserved buildings from the 18th and 19th centuries. Unfortunately, there appears to be no bus service there, which would mean hiring a taxi both ways or possibly hiring a car.

It is a good opportunity though, to see how people furnished their homes as most of the buildings have been left as they were when still lived in. Apart from the smallholdings, complete with preserved interiors, machinery, tools and equipment, there is also a sizeable art museum and several other exhibition buildings focusing on local crafts. There is a shop selling quality handcrafts, books, souvenirs, postcards and ice cream, and a café where you can sit outside or inside and enjoy the unique setting.

The museum is open at weekends from 10th May and daily from 1st June until August 31st between 11am and 5pm. The entrance fee is SEK 80 (£6.50, $8.50, 7.55)

Should you be able to find transport, it would be worth a quick visit to *Ismantorps Fortress*, in the centre of the island.

This is one of several ringforts on Öland and occupied for only a short time between about 200 BC and 650 BC. It comprises a limestone wall approximately 300 metres long. Inside are the ruins of 95 houses around a central open air.

There is no doubt that Borgholm is an attractive and charming town, but whether it catches on as a regular cruise port remains to be seen.

* * *

Visby, Gotland

The Main Attractions

Visby is one of the most attractive medieval cruise towns in Sweden and consequently attracts 90 cruise ships a year – equivalent to some 90,000 passengers. That is partly thanks to a new cruise terminal and a quay that can accommodate two cruise ships of up to 31,115 feet (40 metres) at the same time.

It is also because Visby and Gotland have a unique history. The island is the only place where you can find Viking picture stones and caches of Arab silver coins found on the island underline how important it was in Viking times in terms of trade.

Gotland's strategic position in the Baltic Sea transformed the island into a hive of trading activity, a natural hub between west and east.

A thousand years ago, Vikings left Gotland and Birka (in the Stockholm archipelago) for what are now the Baltic States and the entrances to the Russian river systems. These that allowed them to travel to markets as far east as Tashkent and Samarkhand, which lie on the same longitude as Kabul in Afghanistan.

These epic journeys made Gotland rich. Many traces of the Viking era, from rune stones to grave mounts remain visible to this day.

For photographers, Visby, with its Viking and Hanseatic history offers a picture at every turn, from the old city wall and maze of cobbled streets and alleyways to the ruins of hauntingly attractive 12th century churches. Not for nothing, is Visby a UNESCO World Heritage site.

The summer months are crowded but if you are lucky enough for your ship to dock during Medieval Week, you are in for a real treat.

At this time, residents and holidaymakers don historical costumes and the city is filled with Kings, Queens, knights and peasants enjoying a binge of wining, dining and dancing. Great fun!

Archeological evidence proves that people had settled where the city now stands as long ago as the Stone Age. Viking traders plying the Russian river routes had transformed the settlement into a flourishing town by 900AD.

With just under 25,000 inhabitants today, Visby - or at least its centre - is encircled by a city wall approximately two miles (3.4 kilometres) long.

Probably built in the mid-1100's, it was later raised to its present height. Builders added the towers some three centuries later.

By the end of the 12th century, the population had grown sufficiently to build *St. Mary's Cathedral*, which was consecrated in 1225, although it was not designated a Cathedral until 1572.

Over the years, the church was altered and extended to its current state with its red roofs, triple towers, wooden spires and baroque gables.

Several fires necessitated some changes to it, but these were relatively minor and around 1350, the church was enlarged and converted into a basilica.

Visby thrived principally thanks to the Hanseatic League, which was founded by merchant communities in northern Germany to protect their trading interests. For two centuries. the League dominated all trade in northern Europe, from the mid-1200s onwards.

Each time these traders visited the city, local councilors levied a fee on them. This eventually created a fund that paid not only for St. Mary's but also about a dozen other churches, all of which are now in ruins.

Originally, St. Mary's was intended specifically for use by the German traders. As time passed, however, many Germans settled permanently in Visby and the church eventually opened its doors to locally born residents, as well. As German was spoken as much as, if not more than,

Swedish, this required two priests, one for the Germans and one for the Swedes.

Today, St. Mary's is the only medieval church in Visby that is still in use. The Cathedral is well worth a visit with the carved wooden altar, spectacular stained-glass windows and more exquisite carvings in the chapels.

Visby continued to thrive as the Vikings brought more and more treasure from Arab lands to the city. Viking influence was extensive and foreign ambassadors and traders came to Visby (and Birka further north) frequently.

In the meantime, Valdemar IV of Denmark and his troops had been warring just about everybody in northern Europe and, by 1360, he had conquered the southern Swedish country of Skåne. Now, he wanted to extend his gains to incorporate Gotland and Visby.

In 1361, his army attacked the city and, in the ensuing battle outside the walls, slaughtered nearly 2,000 islanders.

Valdemar breached part of the wall and demanded that the city councilors fill three large beer barrels with silver and gold. Failure to do so, he warned, would result his soldiers sacking and plundering the town of all its wealth.

Literally over a barrel, the councilors denuded the churches of all their silver and other treasures.

Valdemar proclaimed himself King of Gotland and thus triggered a war with the Hanseatic League, of which Visby was a member.

Visby, however, remained Danish and for a while Valdemar benefited from the Baltic trade until the coalition defeated him in 1368.

After that, in the 1390s, pirates attacked the city several times. Teutonic knights destroyed the city in 1398 and, after guaranteeing peace with the Kalmar Union, sold Gotland to Margaret, the Union Queen.

From then on, Visby's fortunes faded. Pirates known as the Victual Brotherhood attacked Hanseatic ships and brought Hanseatic trade to a near standstill. Eventually the League annulled Visby's membership.

As if that was not enough, during a spat over the Danish throne in 1525, an army from Lübeck a leading member of the Hanseatic League, attacked Visby, set the city on fire and burned down three of its churches. The rest were closed after the Reformation so that by 1535 only St. Mary's church remained in service.

In 1645, the Swede's re-took Gotland and it remained in the doldrums for a long time. Worse, in the mid-18th century, the plague that had already savaged the populations of Karlskrona and Kalmar and now arrived in Visby, which suffered similar casualties.

Finally, in 1808, Russia attacked and captured Gotland, although the Swedes took it back a few months later. Not until the early 19th century, did Visby Harbour attract ships and commerce again.

Today, Gotland survives on agriculture, food processing, IT, some heavy industry and tourism.

The Tourist Office in Visby is located at No. 1 Donners Plats, next to Almedalsbibliotek (library) opposite to *Almedals Park,* which conveniently is usually the stopping off point for ships' shuttle buses.

Walk up the slight incline with the park on your left to the yellow houses, where you will find a yellow painted archway. This is the gateway to *The Old Town.*

Visby is a dream for those who like nothing more than to wander wherever their noses take them, ambling down narrow alleyways, diving into quaint shops and perhaps stopping for a cup of coffee at a roadside café and watching the world go by.

You could start by walking up the hill until you reach a shop called *(Akantus)* (opposite a small square and yellow building with a sign saying 'Kranku'). Over the centuries, local Visby people built a monastery, a church and the Town Hall

in the main square, *Stora Torget,* and used it for markets and entertainment.

In summer, tourists make a beeline for it. The square is lined with outdoor restaurants and cafes, and sometimes a small market. A much larger market took place in the autumn and at Christmas, residents dance round the Christmas tree and pause for breath at stalls selling hot *glögg,* a warming Swedish mulled wine.

Dominating the square is the imposing ruin of *Sankta Karin's Church,* the first Franciscan monastery founded in Sweden in 1233. The friars began building the church in the 1250s, a task that continued until 1391.

It had large stained-glass windows, seven altars and an organ that was installed in 1404, making St. Karin's the richest Church in Gotland.

In winter, the ruins are a popular venue for children who go there to skate on an artificial ice rink inside the walls.

A five-minute walk from St. Karin's ruins are the remains of another medieval church, that of *St. Nicolai.* In 1226. Dominican friars, also known as the 'Black Friars', arrived in Visby and, four years later, they built St. Nicolai's monastery. This was one of many churches destroyed by the Lübeck army in 1525. Its most distinctive feature is its large rose window.+

Perhaps the most interesting way of delving into Gotland and Visby's history is to visit the *County Museum of Gotland* on Strandgatan (No 14). It's a great starting point and attracts some 250,000 visitors each year. Founded in 1875 by Association of Gotland Friends, it comprises

Gotland's Art Museum, Fornsalen (the Museum of Cultural History), Visby ruins and three museum farms.

In **Fornsalen,** you can see the 'hedgehog girl' from the Stone Age, Viking picture stones unique to Gotland, Viking

age silver jewellery and such other treasures as church sculptures, medieval armour from the Danish invasion of 1361 and a great deal more. Gotland, it seems, was created on a coral reef and in Fornsalen you can follow the lives of people who lived on the island 9,000 years ago.

The Fornsalen Museum, which has a café, is open daily from 10 am until 6 pm. There are guided tours at 11am Monday-Friday.

Admission is SEK 150 (£12.20, $16.20, €14.30 June-August) and SEK 100 (£8.15, $10.80, €9.50 Sept-May)

Gotland Art Museum (Konstmuseet) located at St. Hansgatan 21, comes under the Gotland Museum umbrella and stages permanent and temporary exhibitions, the latter mostly displaying contemporary art, applied art and design. These may be local, national or international.

The permanent exhibitions on the top floor display works by different artists whose work focused on Visby and Gotland.

The Art Museum is open at different times according to the months of the year. In June and July, when most cruise ships arrive, it is open daily from 10am until 6pm. At other times of year, it opens at 1200 and closes at 4pm except for Thursdays when it remains open until 8pm.

The admission price is SEK80 (£6.50, $8.60, €7.60).

For anyone – and Americans particularly – who has roots in Gotland, the Svahnströmska Room will be of special interest as it contains the museum archives and reference library.

These tell the story of Gotland and Visby through photographs and documents relating to farms and real estate, people and archaeological reports, inventories, newspaper articles and maps.

This is open from 1pm until 4pm Tuesday-Thursdays. Entry is free.

For those with a scientific bent, the *Phenomenal Science Museum (Fenomenalen),* offers 'something for everyone' – from three-year olds to the 72-year-old, according to its website, which adds: 'Challenge each other in games and cope with cunning problems together… Examine the lifting force in the wind tunnel and discover how your brain can trick you. All that and much more you can do with us.'

Some people may feel that the exclusion of everyone over the age of 72 is not only arrogant but also an insult to those passengers who are of a certain age. It may come as a surprise to the curators that they have not all been gathered or gone ga-ga yet!

The museum is open between 12 and 4pm Thursday and Fridays, and 11am to 4pm at weekends. Admission is SEK 70 (£5.70, $7.55, €6.70).

Visby's *City Wall* is arguably the most invincible, longest and best-preserved medieval city wall in Scandinavia. Originally 2.2 miles (3.5 kilometres) long but now slightly

shorter, it had 51 towers. Of these 36 remain (27 large and 9 small). Construction began in the mid-1200s with a defensive tower known as Kruttornet *(The Gunpowder*

Tower), at the entrance to what was then the harbour and which now is Almedalen Park.

Work on the wall itself did not begin until the 1270s and most of the towers were built at the end of the 13th and beginning of the 14th centuries.

This was a period when disputes arose between the people of Visby and the Gotland Assembly eventually leading to a civil war in 1288.

The mere fact that residents felt it necessary to build a city wall points to the commercial importance of Visby at the time. Stockholm and Kalmar were the only other Swedish cities enclosed by a defensive wall.

Maybe the curators of the 'Phenomenal' Science Museum believe that the over-72s are better off wandering around the **Botanic Gardens** where they can come to no harm.

Certainly, the gardens lie along the beach just to the north of the Gunpowder Tower and Almedalen Park and are worth a visit, not least in Spring when the city wall protects them from storms and salt spray, and they are ablaze with flowers.

Visby has temperate, if not an almost Mediterranean climate, which means that many unusual trees, shrubs and plants grow well there.

Some of the more exotic trees include the tulip tree, empress tree, Pride of India tree and the handkerchief tree, into which we oldies can cry into, having been excluded from the enjoyment of the Phenomenal Museum.

The leafy Botanical gardens are not large – just six acres (two and a half hectares) but the combination of plants, trees, open lawns and pleasant pathways make them a tranquil and very beautiful place to visit.

Even better, they are always open and there is no entrance fee!

* * *

Nynäshamn

The Main Attractions

Hamnbodar
Sjötelegrafen (Marine Telegraph)
Nynäshamn Church
Nynäs Havsbad (Sea Bathing)
Strandvägen
Lövhagens Reacreational Area
Ångbryggeriet (Steam Brewery)
House of Chocolate
Mopedum Nostalgia Museum
Railway Museum

Cruise ships tend to use Nynäshamn *(pronounced Knee-ness-hamn)* as an alternative port for Stockholm, an hour's train journey away, probably because it is almost certainly cheaper.

Nynäshamn is an anchor port, but there is a 250 metre (273 yard) extendable floating pier that connects with cruise ships directly, making it possible to disembark and walk into town. This is retracted when the ship leaves.

Surrounded by beautiful countryside and several thousand islands in its archipelago, Nynäshamn is an attractive, vibrant town that is home to some 13,500 souls, of whom approximately 5,000 are non-Swedes.

There are not many attractions in terms of castles, churches, museums and so on, but for passengers not planning to go to Stockholm, Nynäshamn is a pleasant place in which to spend a day.

It is known principally for its summer homes, seaside hotels, spas and sailing centres. During the 1912 Olympic Games, the sailing events were held here in what are still among Sweden's best sailing waters.

However, Nynäshamn is unquestionably a small provincial town and like many others, exudes charm. A mini-village of chalets known as **Hamnbodar** (lit: harbour stores), comprises enticing shops, cafes and restaurants painted in the traditional Swedish Falu red colour. It is a great place to amble round, stop for a Swedish *fika* (coffee, buns and or cake) and generally relax after meandering round the marina.

Until 1900, Nynäshamn was a town known mainly for its spas, most of which have now closed. It did not become remotely significant until construction began on the railway to Stockholm in 1901.

After that, more people came, the population grew, the harbour expanded into a port and that in turn attracted commerce and industry. Today, it is also a ferry port for Gotland and Gdańsk in Poland.

The modern part of the town is pleasant but not in any way noteworthy. Most Swedes live in apartment blocks, none higher than ten storeys and there are many detached villas dotted around the town and countryside. So, it is a tranquil, relaxing port of call, ideal for walking along the promenade, around the harbour and enjoying the fresh, sea air. That means that there is also plenty of time to see the few attractions on offer.

A short distance from the extended cruise ship pier is a shopping centre known as **Sjötelegrafen** *(lit: Marine Telegraph),* telecommunications workshops from 1910 until 1980. This is useful if you don't feel like walking or taking a shuttle bus into town.

There are two ways to see both the town and its surrounding countryside. Firstly, you can rent a bike. These can be picked up at and returned to the Tourist Information Office at the cruise ship pier or at the Tourist Centre in the Fishing Harbour.

Prices include a helmet. There are 14 28-inch bikes available as well as four 26-inch bikes, two 24-inch and two 22-inch bikes. Prices are SEK 60 (£4.90, £6.50, €5.75) for two hours or SEK 150 (£12.20, $16.25, €14.35) for a day.

The pier is also the starting point for the Hop on, Hop Off bus, which stops in about ten carefully selected places. The guided tour takes just under an hour and is undoubtedly the best way to see the town and surrounding countryside and archipelago.

You can buy tickets at the Visitor Centre (at Fiskegränd No.5). Please note that you can only use Visa, MasterCard, American Express or Diners to purchase the tickets, which cost SEK 100. ((£8.15, $10.80, €9.50).

The second stop (the pier counts as the first) is at the Visitors Centre, which is a three-block walk from the city centre and **Nynäshamn Church**, completed in 1930 and overlooking the town from its cliff top site.

There was once a lighthouse on the site and mariners still reference the church as a navigational aid.

The third stop on the Hop On, Hop Off bus is *Nynäs Havsbad (Sea bathing)*. The website describes it as a 'health resort for the soul!' After lying dormant for nearly 80 years, the spa re-opened in 2003. With wonderful sea views, it is a place for relaxation and well-being.

Oddly, perhaps, it offers not only views, 'culinary experiences', spa treatments and superb bathing facilities but also a cigar room, which you might feel is not quite as healthy as the other items on offer.

Nynäs Havsbad lies at the southern tip of an island called Trehörningen (meaning 'three-cornered island'*)* and became a seaside resort in the early 1900s, when there were several large hotels, cold baths and a casino.

Once frequented by royalty and Swedish celebrities, *Nynäs Havsbad* is arguably Sweden's most exclusive spa with a unique location on the water looking out to the horizon. Here, you can relax in the spa and enjoy a two-course lunch with a fantastic view of the archipelago. Or just wander around for an hour checking out the luxurious holiday villas.

Trehörningen was first mentioned in the 1780s when it was just a farm. Not until the early 1900s did it benefit from the railway connection to Stockholm and become an offshore island for holiday villas and a health resort.

Those early – and wealthy – holidaymakers arrived to enjoy the archipelago with its granite skerries and rocks dotting the waterways. Today, the island consists mainly of landscaped gardens but is still only accessed by boat, a pedestrian bridge or Oscars Bridge, which was built to allow vehicles to cross to the island.

Next, the Hop On, Hop Off bus doubles back on itself and once back on the mainland heads south along **_Strandvägen_,** a narrow, wooded coast road that has become increasingly popular as a tourist attraction in its own right, offering as it does some lovely views of the fjord.

Stop No. 3. is at Hembygdsgården but there is not much to see here – just a restaurant which, judging by the reviews on TripAdvisor is not especially noteworthy.

Stop No.4. is the tour's southernmost point, **_Lövhagens recreational area_** and café. This is a favourite picnic spot for the local people with forests, grassy meadows and both rocky and sandy beaches.

Swedes always say: 'There is nothing like a Swedish summer' and they are right; when the sun shines, places like this are sublimely beautiful.

Lövhagen means 'The leafy meadow' and here there are any number of walking, cycling or jogging trails. Sitting on the smooth granite rocks sunbathing for a while is to enter the Swedish summer world.

In the woodland, you may see here you may see deer, elk, mink, fox or even wild boars, and pick blueberries and mushrooms (if you know what you are doing!) or fish from the rocks and grill your catch on one of the barbecues provided. There is also a café where you can _fika_ or have a light lunch.

Even a short stay here, an hour perhaps, will explain better than any words what is meant by Sweden's 'Affinity with Nature'.

Next, the Hop On, Hop Off bus drives through the woodlands back to town via a different route, stopping at the town centre. Stop No. 7 is where you would get off if you wanted to see *Nynäshamns Ångbryggeri (Steam Brewery)*, located at Lövlundsvägen No.4. The owners started to brew beer here in 1997 and have since won several national prizes. On a short tour, a guide explains the basics of beer brewing, and discusses the issues micro-brewers face in Sweden where a couple large brewers have a semi-monopoly.

Steam beer was invented about 150 years ago in California, probably during the gold rush. It is extremely effervescent and is made by fermenting the yeast used to make lager without refrigeration and at a warmer temperature used to ferment ale yeast.

For those who love their beers, there is a small outdoor patio where you can sample a dozen or so of the different brews.

If beer is not your choice nourishment, the *Chokladhuset (The House of Chocolate)* at Hamngatan No 5, may appeal. This is the only bakery in Sweden chosen to produce the special Nobel Nightcap Party praline. The shop also offers truffles, chocolate bars, marzipan, cakes and much more.

Stop No. 7 is also where you will find the somewhat quirky *Mopedum (The Swedish Nostalgia Museum)* at Vikingavägen 39.

As the name suggests, this is a museum for mopeds, but it is more than that. It is also a fun and nostalgic way of getting an insight into Swedish history between 1952 and 1979.

It is in a great setting and displays toys, household goods and many more fascinating objects showing how society changed over the years. The curators have given great attention to detail with an engaging narrative following the life of a couple through the three decades.

The café is also 'strewn with nostalgic set pieces', as one TripAdvisor contributor put it.

The museum is closed on Mondays but open from 11am to 4pm daily including Sundays except for national holidays. There is a lift to accommodate wheelchairs. The entry fee is a relatively modest SEK70 (£5.70, $7.60, €6.70) with an SEK 10 discount for oldies.

Nynäshamns Jarnvagsmuseum (Railway Museum) at Nickstabadesvägen No. 9, which is about 200 metres from the railway station. It contains five steam and six diesel locomotives with accompanying passenger carriages and goods wagons.

These were all built after 1900, when the museum was founded. A year later, local officials inaugurated the line from Stockholm.

Unfortunately, the area is not suitable for wheelchairs or those who need Zimmer frames (strollers). This is because the buildings are listed and cannot therefore be changed in any way.

The museum also serves as a workshop and can be very busy, with some items not in their usual places.

Opening times are every Sunday from 1pm to 4pm in July and August, and at other times of the year (apart from December and January) at the same time on the last Sunday of the month. The entry fee is a modest SEK 20 (£1.60, £2.15, €1.90).

Stop No. 9 on the Hop On, Hop Off bus is at Malmtorget, but there is nothing much there apart from half a dozen shops, so if you need to go shopping, Stop No. 10 takes you to the Sjötelegrafen Shopping centre. From there it is a 10 minute walk back to the Cruise pier, which is also the final stop for the Hop On, Hop Off bus.

Whatever you do in Nynäshamn, have a great day!

* * *

Stockholm

The Main Attractions

Old City *	14,120	Grand Hotel	125
Riddarholm Church	120	Strandvägen	126
City Hall	14-16	Djurgårds Bridge	127
Royal Palace *	121	Vasa Museum *	127
Opera House	122	Abba Museum *	127
Sergels Torg	123	Nordic Museum *	128
Hötorget	123	Gröna Lund	128
Concert Hall	123	Skansen *	128
Royal Dramatic Theatre	124	Rosendals Palace	132
National Museum *	124	Milles Sculpture Garden *	135
Af Chapman	124-5	Drottningholm Palace *	136
Modern Art Museum*	125		

* Top Attractions

Stockholm is probably more deserving of the ubiquitous label 'Venice of the North' than any other capital that claims it, built as it is on 14 islands that are stunningly beautiful in summer or winter. This is a fabulous city from every perspective, whether it be parks, museums, shopping, attractions, history or culture. Stockholm has it all!

With a population of just under one million in the city itself and 1.5 million including its suburbs, it lies at the junction of the Baltic Sea and Lake Mälaren, which with an area of 440 square miles (1,140 square kilometres) makes it the third largest lake in Sweden.

Sailing into the city through Stockholm archipelago, a cluster of some 30,000 islands, skerries and rocks, is one of the truly great voyages as your ship passes within a stone's throw of luxury villas and tiny holiday cottages  perched on granite, grass and tree-laden islands and islets.

Most ships dock at about 8 a.m. which means you can either get up at 6am to enjoy the early morning light as you sail through the archipelago or sleep on and enjoy the sailaway in the late afternoon/early evening. In both cases you will have the sun behind you.

Ships berth in one of three places. Larger ships usually dock at Frihamnen (The Free Port although anything but as far as port fees are concerned). Some, however, tie up on the southern side of town. Smaller ships, if they are lucky, can dock on the edge of Gamla Stan (The Old Town).

Passengers should be aware that Stockholm is a quite large city with far too many attractions for a one-day stay. Indeed, it is a city in which you could easily spend a long weekend or four days and still not see it all.

Primitive people are believed to have settled in the Stockholm area as long ago as 8,000 BC, but it was not until about 1000 AD that Vikings settled there.

One suggestion is that they arrived from Sigtuna, a small town north of Stockholm on the banks of Lake Mälaren, which is actually not a lake but part of the Stockholm archipelago, albeit linked only by an extremely narrow channel.

In those days, Sigtuna was an important trading centre, especially for the iron ore industry further north. Consequently, pirates plying the Baltic Sea, the Gulf of Bothnia and the inland waterways realized it offered rich takings.

In 1187, they pillaged the town and burnt it down, leaving the Viking residents homeless and without food or sustenance.

For this reason, legend has it that they loaded their few remaining belongings into dug out logs and decided to settle wherever the winds and tides took them.

They apparently made land on the small island of what today is known as Riddarholmen, just opposite the Town Hall.

The Swedish word for log, incidentally, is 'stock' and it is suggested that this is how Stockholm was named ('holm' meaning islet'). Another suggestion is that 'stock' derived from the German word meaning fortification.

It is a good yarn and may or may not be true. What is true is that Stockholm is mentioned in 1252 in a collection of sagas called *Heimskringla* about Swedish and Norwegian kings. These, the oldest chronicles in Sweden, are written in rhyme and state that Stockholm was founded by the Swedish ruler Birger Jarl.

In the latter years of the 13th century, Birger Jarl invited German merchants to the city in order to strengthen the trade between Lake Mälaren and the Baltic sea.

The King sanctioned tariff free trade with the Germans and allowed them to settle if they so wished, provided that they obeyed the law and integrated with the Swedes.

Mostly they did, but at one stage between 1364 and 1389, the Germans took control of the city and introduced German as the official language.

After that, the German influence waned although traces of it exist even today. One could speculate that Birger Jarls' decision to trade with the Germans was the reason the Swedes remained neutral – with a large proportion of the population pro-German – during the Second World War.

By 1400, Stockholm was the largest city in Sweden. That said, it would be another 100 years before the population grew to more than 5,000 souls.

These, of course, were violent times. In 1519, the Danes invaded Sweden and a year later captured Stockholm and executed 80 Swedish nobles for heresy. However, the Swedish King, Gustav Vasa re-captured the town in 1523.

Under Gustav Vasa's rule, Sweden evolved into a major power, its reach extending across Finland, the Baltic States and into Poland. Indeed, you can visit the old parts of Warsaw (rebuilt after the Second World War) and easily imagine yourself in the Old Town of Stockholm, such is the similarity of architecture and design.

By the 17th century, Stockholm's population had grown to some 50,000 people. This was somewhat depleted by an outbreak of the plague, which had spread from southern Sweden between 1710 and 1712.

Nonetheless, the capital flourished throughout the 18th century and in the 19th century evolved from a largely agricultural country into an industrial one.

As Sweden remained neutral in the Second World War, Stockholm remained undamaged by bombing, but in the 1960s, the city fathers decided to embark on a modernization programme.

They ordered large sections of the Old town (Gamla Stan) to be torn down and replaced with skyscrapers, modern apartment s and shopping centres. At the time, it was seen as an unforgiveable act, but in retrospect probably a good decision.

Today, Stockholm is the cultural, political and economic centre of Sweden. The greater Stockholm area alone accounts for more than one-third of the country's GDP. Unusually, approximately 85% of Stockholm residents work in the service industry. There is very little heavy industry. Instead, the focus today is increasingly on the high-tech and IT industries.

Since the 1960s, tourism has become increasingly important. In 1963, the first cruise ship appeared and hundreds of people turned out to see it. The newspapers splashed the story, noting that it was the most luxurious ship in the world.

The cost of the cruise was said to be between 6,000 and 8,000 dollars (an absolute fortune in those days). Almost all the male American passengers remained on board their ship playing poker, while the women stepped ashore and immediately wanted to know 'where can we buy Swedish glass'.

The answer, then, was at NK, the main shopping store, not far from *Gamla Stan (The Old City*).*

The oldest surviving building in Stockholm is *Riddarholmen Church,* a former monastery built in the late 1200s more or less on the spot where the Sigtuna refugees landed in 1187-88.

It is the last resting place of the Swedish monarchs and aristocracy, including Gustaf II Adolf, Karl CII, Gustav V and their consorts, although today, it is no longer used as a royal burial site.

Gamla Stan*, previously mentioned in the opening chapter, is one of the largest and best-preserved medieval city centres in Europe and arguably the most popular attraction in Stockholm.

Lined with buildings painted in warm yellow and rich ochres, it has a unique ambience. The cobblestone streets are

sometimes so narrow that you can touch the walls with outstretched arms. One alley is only 35 inches (90 centimetres) wide!

Quaint shops display curios. antiques, handicrafts and souvenirs. Restaurants occupy ancient cellar vaults with walls adorned with frescoes.

Away from the main squares in the Old Town, there is an air of magical tranquility as you wander through the maze of pedestrian streets. This is an artist's heaven, a drawing or painting at every corner.

Gamla Stan, Stockholm

Across the water from Riddarholmen is the **City Hall (Stadshuset)***, also previously described in the opening chapter. A short, five-minute walk from the church is the **Royal Palace (Kungliga Slottet)***, which boasts no fewer than 600 rooms on 11 storeys, one of the largest palaces in Europe.

This is the King's official residence and venue for most of the monarchy's official receptions.

However, none of the members of the Royal Family live there, although they do all work there.

Designed by Nicodemus Tessin and based on the design of a Roman palace, it is in a baroque style and is home to three museums.

These comprise the Tre Kronor Museum which focusses on the palace's medieval history, the Treasury with the royal regalia and Gustav III's Museum of Antiquities.

The palace was built in the early 18th century on the site of the previous Royal Palace, Tre Kronor, which was destroyed by fire in 1697.

Apart from being the King's official residence, the palace is open to the public year-round – from 10am to 4pm on Tuesday to Sunday in October-April and 10am – 5pm April-September.

The Royal Apartments open at 9am July-August., although they may be closed if an official reception taking place. Admission is SEK 160 (£13.10, $17.35, €15.30).

Across the Norrbro bridge from the Palace is the *Opera House,* which was founded by King Gustav III and saw its first performance in January 1773, the first opera ever performed in Swedish.

The building also houses Operakällaren (The Opera Cellar Restaurant), which is the absolute best place to go if you want fine dining in a lavish setting. On Sundays, the restaurant offers arguably the best example of a true Swedish smörgåsbord anywhere.

The Opera House, one of the terminals stops for shuttle buses, lies on the southwest corner of *Kungsträdgården,* a rectangular park lined with restaurants that are mostly ,but not all, touristy.

In winter, a large section of the park is transformed into an open-air ice rink in winter.

Walk to the 'top' end, turn left and you come to *NK (Nordiska Kompaniet),* a venerable 1915 department store known locally as 'N-Kaw) and the main shopping area of Stockholm.

If you continue walking past Regeringsgatan, you will come to **Sergels Torg,** nicknamed 'Plattan', which means 'The Platform'. This is a large public square with a sunken pedestrian shopping area and the **Kulturhuset (House of Culture).**

In recent years, this area has become a place of drug trading and beggars. The police recently evicted 50 of them and continue to police the area continuously.

If you continue to walk up the pedestrianized Sergelsgatan you will come to **Hötorget (Haymarket)** and the famous neoclassical Stockholm **Concert Hall**, on the

steps of which is an equally famous 1936 bronze statue **The Orpheus Well** by Karl Milles, the Swedish Sculptor.

The five skyscrapers in Hötorget mark the beginning of the area of the Old Town that was ripped down in the early 1960s in order to modernize the city centre. Today, it continues to be a marketplace and is lined with outdoor restaurants in summer.

The building with the legend 'Haymarket' was where the Hollywood star, Greta Garbo, first worked as a shop assistant before she was discovered and became so famous, that she was almost forced into becoming a recluse.

Ingrid Bergman, Max von Sydow and Ingmar Bergman all made their names at *The Royal Dramatic Theatre* at the junction of Birger Jarlsgatan and Strandvägen. Commonly known as *'Dramaten'*, the theatre was founded in 1788 and is Sweden's National Theatre.

The current art nouveau building has been the theatre's home since 1909 and is remarkable because it has not one, but five separate stages. The main theatre seats nearly 800 theatregoers.

Not far away on the Blasieholmen peninsula is the newly-furbished *National Museum**, which stages both permanent and temporary exhibitions of paintings, drawings, prints and sculpture ranging from 1500 until 1900, and includes works by Rubens, Rembrandt, Goya and other leading international and Swedish artists of the time.

A collection of applied arts and design covers the late Medieval period until the present day.

The museum is closed on Mondays, but open from 11am -7pm daily including Sundays and from 11-9pm on Thursdays. The museum restaurant, bar and café open at the same times but serving stops one hour before closing time.

The museum is also closed on Easter Monday and Midsummer's Day, which suggests staff might be suffering hangovers from the revelries of Midsummer's Eve!

Admission costs are SEK 150 £12.25, $16.25, €14.35) and for seniors SEK 120 (£9.80, $13.00, €11.45). Free admission for visitors under 20 years. Cross over the bridge called Skeppsholmsbron and you will see the three-masted ship, *Af Chapman.* Built at

Whitehaven in Cumbria, England and launched in 1888 as the *Dunboyne*, she sailed to ports in Europe, America and Australia.

Originally Irish owned she was sold first to a Norwegian company and then a Swedish shipping company, who in turn sold her on to the Swedish Navy. The Navy, who used her as a training ship re-named her *af Chapman* after a Swedish admiral. She made several voyages around the world under Navy command. Her last voyage was in 1934.

Having reached her sell-by date as far as the Navy were concerned, the Stockholm City Museum rescued her from the knacker's yard and in 1949 the Swedish Tourist Board took responsibility for her. Today, the ship is a youth hostel with a capacity of 285 beds.

Close by, still on the islet of Skeppsholmen, is the **Modern Art Museum (Moderna Museet)*** at Exercisplan No.4. Here, you will find modern and contemporary art both Swedish and international, including key works by the most prominent artists of the 20th and 21st centuries from Popova, Dardel, Gerhard Richter and Francis Bacon to Andy Warhol, Dali, Picasso and many more.

The artworks - paintings, prints, photographs, films and videos as well as textiles and performance art - are changed and reinstalled continuously. The museum is open every day except Monday from 10am until 5pm or later, depending on the day. Admission is free.

A great place for a break is at the **Grand Hotel,** as all the attractions mentioned so far are in the western areas of Stockholm (Norrmalm and Gamla Stan). The Grand Hotel,

at the beginning of Strandvägen, separates them for the rest of the main attractions, which lie in the eastern half of the city. To sit in the Verandah Café over a coffee and cake, or a light lunch watching the ferry boats plying back and forth is pure joy.

When I first arrived in Stockholm in 1958 practically penniless, I borrowed a bicycle because I didn't have enough money for the tram fare into town (they had trams everywhere in those days).

Unfortunately, the chain broke and being December, it began to snow. The temperature was about minus 10° Centigrade and I did not have an overcoat. It was freezing and I recall standing outside the Grand, looking at people having lunch in the Verandah and swearing that, one day, I would stay in the hotel and eat there.

Not until 20 years later did that dream come true, when my wife and I flew to Stockholm for my son's graduation. Happily, we secured the last room in the hotel.

Refreshed but hopefully not replete, you could do worse than to wander along **Strandvägen***, a wide, tree-lined avenue leading to the island of Djurgården (*lit: animal garden)* that is arguably one of the most beautiful boulevards in all Stockholm.

In 1861, the king gave permission for its construction to go ahead to replace what formerly was a muddy roadway alongside a rotting wooden quay. The stipulation was that it should be better than any other concourse in Europe and be completed in time for a major arts and crafts exhibition due to be held in Djurgården in 1897.

On one side of the boulevard, you can admire the magnificent architecture and palatial mansions, mostly built between 1885 and the early 1900s, some in the Jugend style, others inspired by French chateaux.

On the waterfront side, the floating cafés and boats moored along the quayside are endlessly fascinating. Back in the 1960s, I almost signed onto one boat here as navigator with a skipper planning to sail round the world.

He was fortunate that in the end I didn't do so, as a couple of years later, I was navigating at night with a friend who had a fishing boat in Oslo. I took two bearings on what I thought were two fixed points and gave him the course.

Fortunately, we discovered at the last minute, just before we hit some rocks, that one of the bearings was from the light of a moving boat.

Strandvägen ends at **Djurgårdsbron,** an ornate bridge adorned with statues of various Nordic gods that leads to the island of Djurgården.

This is the site of the now famous ***Vasa Museum*,*** considered to be one of the top ten museums in the world. The opening chapter of this book, *An Affinity with Nature*, tells the story of the Vasa, how it sank and how it was finally salvaged after lying for 333 years on the bottom of the harbour.

Djurgården is also the site of the ***Abba Museum*,*** the slogan of which is 'Walk In and Dance Out'. Essentially, the museum tells the story of the group's formation and how, in 1974, they eventually won the Eurovision song contest with their song 'Waterloo'.

The exhibits include the clothes the four Swedes wore, the instruments they played, their mixing console and a plethora of other memorabilia.

Unusually, the museum also invites visitors to sing and dance along with the group – re-incarnated in the form of a hologram. The visitor thus effectively becomes the fifth member of the group. The museum staff record your performance, which you can download it from the museum website later.

In the near vicinity, The **Nordiska Museet (Nordic Museum)** * is often overlooked. This is the largest museum of cultural history in Sweden.

It covers the lifestyle of Nordic peoples in the past, the present and potentially the future with exhibits of the clothes they wore, the fashions of the day. textiles and jewellery, home furnishings, toys, folk art, glass and porcelain, not forgetting photography.

There is also an exhibition about the indigenous Sami people and reindeer herders of Sweden. The museum is open every day

Just south of the Abba Museum is **Gröna Lund,** an ever-expanding amusement park in which several concerts are held throughout the year by Swedish and international artists.

The park has some 30 rides that are either fast, whirly, thrilling or high. There is even a 'House of Nightmares' although why you would want to see that when you have just been on a fast, whirly and high ride is anybody's guess.

Admission is SEK 120 (£9.80, $13.00, €11.50) and free if you are more than 65 years old and in need of an adrenalin rush. The main attraction – other than museums – is

Skansen, said to be the world's oldest open-air museum.

Here, there are imported houses, farmsteads and churches from

every corner of Sweden, some decorated with original peasant paintings.

Here you can discover how Swedes once lived according to the changing seasons, through the customs and traditions, work, celebrations and everyday life of times gone by.

Festive events take place throughout the year. These include singing, dancing and concerts in the summer and, in the winter, Christmas markets with dancing round the Christmas tree and special concerts at the Seglora Church.

Not only is Skansen an historical venue, it also claims to be the world's only open-air museum with wild animals. I suspect other similar open-air parks might contest the claim, however.

That said, Skansen probably has more examples of Nordic wildlife, rare breeds and other exotic creatures. A smaller, children's zoo is home to several domestic animals such as cats, rabbits and guinea pigs as well as some smaller wild animals.

The good news is that all these animals are in quite large enclosures apart from the seals in the *Skansen Aquarium.* Another feature is the *Our Africa* enclosure in which there are monkeys, birds, reptiles and insects.

There is also a park area with a wide diaspora of plants and gardens, while the *Skåne Farmstead* and the *Skogaholm Manor* both have large and historic kitchen gardens containing the kinds of plants grown in their time.

In a way, Skansen is a little like a time machine, transporting visitors from the early 1700s up to the present day. In all the houses, workshops and shops, there are people

wearing authentic costumes of the day to explain what life was like in the 'good old days'.

Skansen is a large area and with restaurants and cafés available, you could easily spend an entire day there. There are several entrances all of them open from 10am. The park remains open from 10am until 1600 in April, until 6pm in June and 8pm in July and August.

Ticket prices are dependent on the time of year and vary from SEK 125 (£10.0, $13.50,€11.95) in January to SEK 140 (£11.45, $15.10, €13.35) February-May, up to SEK 170 (£13.90,$13.35, €16.25) in May SEK 195 (£15.90, $21.05, €18.60) in June and SEK 220 (£18.00, $23.75, €21.00) June 21st to August 18, when the prices gradually diminish as ach month passes.

Given the huge variety of what is on offer, the prices are quite reasonable when compared with other museum prices elsewhere in Scandinavia. And it is a good day out, with great views of the Stockholm skylines!

Gamla Stan as seen from Skansen

Gröna Lund and Skansen account for approximately one-third of the island of Djurgården. The rest of the island is parkland, much of it woodland with a few scattered houses.

To walk along the waterside pathways is a wonderfully peaceful way of spending an hour or so, especially on a sunny day, when the Swedes rightly claim there is 'No summer like a Swedish summer'. Mind you, that idea is probably spawned from the awful, long dark winters!

In the centre of Djurgården, ***Rosendals Palace och Trädgård (Rosendals Palace and Garden)*** are one of the best ways of avoiding the bustling city and (possibly) other cruise passengers. This is the ideal place to get away from it all.

The Palace, one of the eleven royal palaces, is largely unchanged since it was built between 1823 and 1827 for King Karl Johan, the first Bernadotte King of Sweden.

Despite being built in the European Empire style with mahogany furniture, wall to wall carpeting and magnificent curtains with richly colourful curtains, the palace was never intended to be lived in – merely as an escape from the busy and formal life at court. In other words, an extravagance *par excellence!*

The palace was transformed into a museum in 1907 on the death of King Oscar and is now open for guided tours between 12-4pm in June, July and August only.

Adjacent to the palace is the ***Palace Garden***, home for more than 30 years for the Rosendal Garden Foundation, renowned for cultivating and spreading biodynamic farming practices. Here, gardeners grow vegetables, herbs, flowers and fruits, many of which are used in the garden café and woodfired bakery.

During the summer months, there is hardly a better way to spend a few hours, sitting on the grass with a picnic under the apple trees in the orchard or wandering around the flowerbeds, herb gardens and rose garden. There is even a wine garden and an outdoor bar.

If you don't have a picnic, there is a café and a bakery in which delicious breads are made in the wood-fired stone oven.

This is one of Stockholm's true gems. The café uses organic and biodynamic ingredients from the gardens and offers salads, soups, sandwiches and pastries made in the bakery.

Before you leave, don't forget to visit the boutique shop, filled with wonderful produce, tools, books and crafts.

The most enjoyable and probably best way to get there is to take the tram (or walk) to *Djurgårdsbron (Djurgårds Bridge)* and walk along the canal pathway where you will see signs directing you to the palace and garden.

Alternatively, you could take tram number 7 from central Stockholm to Waldemrsudde. The next stop after that is Bellmansbro, where you get off. The palace and garden are a five to ten minutes' walk away and signposted.

Also, out of town is *Millesgården*, (Milles Sculpture Garden)* on the island of Lidingö, which, if your ship is berthed in Frihamn, lies on the island opposite the cruise terminal.

Millesgården is an oasis just 20 minutes from the centre of Stockholm. This was the home of the sculptor Carl Milles and his wife, the painter, Olga Milles. Today it is a museum with a collection of antiques, an art gallery, a large sculpture garden, a shop and a restaurant.

A figurative and often narrative sculptor, Carl Milles dominated the Swedish art world throughout the first half of the 20th century.

He was inspired by ancient Greek, Roman and Christian mythology as well as Swedish history. Perhaps his greatest achievement was his own sculpture garden, inspired by Mediterranean and especially Italian gardens and which took him 50 years to complete.

There is one other out of town escape: **_Drottningholm Palace*_**, idea for passengers who may have been to Stockholm several times before.

This is almost certainly Stockholm's best-preserved palace, designed by Nicodemus Tessin the elder and built in the 17th century. Various members of the royal family left their mark on it from then on and the Royal family have used it as a permanent residence since 1981. The palace is also one of Stockholm's three World Heritage sites.

It's a great day out, beginning with a boat trip lasting for about an hour through some magnificent scenery.

Depending on what you want to do, the cost of the trip ranges from SEK 230 (£17.95, $23.70, €21.00) for the return trip, to SEK340 (£27.75, $36.65, €32.45) for the return trip plus entrance the palace. Add to that the Chinese Pavilion and the Court Theatre and it will cost SEK 490 (£40.oo, $52.85, €47.75).

There is a lot to see and you will need to take a mid-morning trip at the latest if you opt for the most expensive deal. Compared with the price of some cruise ship's excursions, it is a very moderately priced day out.

The palace features fabulous 17th, 18th and 19th century salons, and a marvelously well-preserved theatre that is the only 18th theatre in which stagehands still use the original stage machinery on a regular basis.

The palace is richly decorated and furnished, and it is easy to forget as you wander from room to room that in the southern part of the palace, members of the royal family may be working, resting, reading a book or having an afternoon nap!

Apart from the Chinese Pavilion, there are also wonderful gardens, both natural and Baroque formal. These were designed by Tessin the Younger.

The palace and gardens are open from 10am until 4pm year-round.

Back in town, there are many other attractions to see and visit – The Historical Museum, the Technical Museum, the Maritime Museum and a host of others far too numerous to mention, given that most cruise passengers have only one or two days to spend in what is undoubtedly one of the most attractive cities in Europe, if not the world.

* * *

Örnsköldsvik

The Main Attractions

Paradise Park
Örnsköldsvik Museum & Art Gallery
Hand Hedberg Museum
Eagle Park
Genesmons Iron Age Village

Örnsköldsvik   *(pron: Earn-shirlds-veek)* is not the brightest firework in the box when it comes to Swedish ports of call, but it does have some merit – a good shopping centre with some very sophisticated design shops, a beautiful park in the city centre, lots of waterways, a museum, an art gallery, leisure centre and a large water park.

Candleholders designed by Lara Bohinc

Ship's crews especially should always remember that the libraries (*Bibliotek*) in all Swedish, Norwegian and Finnish towns offer free Internet facilities.

If you are into ski-jumping, a couple of ski jumps are visible from the ship. These lie on the perimeter of the town,  which, with a population of only about 9,200, is not exactly huge.

Ski jumping is a great spectator sport; for participants it calls for a considerable degree of insanity and courage. One look at a ski jump is enough to convince anybody of sound mind not even to contemplate it!

Örnsköldsvik is blessed because wherever you are, you are always close to nature. Woodland paths and trails, ski trails and ski slopes abound and the sea, archipelago, lakes and rivers are ideal for fishing, bathing and messing around in boats.

The High Coast Art Valley outside the town limits runs along the Nätra river, exhibiting artworks in natural surroundings.

Örnsköldsvik city fathers are environmentally conscious and despite the town's principal industries being paper and pulp exports and heavy machinery, the town and its environs are pristine. The town has also been a testing centre for vehicles powered with ethanol.

Bronze Age people lived in the area of the town between 1700-500BC, although there were no villages or towns as such, just individual farmsteads. Back then, they grew wheat and barley, kept cattle, sheep and pigs, and were also partially dependent on fishing and hunting elk, deer and wild boar.

Örnsköldsvik, however, was not founded until 1842, when it was a simple market town. It was granted city status in 1894.

Most of the people lead healthy lives, spending much of their free time hiking and skiing along the many heavily wooded trails in the surrounding hills.

Given its location approximately 225 miles (362 kilometres) south of the Arctic Circle, the city is almost in the 'Land of the Midnight Sun', so it remains light until about 11 pm in summer. Of course, this also means 'Land of Long, Dark Winters'.

Not surprisingly, winter sport such as ice hockey, cross country and alpine skiing, ski-jumping and curling are all practised within the town borders.

In summer, swimming off the many beaches close to the town, boating, outdoor barbecues and camping are as popular as football and golf – not to mention basking in the 'Midnight' Sun, which sets only for a couple of hours during the summer months.

Ships visiting Örnsköldsvik usually offer panoramic excursions around the town and surrounding countryside, but the best ones are 'Scenic Skuleberget' and the UNESCO World Heritage 'High Coast' scenic drive during which you will see Europe's third largest suspension bridge.

The land and seascape here are notable for its distinctly red granite cliffs and rocks and spans about 60 miles (100 kilometres) of the Gulf of Bothnia coast. Örnsköldsvik lies at its southern end.

For cruise ship passengers the only way to see this part of the coast is by ship's excursion or by renting a car, which could work out more expensive.

The Skuleskogen National Park is located at the centre of the High Coast. What makes it interesting is that, thanks to glaciation and a glacial retreat after the last Ice Age nearly 10,000 years ago, the wild and unsettled landscape was once an ancient seabed.

Now, the forests, lakes and inlets, once compacted due to the pressure of the ice, are rising again. It is known as the post-glacial rebound.

Incredibly, the entire landscape has risen by approximately 968 feet (295 metres) in the past 9.600 years, a vertical movement that accounts for the steep granite cliffs and rocky islands.

Back in town, especially if it is raining, passengers fond of swimming and spas may like to visit *Paradiset (The Paradise Water Park),* a large 1,435 square yard (1,200 square metre) spa, that is said to be one of Sweden's best waterpark experiences and is located in the heart of the town. Its main feature is the 'Magic Eye', Sweden's longest water slide.

Aside from the slide, there are wild rapids, hot tubs, the largest wooden sauna in Sweden with a resting room, green room, salt cave, meditation and massage stations. All in all, it is a great place to relax and rejuvenate the old phagocytes!

Paradiset is open from 10am -5.30pm every day and costs SEK120 (£9.80, $12.95, €11.45).

Örnsköldsviks museum and art gallery, a Jugend (Art Nouveau) style building located at Läroverksgatan No. 1 was completed in 1905 and presents a wide range of historical and cultural exhibitions as well as national and international art exhibitions.

Previously used as several different schools, it was rebuilt in 1977-78 so that it could function as a museum. Later, in 2005, the art gallery was moved from the Town Hall.

Exhibitions have mainly focused on the history of the city and its surroundings, but from time to time the curators stage temporary international exhibitions. These have included such subjects as Elvis Presley, Andy Warhol, Star Wars and even one about ice hockey.

The museum is open from 11am until 4pm every day except Sunday and Monday. Entrance is free.

The ***Hans Hedberg Museum*** at Strandgatan 21 is devoted entirely to the artist, sculptor and ceramics artist Hans Hedberg, who was born in 1917 a few miles south of Örnsköldsvik.

Known especially for his huge sculptures of eggs and fruit, he studied under various Swedish artists before continuing his studies at the Royal Danish Academy in Copenhagen in1945-1946 and subsequently at the Colarossis School of Painting in Paris in late 1946 and at the Instituto d'Art della Ceramica in Faenza, Italy in 1947-1948.

With bold colours and strong luminescence, the glazes on his eggs and fruit sculptures soon became known internationally and are now available in more than 30 leading collections.

In his early days, he was colleague of Matisse, Picasso and Chagall, and lived half his life in France. The museum in Örnsköldsvik was inaugurated in October 1988. Hedberg, died in March 2007 at the age of 89 years.

The museum is open every day between 8am and 5pm, and there is no admission charge.

In between museum visits, it is well worth strolling through **Örnparken (Eagle Park)** and the adjoining Lungviksparken.

A 20-25-minute (4.3 mile, 7km) bus trip out of town is the re-constructed **Genesmons Iron Age village**, which shows how people lived in the year 500AD. (Buses run approximately every 20 minutes).

The village, which also exhibits clothing, food and crafts of the period, was reconstructed following excavations of an iron age farm a short distance away. Apparently, it had been used for about 500 years, beginning in the first century.

The farm comprised several homes and one large house that probably belonged to a local chieftain.

There was a forge where the iron page people cast jewellery, made keys and gilded bronze.

Archeologists believe that a family of some 10-20 farmers lived here for several generations, cultivating grains and oats on approximately 7.5 acres (three hectares) of arable land. The middens also show that they supplemented their diet by hunting game in the forest, fishing and seal hunting.

The excavations also showed that they had a herd of about 8-10 cows, 20 sheep or goats, pigs, a horse and a dog. The museum website does not post opening times. It is staffed only during the summer months. At other times, visitors are free to roam around on their own.

Finally, as your ship leaves Örnsköldsvik, don't miss the sailaway – or, if you are sailing further north, the late evening sun if the sky is clear.

* * *

Umeå

The Main Attrations

Umeå is a vibrant, fast-growing university city with a population of just under 85,000, some 30,000 of whom are students. Those figures make it the fastest growing city in Sweden.

Lying just 189 miles (304 kilometres) south of the Arctic Circle, it enjoys almost 24 hours of sun in the summer.

Umeå was also the European Capital of

Culture in 2014, and it is not difficult to understand why; Dance, theatre, sports and concerts with famous national and international artists occur almost every week throughout the summer. There are annual film and music festivals each year.

In winter, the local people celebrate an annual Sami week, a celebration of Sami culture in which Sami art, music, culture and language are all open for everyone's appreciation. Umeå is the unofficial capital of Norrland County and thus of the northern part of Sweden. Should you wish to sum it up in a sentence you would have to say it is a buzzing city with trendy shopping, great design hotels and first-class restaurants.

Additionally, being surrounded by Europe's last great wilderness, tranquility is never far away and there are always great opportunities for all kinds of sports, too.

With nearly 500 miles (800 kilometres of winding coast, beaches, islands and beaches, it is a haven for hikers, campers, cyclists, sailors and skiers. In winter, there are locations and facilities for every kind of winter sport, including dog sledding.

Four mighty rivers (Öreälven, Lögdeälven, Vindelälven and Umeälven – 'älven' simply meaning 'river') cut through the county offering rapids and white-water rafting, peaceful rafting, canoeing, beaver safaris and endless scenic walking trails dotted with barbecue sites and cabins for overnighting.

Umeå lies at the mouth of the Umeå River and because of the plantings in the pedestrian areas, residents refer to it as the 'City of Silver Birches'.

When fire destroyed the city in 1888, *Umea Town Hall (Umeå rådhus),* a 17th century wooden structure was among the casualties, so work began immediately to erect a new Town Hall.

This building was also subsequently replaced and the city fathers commissioned the architect, Fredrik Olaus

Lindström, who had designed Umeå Church to design a new Town Hall.

Built with red bricks in the Dutch Renaissance style, Lindström was extremely conscious of the location, so he designed the small park to give emphasis to the building and make the most of the views of the river.

Unusually, the Town Hall has two main entrances. Originally, the main entrance faced the park and the river. When the mainline railway reached Umeå in 1890, planners intended to build the railway station at the back of the building facing the town square

However, the city fathers pointed out that this would be extremely embarrassing because when King Oscar II arrived to inaugurate the railway station in 1896, he would essentially be looking at the backside of the Town Hall.

This, they said, was simply not on. So, prior to the King's arrival, builders hurriedly created a second main entrance overlooking what is today the Town Hall square *(Rådhustorget).*

Väven Cultural Centre, *(lit: 'the weave'),* on the riverbank, has become the hub for everything from the city library, theatre, art house and gallery to a cinema, museum, market and cafés.

Built between 2011 and 2014, the streamlined building, which appears similar in design to the upper decks of a cruise ship, won the Kasper Salin Prize, Sweden's most prestigious architectural award. Coincidentally, this was presented in November 2014, a week after the Centre was inaugurated and in the same year that Umeå won the European City of Culture status.

Väven is described as a platform for culture and experiences 'in which people and ideas are woven together' – hence the name.

This is a place for a broad spectrum of culture, from music to food, lectures to recreation, the spontaneous to the organized and private to business.

In the indoor courtyard (*Torget*), are two hotels and several restaurants. The British newspaper, *The Guardian* named **Gotthards Krog,** Stora Hotellet's plush restaurant, one of the top ten 'coolest' restaurants in the world – and it wasn't referring to the temperature, either!

The décor is stunning with wallpaper featuring giant fish and octopuses and seats shaped like seashells, all lit with ship's lanterns.

The restaurant is named after a Swedish adventurer called Gotthard Zetterberg, the original owner, who in a flash of irrationality decided to sail to Greenland with explorer Adolf Nordenskjöld to see if it was really green (the coastline is, but 90 per cent of Greenland is ice – at least for the time being. A century on and the chances are it may well not be!)

Gotthards Korg comprises a bar, dining room and restaurant on the continental indoor square of Väven and specializes in fine dining and lunch dishes using local ingredients flavoured with spices from port cities around the world. Gotthards Krog is open daily from 7am until late.

Två Fiskare (Two Fishermen) is a different kettle of fish, if you will excuse the pun. This white-tiled establishment takes Nordic fish extremely seriously. Not only does it sell fresh fish and shellfish from its fish counters, it also prepares several seafood dishes from smoked shrimp and crab cakes to fish soup, classic fish 'n' chips and whatever is 'flapping fresh' that day.

Två Fiskare is open 10am -6pm Monday-Friday, until 4pm Saturdays, and closed on Sundays.

Above the inner courtyard and restaurants, Umeå City Library is located on three floors (open 9am-6pm daily, 10am-4pm on Saturdays and 12am-4pm on Sundays) together with several creativity workshops, cinemas, venues for art and the *Museum of Women's History*.

This small but important museum is the first of its kind in Sweden. Opened in 2014, the idea was to give a new perspective on history, which rarely mentions women. The museum hopes to change that.

Noting that women in most places and at most periods of history have been excluded from various social arenas, the museum asserts that, as a result, women were able to make fewer important inventions or voyages of discovery. They painted fewer great paintings, built fewer houses and wrote fewer books.

Although, clearly, some women made the history books, most women's knowledge, skills, interests, activities and memories were considered unimportant, less interesting or less worthwhile to document.

The path of history has been a chronological story of war and politics, economics and ideas shaped by male actions. The museum breaks the silence woven around women in history.

It is, the museum suggests, one of the greatest democratic problems of our time nationally and globally. It states its purpose is to become involved in discussions on how society should look in the future and how equal opportunities, power and influence between women and men could evolve.

The museum is open 10am-5pm Tuesdays-Fridays, 10am-4pm on Saturdays and 12-4pm Sundays. Closed on Mondays. Entrance is free.

Bildmuseet (University Contemporary Art Museum) at Östra Strandgatan 30B is undoubtedly one of Sweden's most interesting international contemporary art museums.

Spanning seven floors of ultra-modern architecture, the museum's programme spans existential, political and philosophical issues through exhibitions produced in collaboration with artists, museums and universities around the world.

Adjacent to the Umeå Academy of Fine Arts, the Institute of Design and School of Architecture, the building has been named as one of the world's most beautiful university museums.

Apart from the wide range of exhibitions, the interior design of the museum is worth a visit in its own right.

Entry is free of charge, the museum is open every day, offering guided tours, from 10am-5pm except for major public holidays, which include Midsummer Eve and Midsummer Day. There is a museum shop, restaurant café, and wonderful views across the Umeå.

The museum is free of charge, open all year and offers guided tours. Museum shop, restaurant café and sparkling views across Umeå and its river.

For any musically minded cruise passengers with a passion for electric guitars, The *Guitars Museum* at Umeå Folkets Hus, Vasaplan (Skolgatan 59) is a must, claiming to have one of the world's largest privately-owned collection of guitars.

The brothers, Mikael and Samuel Åhdén, assembled this unique collection of more than 500 guitars, basses, amplifiers and musical props from the 1970s onwards.

The collection consists mainly of electric guitars from the 1950s and 1960s and, for *aficionados*, includes a 1958 Gibson Flying V, a 1960 Les Paul and a 1950 Fender broadcaster.

Umeå City Church *(Umeå stadskyrka),* located at Västra Kyrkogatan 3, was inaugurated in 1894 and was preceded by the original church, which the Russian Army destroyed in 1770, and the second church, which was burnt down in the great fire of 1888.

Construction on the current brick built, neo-Gothic church began in 1892 and it was completed two years later. The church underwent a major restoration in 1929-30, primarily because of water damage to the ceiling.

In 1935, the church council authorized further work to be carried out, including the addition of an aisle and the expansion of the organ gallery and choir.

When city councilors decided to add a third bridge across the river, construction works discovered a previously unknown graveyard. Under Swedish law, this means that all work on the site had to be halted until archaeologists could excavate it.

There were no gravestones, but the dig nonetheless revealed 40 graves containing some 60 skeletons. One grave also uncovered a name plate showing that it was a family grave. Surprisingly, there was no tomb or tombstone so all details about the family – that of a former city governor – were lost.

When the archaeologists had finished examining the skeletons, they returned them to the church wrapped in plastic carrier bags. Unfortunately, the church warden buried these but failed to tell anybody where they were, and died soon afterwards, so once again, the family ended up in an unmarked grave.

Västerbotten County Museum on Helena Elisabeths väg, northeast of the city centre, comprises the Gammlia open-air museum and exhibitions from the former Fishing and Maritime Museum, which focuses on the history of Arctic seal hunting, and the Swedish Ski Museum, the latter displaying what is claimed to be the world's oldest ski, predating the pyramids in Egypt.

In the 1920s, museum officials oversaw a diverse range of buildings, including a church, a manor house, a windmill, an 18th century farmhouse and various sheds, cowsheds, bakehouses, barns and mills, all of which had been moved from all over Västerbotten county to the museum

Not satisfied with that, they subsequently added a school, a blacksmiths forge and Sami camps, thus giving the museum an extraordinarily vivid idea of life in northern Sweden during the 18th and 19th centuries.

In the summer months, there are horses, cows, sheep, pigs and chickens on display, and local people in period clothing demonstrate such arts as butter churning, baking the traditional Swedish thin bread *(tunnbröd)* and other crafts.

There is a well-stocked museum shop and a cosy café. Entry is free and the museum will probably be open Monday-Saturday from 10am until 5pm and closed on Mondays, although no times have been announced at the time of writing.

Having wandered around the town, you may feel like a little lunch and, if you opt not to eat in the Väven Culture

Centre restaurants, a good alternative is the floating restaurant, Vita björn, a short walk from the Culture Centre.

Here, you can choose from a casual international menu of Caesar salad, vegie burgers, baked salmon, beef tenderloin or fresh grilled herring. Alternatively, a traditional Swedish open sandwich piled high with fresh shrimps, cucumber and mayonnaise takes some beating.

For passengers who prefer to get out of the town, the **Umeådalen Sculpture Park (Skulpturpark)** is only 4.3 miles, a little over seven kilometres west-northwest of the town and accessible by the No.1 bus from Vasaplan (alight at the Glädjens gränd stop).

Although the Sculpture park contains one of Northern Europe's leading sculpture collections with more than 40 works by various international and local sculptors, including Antony Gormley, it has received mixed reviews on TripAdvisor, and passengers may wish to do more research before deciding to go.

The park is open all day, every day of the year and there is no admission fee.

An alternative out-of-town attraction for those wishing to swap blue water for green woodland is *Nydalasjön (Lake Nydala, formerly Lake Tavlesjön).*

This is a two mile (three kilometre) long lake running north to south and a 5.6 mile (nine km) drive east of the city centre – approximately a 20-25 minute journey.

Adjacent to the beach at the northern end of Nydalasjö, there is a large temperate outdoor pool with natural lake baths, water ramps, open grass areas, saunas and cafés. Open from June 15th.

Here, you can also stroll along the lakeside paths, swim and have a barbecue in the bays and on the promontories around the lake. The community even supplies the wood!

If you wish to walk round the lake, the distance is approximately 5.3 miles (8.5 kilometres).

In the autumn months, you might even like to pick blueberries, lingonberries and mushrooms in the wooded banks of the lake. You can also fish for rainbow trout, brown trout, perch, pike and roach, although you will need to buy a rod license at First Camp, Umeå. Tel: +46 (0)90-702600. Email: umea@firstcamp.se.

To get to the lake, take Bus No 1 towards Östra Ersboda or Bus No 2 towards Ersboda. The journey takes about 15 minutes and there are several departures an hour. A one-way ticket is SEK 26 (££2.15, $2.80, €2.50) or SEK36 (£2.95, $3.90, €3.45) respectively.

* * *

Luleå

The Main Attraction

With a population of some 75,000 inhabitants, Luleå is the largest city in Swedish Lapland with a climate that is sub-Arctic, whis is to say it has short, cool summers and long, cold, snowy winters.

That said, the Gulf Stream ensures that in summer it is relatively mild, although in June and July the temperature can reach +30° Centigrade. That, however, is by no means the norm. What is normal is that Luleå is the sunniest city in Sweden.

Only 95 miles (152 kilometreses) south of the Arctic Circle, the sun does not set on Midsummer's Eve until five minutes to midnight. It rizes again just 65 minutes later at 1 am.

Winter is a different story. On December 21st, the city remains in darkness or semi-darkness for all but three hours and 20 minutes, rising at 9.50 am and setting at 1.10pm

In winter, snow carpets the landscape with deep snow and the sea freezes. At this time of year, temperatures average minus 13° Centigrade (8.8° Fahrenheit) with a record low of minus 42.3°C (44.1° F). The lack of sun between September and March, however, make it a perfect venue in which to see the Northern Lights *(Aurora Borealis)*

Luleå is a beautiful city with so much to offer that it is difficult to know where to begin. Surrounded by the majestic Lule river and with an archipelago comprising 1,312 islands just a short hop from the harbour, the town is comparatively small. You can be anywhere within 'The Nature' in ten minutes, whether you are working, at home or at school. Yet Luleå has everything you could need from a big city; excellent and sophisticated shopping, music, festivals, sports, theatre - you name it.

Like Umeå, the town is growing rapidly with more and more people opting for the benefits of life in smaller town; relaxation, hiking, skiing, swimming, watersports and blissful tranquility. Conversely, the town has a sizeable steel industry and the seventh largest and busiest harbour in Sweden, exporting iron ore from mines in Gällivare nearby and timber, which is floated down the Lule River in huge quantities.

From the first small industries to start up in the 1860s, Lulea has expanded into an industrial power house. Innovation and technological advances were the engine driving the development of modern blast furnaces and steel works.

The city is alsoa major centre for technological research with three technology universities and a dedicated Science Park. More than 800 scientists from around the world are currently developing new techniques and technologies in the fields of mining, metallurgy, renewable resources and communications.

This is where some 100 companies are developing and expanding, primarily in IT and the energy fields. Working closely with Luleå University of Technology, the Park consists of several office buildings in an area of more than 23,920 square yards (20,000 square metres).

Here, a company can start up in a tiny office room and in six months switch to a space ten times as big, complete with its own building.

The city's IT (Information Technology) industry employs more than 2,000 people.

The management of Facebook were so impressed that they decided to set up Europe's largest data centre in the city, the first to be built outside the United States. They were attracted there by a combination of reliable low-cost electricity supplies from renewable sources and a climate ideal for cooling its servers,

As a result, Luleå is now the nucleus for data traffic in Europe, earning it the nickname 'The Node Pole'.

Not surprisingly, Facebook's arrival has had a knock-on effect, boosting both university applications by nearly 20% and attracting scores of new companies to the Science Park, which has been described as a meeting place between 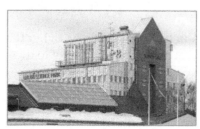 technology, people, knowledge and creativity'.

King Gustavus Adolphus granted Luleå's Royal Charter in 1621 despite it having a population of only 200-300 inhabitants. Even by 1805, there were less than a thousand people living there.

As with so many other towns in Sweden, fire ravaged the town several times, in 1653, 1657 and again in 1887, the latter blaze destroying almost the entire town.

The **Old Church Town (Gammelstad)** is one of the survivors, now a UNESCO world heritage site and Luleå's No.1. tourist attraction.

Dominated by a 15th century stone church, its medieval streets are lined with 424 wooden houses making it the largest and best-preserved example of a 'church village' in Sweden.

Church villages were first established in northern Scandinavia because the combination of large parishes, difficult terrain and weather conditions made it extremely difficult for people to go to church.

Result: They built villages round the churches. These consisted of small houses in which parishioners could sleep overnight or for a weekend festival. The cottages continued to be used for this purpose until the 1950s and some still are used for major seasonal church celebrations.

However, nobody lives in them permanently and in this day and age, it is unlikely that anybody would want to do so because although they have electricity, there is no running water or sewage facility.

Many of the cottages are still furnished as they were in former times and tourists can visit these, learn about traditional cooking, butter churning, bread baking and candle making – or take a quaint lantern guided tour, have a horse and sleigh ride in the winter snow and try a range of handicrafts.

Luleå is home to two majestic churches and both, in their own ways, have helped put the city on the map and played a pivotal role in its development.

The first and oldest of these is ***Nederluleå Church (Lower Luleå Church)*** is the largest medieval church in the county of Norrland and forms part of the UNESCO World Heritage Site.

Archbishop Jakob Ulfsson consecrated it in June, 1492, in the same year that Columbus set sail for America (although he never found it!).

When the parish authorities decided to re-plaster the walls in 1954, the work revealed stone walls consisting of some 40 different types of rock.

In the choir, there are paintings from the beginning of the 16th century. The altar cabinet was made in Antwerp around 1520 and the heavily decorated wooden pulpit was carved in 1712. The organ weighs 25 tons and has 4,200 pipes varying in length from 2/10ths of an inch to 20 feet (five millimetres to six metres).

With the red-painted cottages all around it, the church, dedicated to St. Peter, was the focal point not just for Luleå but for the entire county of Norrland.

In medieval times, national law stipulated that attendance at church services should be mandatory. Distance, weather and terrain were no excuse for non-attendance. Consequently, in order to ensure that the long-distance travellers had somewhere to stay, they were obliged to build temporary housing for them.

The church and village remained the city centre until the 1600s, when retreating inland ice caused the land underneath it to rise up – the post-glacial rebound. This had the effect of making the waters in the harbour too shallow, so the city fathers decreed that the city be moved to its current location.

The deserted cottages remained abandoned for centuries. Today, most of them are privately owned, having been handed down from one generation to another. Now, the Old Town has come back to life, not just in the interests of tourism, but as a wedding venue and for holiday homes.

Luleå's brick-built *Neo-Gothic cathedral* is another church worth visiting. Inaugurated in 1893, it was originally called Oscar Fredrik Church after King Oscar Fredrik II, but was renamed Luleå Cathedral in 1904, making it Sweden's northernmost and youngest cathedral.

It is the highest building in the city, standing 220 feet (67 metres) high and can accommodate 650 people, of whom 520 can be seated. Preceded by two other churches, both of which were built of wood and burned down during major fires in 1887, the cathedral retains its height and thus its dominance thanks to city planners, who have consistently declined to allow high rise buildings to be erected anywhere near it.

The advent and subsequent growth of industry in the latter part of the 19th century combined with the influx of 17,000 students and new businesses to the city, meant that Luleå has evolved into a thoroughly modern town with superb opportunities for shopping.

The town has the distinction of having opened the world's first indoor shopping mall in 1955. It has several museums, an ultra modern library and cultural events punctuate its calendar on a regular basis.

One such event is *Musikens Makt (The Power of Music)*, a groundbreaking festival held every August since 2009. Named aftger a magazine published in the heyday of the progressive rock movement, it takes place on Gűltzaudden, on the banks of the Lule River.

The organisers pride themselves on the fact that there are no beer tents 'which makes for a more pleasant atmosphere and that at least half of the acts they book are predominantly female.

A new and novel form of concert in the witner is ice music, which requires professional musicians play on instruments made of ice.

These concerts are performed in a huge igloo with a light show bathing the interior with pulsating multi-colours. Whether the musicians wear gloves or not is unrecorded. If not, one can only commiserate with them.

Not all the music concerts are to everyone's taste, however. Luleå is also home to a punk band called 'Raised Fist', which suggests a somewhat anarchistic approach to music, and several heavy metal bands, not least one described as 'Helltrain, the death 'n' roll band'.

A more classic event is the Luleå Harbour Festival, which attracts visitors from all over Sweden. It is one of the largest events in Swedish Lapland attracting around 130,000 visitors each year. The artists and bands are almost exclusively Swedish, market stalls line the streets of the North Harbour, the funfair comes to town and, best of all, there is no entrance fee.

So, that's Luleå, a city of infinite opportunities. But where to start? Let's begin with **shopping and eating**, arguably every cruise passengers' favourite occupations!

The main shopping street is Storgatan on which there are three large shopping malls as well as smaller shops in which you can find a wide range of fashion, beauty, interior design, electronics and so on as well as restaurants and cafés. Free wi-fi is available in all the malls.

If you are looking for souvenirs from Lapland, try Lapland Heartwork at Smedgegatan 13, where you can find art and handicrafts made by local craftspeople. Shop in

Lapland in Gammelstad sells jewellery and selected works of art, Sami crafts and designer crafts

Biergo at Nygatan 10 is a Sami-style wildmeat shop where you can buy wild game products including reindeer fillet, reindeer burgers and different types of sausages as well as berry products from the local forests and local handicrafts.

On Norra Strandgatan (No.1), Hemmagastronomi Deli offers delicacies for those who enjoy the good life – everything from cheeses, dry aged meat, fish and shellfish to hand-painted chocolate truffles, cold-pressed olive oils and Balsamic vinegars,

Bottenvikens Bryggeri (Brewery) at Kungsgatan 32 describes its beers as 'un-filtered, un-boring, un-inhibited, un-mass produced, un-watery, un-artificial', which suggests it might be worth trying!

The brewery began operations in 2013 and is run by two enthusiasts, Mattias Bergström and Joakim Nilsson, who say they have the passion and the desire to create beer 'with an attitude inspired by nature's changes'.

What is unique about them is that they only brew a beer once. Each beer – and there have been more than 60 of them since 2013 – has 'a unique name, unique label and unique poetry', they say.

Among the unique names are Dewlap, Dusk-bite, Skerry and Biting Wind, which once again shows how close the Swedes are to 'The Nature'.

The two brewers add that they do not really feel at home in the microbrewery definition. Rather, they define themselves as 'an artist brewery with liquid lithographs'. That is what makes them different!

You can book a beer tasting on the internet at *www.botttenvikensbryggeri.se*. Alternatively, you can sample their various brews at Hemmagastronomi Deli or Bistro Norrland (at Norra Strandgatan 3-7 and open for lunch from 11am until 1.30pm).

For passengers who like to rummage through ***antique and second-hand shop***s, Luleå is bristling with them. Here are some: Fyndhörnan at Köpmansgatan 60, open 12-5pm except Sunday and Monday: Antiques, retro, collectibles, vinyl, glass, and porcelain, lamps, paintings and more.

Kyrkbyn, Gammelstad: Gammelstads popular flea market is open every Saturday from June August 11:00am except for Midsummer's day).

Latinamerikakommiténs loppis at Kronan hus C7. In addition to flea market gadgets, there are Fairtrade goods and crafts from Ecuador and Guatemala. Open every Saturday 10am – 2pm from August.

Rädda barnen (Save The Children) Second Hand Shop) at Repslagargata 16: Clothes for children and adults, books, furnishings and household items.

Röda korset Red Cross at Småbåtsgatan 5. Smart second-hand shop selling clothes, kitchenware, glassware, household ornaments and much, much more.

More athletic passengers and crew will likely be more interested in the city's main *jogging path.*

The best starting point is outside Norrbottensteatern (Strandgatan No. 3), following the quay away from the city centre, towards the residential buildings by the water.

Follow the walking path and after passing the tip of Gültzauudden and the small boat harbour by the Hälsans Hus sports area, you will eventually reach the Bergnäs Bridge (the arched bridge across the Lule River).

Keep following the trail around the water's edge and you will soon be back in the city again.

The path takes you around Gültzauudden to Oscarsvarv, a distance of approximately 1¼ miles (two kilometres). The route is mostly flat and the surroundings are scenic, and close to both the river and the sea – a perfect way to enjoy 'The Nature'.

Luleå's principal museums are located in **Norra Hamn (North Harbour).** These are **Norrbottens County Museum** and the main art gallery, **Kulturens Hus Art Gallery,**

The former, located in opened in 1967 and was the first county museum in Sweden (Norrbotten also being Sweden's largest county). It focusses primarily on the county's heritage, culture and art.

Norra Hamn (North Harbour), Luleå

Norrbotten stretches from coast to mountain and has a cultural history of more than 10,000 years. It is also multi-cultural having been populated by Sami people, Finns, Swedes and Finnish Tornedalians, the descendants of Finns who, in the 14th century, migrated from the Karelia peninsula and southwestern Finland and settled near the Torne Valley at the northern end of the Gulf of Bothnia.

The museum covers archeology and ethnology with documentary exhibitions based on historical stories, culture, crafts, art, society and industries as well as Sami and contemporary art.

There is a café with coffee and home-baked goodies, sandwiches and free Wi-Fi. The museum shop is packed with Norrbotten crafts and literature.

The museum is closed on Mondays and open from 10am -4pm on Tuesday-Friday, and from 11am at weekends. It is also closed on public holidays. Admission is free.

The Kulturens Hus Art Gallery, right next to the Tourist Information Office in Kulturen's Hus (House of Culture) curates several different exhibitions each season covering sculpture and various art genres, although mostly of contemporary art.

These include works by well-known artists who depict in various ways the distinctive, natural environment surrounding the city centre and who, through their work, have put Luleå on the map.

There is a café and a 4th floor restaurant with superb views of the Northern Harbour.

The gallery is closed on Mondays and open from 11am–5pm on weekdays and until 4pm at weekends. There is no admission fee.

Another fascinating museum is the *Norrbotten Railway Museum* at the junction of Karlsviksvägen and Arcusvägen 95, one of Sweden's largest railway museums. It is located in a scenic area of the old industrial community in Karlsvik, 3,7 miles (6 kms) from Luleå city center.

The main focus of the museum is to preserve and display objects that are related to Malmbanan *(the Iron Ore Line)* which runs from the Norwegian-Swedish border to the iron ore mines in Kiruna to the Port of Luleå.

The museum also owns about 140 vehicles and 10 different buildings, including a large, newly built exhibition hall with four tracks of 230 feet (70 metres), a station house from Kos and a switchgear taken from Svartön in Luleå. During the summer, scheduled trains run on the Gammelstad-Karlsvikshytan railway.

The museum opening times are not published. Admission is SEK 60 (£4.95, $6.50, €5.75). If you are fortunately enough to visit the museum on a Wednesday or at weekends, you can take a 45-minute journey on one of the trains, departing at 12.15pm, 1.30pm and 2.45pm. The cost of this is the same as the museum entrance fee.

Maybe, if it is a gorgeously sunny day, you would prefer to sunbathe on a beach and take a cooling dip? No problem. Luleå has it all and there are many excellent **bathing beaches** from which to choose.

Within walking distance from the city centre, Gültzauudden is the most convenient. There is a café nearby and toilet facilities.

A well-preserved jewel, Svartöstaden Beach, is just 2.5 miles (four kilometres) from the city centre. You can take the LLT7 bus from the bus station on Skeppsbrogatan 54 to the Laxgatan stop at Svartöstaden. The journey takes 26 minutes and costs SEK 35 (££2.90, $3.80, €3.35). The beach is popular with local people and the best part of it is next to an old stone pier reaching out into the river.

The real gem though is First Camp, a fabulous, sheltered sandy beach with clear water and an amazing view of the river.

Take the bus from the LLT8 or LLT104 bus from the bus station on Storgatan. The journey time is 48 minutes and the cost is the same as for Svartöstaden.

If you wish is to enjoy the archipelago close up, why not book a buffet lunch on board the tour boat **m.s. Laponia**. You can pick wild blueberries, cloudberries, sea-buckthorn, arctic raspberries and mushrooms on the

islands, or just wander around a couple of islands and enjoy the views.

In summer, you may well see roe deer, elk, sea eagles and reindeer. Farthest out, seals are a more common. On the island of Sandön you will find the popular Klubbviken, with its two entirely different sides: one idyllic and simple with sandy beaches, restaurants and fun activities, one untouched and facing the sea.

On the tourist boat, you can reach the outer rim of the archipelago to Rödkallen, Kluntarna, Småskär and Brändöskär – islands that have been inhabited for hundreds of years.

Kluntara

Here, you can walk inside 18th century log chapels, see fishermen's huts, lighthouse keepers' cottages, sea pilots' cottages and lighthouses.

A day trip to the archipelago on a sunny, Swedish summer's day, when the air is pristine clear and the breeze fresh, is one of life's truly great experiences.

The **Grand Archipelago Cruise** with Laponia Rederi departs from North Harbour at 11 am and includes a lunch buffet, choice of soft drink with approximately one and a half hours on each of the islands of Junkön and Kluntara, returning at 5pm. Guided tours, museum and gallery entrance fees are also included. The price for adults is SEK 550 (£41.20, $53.80, €47.95)

There are many other ferry trips on different ships costing between SEK 75(£6.05, $7.90, €7.10) and SEK 150 (£12.10, $15.80, €14.20), depending on the destinations.

Just be sure to check the return times and be conscious of your ship's all-aboard time, too! Don't forget to enjoy the sailaway through the archipelago – and after dinner perhaps enjoy the midnight sun.

* * *

FINLAND

Living with the Bear

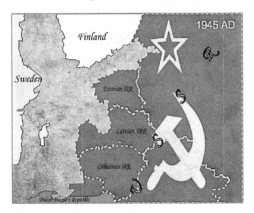

In 1824, the writer, E. D. Clarke, described the night he reached a town called Korpi-kyla in Finland.

'Not being able to find a human being, we began to suspect that the place was deserted,' he wrote.

'But when our boatmen, knowing better where to look for people, opened one of those little steam baths – for all the world like a cow house – out rushed men, women and children, stark naked with dripping locks and scorched skins, and began rolling about upon the grass.'

That is an image that you might just as easily come across in Finland today. If you happened to be there in deepest winter, those naked people with scorched skins might well be rolling about in the snow or, even jumping through a hole in the ice of a lake. Perhaps it is not surprising that the Finns are among the least understood people in Europe.

Despite having steeped themselves in the worlds of industry, high-tech and hard-nosed global competition, the Finns, like the Swedes remain as close as ever to what they call 'Naturen' – 'The Nature'.

The Finns yearn to spend their summers by the sea or in a wooden cabin on the shore of a lake, where they are likely to be bitten, I have to say, by some of the most vicious mosquitoes on earth. Like the mosquitos in Lapland and Greenland, these little dive-bombers don't take prisoners!

Finland has more lakes than any other country in the world – 187,910 of them. Of these, 22 are more than 77 square miles (200 square kilometres) in area and the water in them is so clean that in many places residents still drink it. There are also 98,000 islands in this maze of inland waters.

What is more, Finland is getting bigger. The landmass is still rising by between one and three feet (30-90 centimetres) every hundred years, creating new low-lying islands. That is equivalent to an extra two-and-a-half square miles (seven square kilometres) of new land each century.

About 70% of the land surface is forest. Only 15% is cultivated. The rest is wasteland such as swamps, arctic fells and sand.

Bordered by Sweden to the west and Russia to the east, and cradled by an arm of Norway to the north, the Republic of Finland is the sixth largest country in Europe. About one third of the country lies above the Arctic Circle, the home of the Sami reindeer herders. Today, there are approximately 300,000 reindeer in Finland, 46 times as many as there are Sami people.

As in Sweden and Norway, theirs is an extremely hard life. Their culture is threatened, their language is gradually becoming extinct and the voracious forestry industry is depleting the animals' food sources. Reindeer herding is no longer economically viable unless you own at least 350 animals and very few families can afford that.

Yet, the Sami hang onto their culture with passion, the beauty of their northern wilderness tethering them to the north. Who can blame them for wanting to stay there when, in summer, the sun can shine for 24 hours a day for as long as 70 days?

In the autumn, the fells are ablaze with colour. It is known as the *ruuska* and is arguably even more colourful than in New England.

In winter, there is no sun at all for 70 days, just an eerie half-light reflecting off the snow. This semi-darkness is a small price to pay for the joys of Spring, Summer and Autumn.

From the Sami point of view, who would want to live like the rest of the Finnish population, now numbering 5.5 million, 70% of whom live in towns and cities? Approximately 600,000 Finns live in Greater Helsinki alone.

This means that the overall population density is only 40 people per square mile (17 per square kilometre). To put it another way, 70% of the population live on just two per cent of the land.

Finland was a part of Sweden for six-and-a-half centuries. To begin with, this was more a merging of the two countries than a conquest, but later, as Swedish power and influence grew, the Finns became a vital part of the Swedish army, comprising one third of the foot soldiers and cavalry.

Eventually, Sweden became immersed in a litany of wars. By the mid-17th century, it had become a Great Power with territory encircling the Baltic as far south as Poland.

In Finland, the Swedes pushed the eastern border further and further east, so it was Finland that bore the brunt of the fighting, a plight worsened by severe famine at the end of the 17th century when nearly one-third of the Finnish population died from hunger or disease. But then the tide began to turn.

The Swedes lost Finland to the Russian Empire at the conclusion of the Great Northern War in 1721 and again at the end of the Russo-Swedish war in 1743. When Britain then became an ally of Sweden, the Russians grew fearful of losing their naval access from St. Petersburg to the Baltic, so they attacked Finland once more and in 1808, Sweden had no option but to cede Finland to the Russians.

This left the Swedes utterly demoralised and impoverished, and the Finns desperately disillusioned. Yet, under Tsar Alexander the First, Finland became an autonomous Grand Duchy and he treated the Finns well.

The Tsar ordered new towns to be built, and roads and canals to be repaired. He moved the capital from Turku to Helsinki and gave instructions for the construction of magnificent new buildings, which in many cases still house the same state organizations today. The most striking example of the influence of this Tsarist era is perhaps Ouspensky Orthodox Cathedral in Helsinki.

The Tsar allowed the Finns to set up their own Diet, or parliament, and to retain their legal and social systems. Until this time, Swedish had been the dominant language and the language of government, but by 1840, Finnish civil servants had to show proof of their command of the Finnish language, as well.

In 1863, Tsar Alexander the Second made Finnish an official government language and thus, slowly but surely, sowed the seeds of Finnish nationhood.

The Grand Duchy worked exceptionally well for 90 years, until the weak and ineffective Nicholas II threw it all away. He appointed General Bobrikov, a ruthless soldier, as the new Governor General. Finland lost its autonomy and Bobrikov decreed that all Finnish men of fighting age would be liable to conscription into the Russian army.

The Finns were outraged. Half the men conscripted for military service in 1902 refused to report for duty and two years later, a patriotic student assassinated General Bobrikov, then committed suicide and became a national hero.

In the meantime, a bloody war erupted between Russia and Japan, both seeking to develop spheres of influence in the Far East at the expense of China. In 1905, Japan defeated the Russians.

Coupled with the stirrings of revolt in Russia, the trouncing distracted Nicholas II and when the Finns took the opportunity to propose a radical parliamentary reform, he agreed. So, the Finns introduced a single chamber parliament and gave the vote to women, the first country in Europe to do so.

During the October revolution, the Russian army collapsed. Lenin seized power and the Bolsheviks gave the Finns their freedom.

Finland's greatest composer, Jean Sibelius, saw it as a long, hard struggle which he described in his musical suite 'Finlandia'. It's rousing notes tinged with the ominous tones of the Russian bear stirred the hearts of the Finns and helped to spark in them the spirit of nationalism.

On December 6th 1917, Finland declared Independence. Soviet Russia recognised the move officially one month later.

Unfortunately, Independence triggered a bitter civil war. Pro-Russian Social Democrats and contingents of Russian soldiers known as 'The Reds' wanted a Russian-style revolution in Finland and, with Russian assistance, they quickly took over the whole of southern Finland, forcing the Senate to flee to the west coast.

Here, it appointed General Carl Gustaf Emil Mannerheim, an inspired military leader, to head up a non-existent army. Mannerheim quickly raised an army that would in future be known as 'The Whites'.

With help from the Kaiser's Germany, the Whites disarmed Russian garrisons and re-took the capital and other towns. After a last stand on the Karelian Isthmus, the 'Reds' capitulated but the conflict left the Finns insecure and fearful. The majority had developed a pathological hatred and distrust of all things Russian.

They were ever conscious of being wedged between Communist Russia and neutral Sweden and to the south by Germany, which was becoming increasingly militaristic.

Worse, in the 1920s famine was widespread. Finns were looking to the New World for opportunities and by 1930, one-tenth of the population had emigrated, mostly to the United States.

As mentioned earlier, Finland had been a part of Sweden for 650 years and as a result is officially bilingual and just to make things really complicated, there are three groups of Finns living in Finland and Sweden.

There are the Finn-Finns, whose mother tongue is Finnish; the Finn-Swedes, whose mother tongue is Swedish and the Swede-Finns who are Swedish citizens with Finnish as their mother tongue.

It's a nightmare. Having two official languages is costly, too. Radio and television programmes, for example, have to be broadcast in both languages.

The government has to publish all government documents in both languages. The same applies to street names and traffic signs, and so on. It is an expensive business, especially as today only about six per cent of the population speak Swedish on a daily basis.

Nonetheless, the ties between the two countries remain strong. Swedish is taught as a compulsory language to every Finnish child at school. Education in Finland begins at Kindergarten at the age of five and continues uninterrupted for all students free of charge until they are 16 years old.

There is no elite choice and no working-class choice. Everyone receives the same opportunities. Consequently, reading and writing skills are the highest in the world and 15-year-old Finnish schoolchildren represent the very top in mathematics, natural sciences and problem solving. Not surprisingly, perhaps, an international survey by the OECD places Finnish education as one of the best in the world.

The University of Helsinki has one of the world's most significant university libraries. Indeed, Finland is recognized internationally for its extensive network of libraries covering the entire country. There are 20 university-level educational establishments and 22 centres for science and technology focusing on research and development. The number of young people with degrees in Finland is amongst the highest in the world.

Indeed, education, research and the arts are the cornerstones of Finland's cultural and economic competitiveness.

Finnish towns and cities are also considered the safest in the world together with those in Luxembourg. That means, for example, that school children can still travel alone between their homes and schools, and to after-school activities.

So, in a country in which gun crime is extremely rare, it came as a terrible shock when, in November 2007, an 18-year-old gunman opened fire at his high school just north of Helsinki. Sadly, he killed seven other students and the principal before mortally wounding himself in a rampage that stunned the nation.

Still, crime and corruption rates are very low. Equality and the absence of discrimination are taken for granted.

Finland leads the world not only in many industrial, scientific and medical fields but also in the arts and humanities. Many Finns begin music lessons at nursery school and there are waiting lists for orchestral conductor training courses.

The Finns are considered to be reserved, stoic and enigmatic, but that's only half the story. Collectively, they are innovative, adapting quickly to change. One of their favourite sayings is that change is the only constant in their lives. They are particularly open to outside influences. Fast foods outlets and immigration have transformed the capital, Helsinki.

Today, there are approximately 402.600 foreigners living in Finland, mostly attracted by the very high standard of living and social benefit schemes. That is 7.3% of the population. It may not seem very many and, in fact, it is one of the lowest influxes of immigrants in Europe, but with the influx of Russian, Estonian, Chinese, Vietnamese, Turks and Somalis, and more recently Iraqis and Syrians, Helsinki has evolved into a thriving, vibrant city with a plethora of ethnic restaurants.

The Finns still like their own food, of course, but their staple diet of reindeer and other red meats, potatoes, and creamy sauces, was very high in fat and cholesterol, and led to one of the highest heart attack rates in Europe.

Nor was this alleviated by the Finns' taste for alcohol, which is very expensive in both Finland and Sweden, but in the Nordic countries, people always seem to find an answer where alcohol is concerned. In this case, the answer lay with the ferries that cross the Baltic between Finland and Sweden.

Popularly known as gin palaces, these luxury floating hotels do a roaring trade, not because alcohol is cheaper on board, but because they call in at the Åland Islands, about half way between the two countries.

Although the islands are Finnish territory, the Ålanders' history and culture is more closely allied to that of Sweden, so when Finland became independent in 1917, the authorities agreed that the 25,000 islanders should receive 'special status'.

Now, they have their own parliament, flag and postage stamps, and thanks to their 'special status', they are technically outside the European Union.

That meant that when the bureaucrats in Brussels banned all tax-free sales in Europe, the islands remained unaffected. That is why the ferries make a point of calling at this convenient tax-free haven.

Many Finns and Swedes own summer cabins in the archipelago and on the lakeshores, and it is said that when they build one, they always build a sauna first!

Back in the 1960s, an OECD report on cleanliness in Europe placed the Finns at the bottom of the list because so few Finnish houses had baths. What the report did not record is that there are about two million saunas in Finland, statistically one for every two-and-a-half Finns.

Essentially, a sauna is a cabin in which the temperature is warmed to an ideal 175°-210° Fahrenheit (80°-100° Centigrade) although among the more sado-masochistic Finns, this can be increased to unbearable levels.

The high temperature coupled with the humidity caused by pouring water onto the coals or stones to create steam induces perspiration. This cleanses the body from within through open pores.

To stimulate the circulation, it is common practice to brush oneself or one's partner lightly with a switch of wet birch.

There are no rules as to how long one should stay in the sauna. The rule of thumb is when you have had enough! To cool down, people either swim in the pool, take a cool shower, roll about in the grass, or jump into a lake or a hole in the ice. That done, it is time to relax, ideally with a beer and a hotdog.

The Finns are a tough people. They even have a special word to describe the most embedded aspect of their character: *Sisu!* It's impossible to translate but essentially *Sisu* means a combination of toughness and stamina.

When those qualities are combined with the Finns' intense patriotism and fierce independence, it makes them a very special people, as we shall see.

In the mid-1930s, the Soviet Union was gripped by a fear that Germany might attack them imminently through Finland. The Finns, meanwhile, had let the Russians know that they had no wish to become a Soviet satellite.

In this scenario, Stalin ordered his top generals to draw up a contingency plan for a war with Finland.

In October, 1939, the Soviets demanded that Finland not only cede to them a group islands in the Gulf of Finland but also lease to them a naval base at Hankö in the south-western corner of Finland.

As if that was not enough, Stalin stipulated that Finland should give up much of their Arctic territory and insisted that they move the border on the Karelian isthmus in the southeast further away from St. Petersburg. In other words, he wanted the Finns to cede part of Karelia.

The Finns declined and prepared for war despite the fact  that they would have to defend 600 miles (1,000 kilometres) of their border with the Soviet Union. It would be a formidable task. They knew, of course, that they could not defeat the Russians in the long term, but they did hope to be able to delay them long enough for sympathetic nations to come to their aid. The Finns did not expect a Soviet attack on the frontier between the northern edge of Lake Ladoga, 140 miles (225 kilometres) north of St. Petersburg, and its Arctic border with Russia more than 500 miles (800 kms) further north. The terrain was too remote; the logistics would be a nightmare.

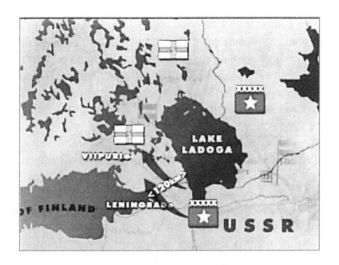

Instead, they prepared for a thrust from Leningrad across the Karelian isthmus, a 75-mile or 120-kilometre neck of land between the Gulf of Finland and Lake Ladoga.

Here, the Finns erected vast fields of barbed wire and laid thousands of mines along the most likely approach routes. They also laid giant concrete tank obstacles across the entire Karelian isthmus. It was known as the Mannerheim Line and the Finns hoped that it might delay the Soviets for a week to ten days.

By the last week of November, 1939, the Soviets had deployed 450,000 men, 2,000 tanks and 1,000 aircraft. As expected, the heaviest concentration of 200,000 men and 1,500 tanks was on the Karelian isthmus.

What the Finns had not anticipated was that the Soviets would deploy troops and tanks along the full length of the border – all the way up to the Arctic coast.

The Soviets had achieved a crushing superiority over the Finnish army. Three to one in manpower, 80 to one in tanks. Five to one in artillery and five and a half to one in aircraft.

The only consolation was that most of the Soviet troops were raw recruits with no battle experience. They were under the command of General Meretskov, who planned to encircle and annihilate the Finnish army with coordinated land, sea and air attacks.

The Finns, who had been able to mobilise only 180,000 men, had no chance at all. They were staring defeat in the face, but what they did have was *Sisu*. Stamina and guts!

On the 17th December, Meretskov launched his main offensive against the Mannerheim Line. It was the heaviest artillery bombardment experienced anywhere in the world since the Western Front in November 1918.

As the tanks pushed forward, the infantry were left behind, leaving gaps between them. It was a weakness the Finns quickly exploited. Finnish machine gunners and mortar teams opened up on the infantry.

The tanks rolled on alone to the line of granite anti-tank obstacles, which pushed them skyward at a steep angle. At this point, the Finnish anti-tank teams struck firing shells directly into the vulnerable bellies of the tanks.

Meretskov was desperate. He had promised Stalin victory by his birthday on 21st December, but on the 20th, Meretskov's armoured commanders reported that the assault on the Mannerheim Line had cost 250 armoured vehicles and horrific casualties.

Despite the Finnish successes, two days before Christmas, the Finns lost 1,500 men in a single day. Elsewhere lightly equipped, half-trained Finnish soldiers were fighting a guerrilla-style war.

One night, 140 Finns, equipped only with 16 light machine guns and personal arms, spread out along a low ridge, looking down onto a Russian battalion encamped around blazing fires.

The Finns opened fire with a withering barrage. Four minutes later, almost the entire battalion had been wiped out. Panic ensued. Russian units to the left and the right began firing wildly and then at each other.

The Finns slipped back across the ice to the sounds of an ever more ferocious battle as the Russians killed each other and so it continued. The temperature sank to minus 13° Fahrenheit (minus 25°C) and the Russians had no skis.

They tried to retaliate with tactical air strikes, but their pilots were mostly unable to locate the well-camouflaged Finns. Again and again, the highly mobile Finns wiped out entire battalions. North of Lake Ladoga the Russians were soon in retreat.

In Moscow, Stalin was beside himself with anger. He ordered some failed officers to be executed, although he was well aware that Finnish successes were due partly to his earlier purge of senior officers.

He appointed General Timoshenko to replace Meretskov and Timoshenko's first move was to assemble 10 infantry divisions, five tank brigades and an artillery piece every 20 yards across a 10-mile (16-kilometre) stretch of land. For Finland, the day of reckoning was approaching.

The artillery opened up on the 1st February, 1940, raining 400 shells a minute on Finnish positions; 300,000 shells in the first 24 hours.

Inevitably, the Finns began to crumble. They were running out of ammunition and battery commanders were ordered to fire only in cases of dire emergency. They now had to rely on machine guns, rifles and mortars to prevent a breakthrough and still the Mannerheim line held.

The Russians sent columns of infantry across the ice of the Gulf of Finland and Lake Ladoga in a bid to outflank the Mannerheim Line. But Finnish coastal batteries sent armour-piercing shells smashing into the ice. Hundreds of Russian troops drowned.

Next, the Russians advanced under the cover of thick fog and were within 50 metres of the shore when the fog lifted. Finnish machine gunners cut them down in heaps. The Finns' stamina and courage – *Sisu* – gave them extraordinary successes, but eventually the sheer weight of numbers began to tell. Finnish reinforcements now consisted mostly of 16-year old boys and eventually Mannerheim was forced to order a withdrawal.

Only three things could save Finland now; Spring, melting ice and the intervention of friendly countries. Sadly, the winter of 1939-1940 was one of the coldest and longest on record, and despite desperate appeals to Norway, Sweden, Britain and France, foreign intervention was not forthcoming. On March 13th, 1940, the Finns signed an armistice, which gave Stalin what he had wanted.

The Winter War lasted just 100 days. Finland lost 25,000 men, the Russians quarter of a million. Finnish wounded numbered 43,500 compared with 250,000 Soviet wounded.

Although the Finns were ultimately defeated, they destroyed the reputation of the massive Soviet Army and British, American and German observers were quick to take note.

The Winter War enabled Finland to retain her national sovereignty, but only at the cost of surrendering the Karelian isthmus and various islands in the Gulf of Finland. Despite the peace treaty, the Soviets continued to exert pressure on Finland, whose fears grew immeasurably when the Russians forcibly incorporated the Baltic States into the Soviet Union in 1940.

Isolated from the West and with Sweden staunchly neutral, the Finns realised that if they, too, remained neutral, they would almost certainly be occupied by one or the other of the belligerents. So, the Finns turned towards Germany and when the Germans invaded the Soviet Union in June 1941, the Finns followed suit, not as allies of Germany, but as co-belligerents.

Thus, began what became known as the 'Continuation War' of 1941 to 1944. During this war, the Finns lost another 65,000 dead and 158,000 wounded, but they returned every single body recovered from the battlefields of both wars to their home towns and villages.

There, they buried the dead with full honours. Monuments all over Finland testify to their bravery and resilience. The Finns also had to find new homes for some 423,000 Karelian refugees displaced by the fighting. The process of national reconstruction was long and painful, not least because the Soviets demanded harsh reparations from the Finns, mostly in the form of metal products.

Eventually, in 1948, Finland signed a treaty of Friendship, Co-operation and Mutual Assistance with the Soviet Union. They then followed a policy of active neutrality, but every aspect of life in Finland thereafter was governed by a concern as to 'how the Russians might react.'

Finland turned more and more to the west. The economy revived and then thrived. The standard and cost of living were soon in line with those in Sweden, which at the time were considered the highest in the world.

In January 1995, the Finns joined the European Union and signed up to the Euro. By doing so, they sent an unequivocal signal to the Russians that they wanted to move outside their sphere of influence and who can blame them!

By 2007, Finland had become one of the most prosperous nations in the world. After that, it did become mired in stagnation for three years, but has now recovered. At the time of writing, the economy is in surplus with a AAA rating.

The capital, Helsinki, is a regenerated, vibrant city that seems to be bursting at the seams with optimism.

Of course, the Finns have by no means forsaken 'The Nature' and in Finland, no matter where you are, even in the depths of the country, you will always find the ubiquitous mobile phone.

In 2007, the Finnish company, Nokia, was the world leader in its production, although the advent of the smart phone cast the company into crisis and in 2014, Microsoft took control of it. Notwithstanding this setback, Finland remains one of the world's leading nations in telecommunications, electronics and information technology.

Forestry provides a living directly or indirectly for one in five Finns and the paper and paperboard industry is the sixth largest in the world with 90% of it exported.

The country is also racing ahead with the application and development of biotechnology; plastic screws that melt and become a part of the bone, for example.

So, the Finns have come a long way and although they still face considerable challenges, there is no question that they will approach the future with the same degree of *Sisu* as they did in the Winter War or that 'The Nature 'will always remain closest to their hearts.

* * *

Oulu (Oulåborg)

The Main Attractions

With a population of nearly 205,000, Oulu is Finland's 6th largest city, yet it feels more like a market town with 20,000 residents. Not for nothing has Oulu been described as an 'urban living room'. Almost everything, it seems, is within relatively easy walking distance.

The city is never far from Nature at its best – beautiful parks, activity parks, the most extensive cycle way network in Finland, fast flowing rivers and streams, leafy streets and, of course, seafront restaurants and great places in which to go swimming or fishing. You can take a ferry to the islands of the archipelago in summer or drive to them in winter – across ice roads on a frozen Bothnian Bay.

Founded in 1605 by King Carl IX, Oulu has evolved from an early trading settlement to a thoroughly modern city with thriving businesses, world renowned hi-tech companies, modern shopping malls, department stores and fashionable boutiques, as well as old-style markets and an abundance of culture ranging from museums and art galleries to a multitude of especial events.

The city plays host to several music and film festivals in both winter and summer. They include the International Children's Film Festival, a rock festival, a 'metal' music festival, a festival of Irish music and, not least, the Air Guitar World Championships.

Sometimes advertised as 'the greatest thing you've never seen', you may never have heard of the air guitar, but it is said to be easy to learn and is great fun.

WikiHow describes it thus: 'Possibly the most influential instrument of our time, the air guitar has inspired millions to

pick up rock, all without knowledge of how to play the instrument or even how to read music. It's the spirit that counts and air guitarists worldwide have a meaningful connection through the joy of strumming away at the imaginary guitar.

'Being a tool of the imagination… there is a certain art involved in knowing how to make it look awesome, it's also a total essential to have heaps of fun doing it, either solo or with friends.'

Oulo, which the Finns pronounce with each vowel sounded, as in 'Oh-ooh-low', has no shortage of things to do.

Shuttle buses usually drop passengers off outside the *City Hall,* on Torikatu which began life as an assembly hall, wooden hotel and restaurant. Fire destroyed them all in 1882.

When the new stone palace was built in the neo-Renaissance style, the former assembly hall was re-instated and used for a celebratory banquet in 1886 to mark the completion of the railway line to the city.

It is well worth walking round to the back of the building to see a wall surmounted by a column of wonderful sculptures representing people who have contributed in some way to the creation of the city.

A short walk away, on Kirkkokatu at the back of the City Hall is *Oulu Cathedral*, a Lutheran church built in 1777 and dedicated to Sofia Magdalena, the wife of King Gustav III of Sweden.

The original, mostly wooden church burned down in 1822. The present building was built on top of the old stone walls with its huge dome and a belfry. These were not completed until 1845.

The Cathedral is open every day at 10 am-8pm from 27th May to 1st Sept. Sunday services are at 10am and held in Finnish.

If you continue to walk two blocks further along Kirkkokatu (in a north easterly direction), you will come to the delightful *Ainola Park* on Hupisaaret island.

This urban park is just a few minutes' walk from the City Hall and the Cathedral and was created in the 1860s. It is characterized by several white wooden bridges over the various streams and waterways that divide the park into a series of islands.

For passengers who wish to get away from the hubbub of the city, this is the perfect answer: a place to

be silent and in which to absorb the full beauty of Nature. There is a photograph at every turn, too! There is also a café in one of the greenhouses.

The park is also the home of the *Northern Ostrobothnia Museum* and the *University of Oulu Botanical Gardens.*

The museum was originally located in a late 19th century villa, but when this burned down in 1929, the city authorities acted quickly, calling in the Finnish architect Oiva Kallio. Not only did he design it in record time, but the museum opened two years later in 1931.

The museum covers the city of Oulu from pre-historic to modern times. There is a large-scale model of the city and province of Oulu as they were in 1938. The model measures approximately 545 square metres (500 square metres).

The museum is open Tuesday-Friday, 9am-5pm. Saturday-Sunday 10am-5pm. Admission €6,00 (£5.22, $6.60). Seniors €4.00 (£3.50, $4.40).

On the edge of Ainola Park, just over half a mile (one kilometre) from the city centre, *Oulu Museum of Art (OMA)* focuses on topical contemporary art with an extensive collection that also includes work by local and regional artists. The museum also arranges innovative communal events around the city. Like most art museums, there is a shop selling top-quality and distinctive gift items and interior decoration products.

The museum opens Tuesday-Saturday, 9am-5pm, Sunday 12 noon-7pm, Monday closed. Admission is €8.00 (£6.95, $8.80). Seniors: €5.00 (£4.35. $5.50).

One of the best-known attractions and a household name in Oulu and northern Finland is the *Science Museum (Tietomaa)*, located at Nahkatehtaankatu No. 6., but don't waste time trying to pronounce it! If Danish is a throat disease, Finnish is a language strictly for Finns, who have built-in safeguards against verbal seizures.

Since the museum was founded in 1988, it has received more than a million visitors, attracted by more than 150 hands-on attractions and demonstrations.

There are new exhibitions exploring different areas of science and technology each year, and the highlights of them then become part of the ever-growing permanent exhibition.

Here you can create sandscapes or get your thrills in a speedboat simulator. Or you can watch 3D films on the 1,645 square foot (153 square metre) screen, the second largest in Finland. These breath-taking films will whisk you into the ocean depths, outer space, dense jungles and even back in time to the pre-historic past.

This is a venue that is exceptional in any circumstances. On a rainy day, it is the perfect place in which to spent the day.

The museum is open Monday-Thursday, 9am-5pm. On Fridays, it remains open until 6pm. Saturdays and Sundays 10am-6pm. Admission is €15.00 (£13.05, $15.50). Seniors: €11.00 (£9.60, $12.10), which is money well spent.

Back in the town centre, the ***Kauppatori Market Square,*** located on the seafront, pulsates with energy all day long with locals and visitors alike enjoying the old granaries once used to store such products as salt, but which are now restaurants and cafes, and boutiques selling reindeer pelts, Sami handiccrafts and all kinds of clothing and decorative products.

The focal point here is the statue of ***The Fat Bobby*** in front of the Market Hall. The statue was created to honour one of the police officers who used to patrol the square many years ago.

You can also buy a postcard of the bobby and pop it into the post box in Oulu Market Hall. It will then be stamped with a special 'Bobby the Policeman' stamp.

Built in 1901, the Market Hall has numerous stalls selling fresh fruit and vegetables, meat, fish and cheese, wonderful breads and not least meats that are only to be found in Lapland – reindeer (best stewed), bear salami, moose and so on, all cured, of course, so that they will more than last the journey home.

Oulu Market Hall is open Monday-Thursday, 8am-5pm, Friday 8am-6pm and Saturday from 8am-3pm. All vendors accept credit cards.

Oulu also hoses the International Grand Market which visits most cities and towns in Finland throughout the year, usually for about four days. This is a truly a grand affair with about 130 merchants from 35 different countries, including Asia and America, all exhibiting (and selling) their specialities.

Although the International Grand Market is staged in the centre of town, just behind the City Hall, most events take place in **_Kuusisaari Event Park,_** located at Raatintie No. 7. Not far from the town centre, the park also has a sandy beach, allegedly the best fishing in Oulu, campfire sites and a basketball court. This is also where Oulu Castle used to be. Today, a café called _Linnankahvila_ has taken its place and is open daily during the summer.

Finally, about nine miles (14.5 kms) out of own and located on three islands at Turkansaarentie No. 165, the **_Turkansaari Open Air Museum,_** has a collection of historical buildings relocated from various parts of Finland. They include a wooden church dating back to 1694. The exhibits follow a theme of agriculture and forestry, fishing and Oulu's history of tar production. Exhibitions describe tar burning and how the tar was, and still is, used, not least to create products for the gift shop!

The museum is open Monday-Sunday, 10am-5pm and there is no entry charge.

* * *

Vaasa

The Main Attractions

The city council of Vaasa, on the central west coast of Finland, is comprised of ambitious men and women. They want to boost the population of the city from nearly 68,000 to 100,000 people.

They may well succeed because although first impressions suggest this is a somewhat underwhelming city, built as it is on a grid system with long streets and endless apartment blocks, it is in fact renowned for its entrepreneurs, culture, dual language, international industry, abundant services and proximity to the Kvarken archipelago, which is Finland's only UNESCO natural heritage site!

Around the city, there are nearly 300 miles (473 kms) of coastline, 112 miles (180 kms) of hiking trails and cycle paths, camping and picnic sites, and abundant birdlife.

Vaasa is the regional capital of Ostrobothnia, (East Bothnia) also known as Österbotten in Swedish or Pohjanmaa in Finnish. The capital, Helsinki, is only a 3½ train journey away. Umeå, in Sweden, is a four-hour trip by boat that operates even in winter when the Gulf of Bothnia is frozen.

Vaasa is a city in which 20% of the population are students, the highest percentage per population in Finland. There are seven different institutions providing higher education which, to no small degree, is why 75% of city residents have at least an upper secondary education.

Vaasa is also perhaps best known as the city in which Swedish is spoken more than anywhere else in Finland; around 25% of the population speak Swedish as their mother tongue and nearly 70% Finnish.

Swedes had settled along the southwestern coast of Finland long before the Viking age, which ostensibly began in the 8th century, but it would be at least another 400 years before Finland became a battleground between Russia and Sweden.

Swedish expeditions to central Finland probably took place around 1157, when King Erik arrived to enforce Christianization efforts., but exactly when Finland became part of Sweden is unknown.

What we do know is that Swedish rule was established by the late 13th century and that King Charles IX of Sweden granted Vaasa its charter in 1606 and originally named it Mustasaari.

In those days, the town was situated around the old harbour 4.3 miles (seven kilometres) southeast of the city's current location.

Later, Charles decided to call the town Vasa after the Royal House of Vasa. Thanks to shipbuilding, trade and especially the production of tar, Vasa flourished. By the late 17th century, the population had grown to more than 2,000 inhabitants. There was a school and the citizens established the first library in Finland there.

Unfortunately, in 1808-9, the city was plundered and mostly destroyed with a considerable loss of life during the Finnish War between Sweden and Russia. The Russians eventually defeated the Swedes and Vaasa was absorbed into the Grand Duchy of Finland, which was part of the Russian Empire.

Meanwhile, Vasa was renamed Nikolaistad after the late Tsar Nicholas I. When he was ousted in 1917, the town was immediately renamed Vaasa., this time spelt with two 'a's. (In Finnish, a single 'a' would be pronounced as in 'bad'. The additional 'a' is applied to denote a long 'a', as in 'rather').

In 1852, a farmer is said to have fallen asleep while smoking his pipe in a wooden barn. Whether he lived to tell the tale is open to question. If he did, he would hopefully have had a monumental guilty conscience because the fire that ensued destroyed almost the entire town, most of which comprised wooden buildings. Only 24 of the 379 buildings survived.

WHAT TO DO IN VAASA.

Korsholm Church, (aka Korsholmskyrka or Mustasaari Church) located at Adelcrantzinkuja No.1 about four miles (seven kilometres) southeast of the city centre, looks more like an old manor house with a bell tower attached rather than a church. That is because it was originally built in 1776 as he Court of Appeal, which after the 1852 fire, was converted into a church.

Seating 900 worshippers, the church was renovated extensively.

During June, July and August, the church is open Monday-Friday from 9am-3pm. Other times as agreed by the Pastor's Office, tel. 0400 415008 (Mon-Tue and Mon-Fri 9 am-4pm, Closed Wednesdays).

Approximately 675 yards (620 metres) walk from the church is the *Museum of Old Vaasa,* located at Wasastjerna House, Kauppiaankatu 10. This was the only private stone house in the city to survive the 1852 fire. Built between 1780 and 1881 by a local merchant shipowner, the three-storey museum portrays life in the city prior to the fire.

The first floor is a café, the second floor is decorated in the 19th century Russian style and includes a shipowner and town councillor's office, and the third floor reflects the Swedish period during the reign of Gustaf III and Gustav IV Adolphus, who stayed there in 1802.

Later, the house was used as a savings bank and pharmacy until the 100th anniversary of the great fire, when it opened as a museum.

It is open Tuesday-Sunday 10am-5pm. Monday closed. Entrance fee is €9.00 (£7.75, $10.00). Seniors: €6.00 ($5.15, $6.70).

A further walk of about 250 yards (225 metres) takes you to the *Old Ruins of Vaasa* at Kauppiaankatu No. 5. These are not extensive and there is not a great deal to see except the remaining walls of

the church and bell tower, but it is worth a photograph. There is also a small restaurant on the other side of the road.

Back in the city centre, the **_Ostrobothnian Museum (Pohjanmaanmuseo),_** located at Museokatu No. 3 in Marianpuisto Park, about a 15 minute walk from Vaasa Market Square is a multi-purpose museum founded in 1895.

It features the history, culture and art of the city and also houses the **_Museum of Natural Science in Ostrobothnia_**, and the **_Terranova Exhibition_**, which focuses on the wildlife of the Kvarken archipelago.

Kvarken is the only UNESCO Natural Heritage site in Finland and was granted the status because of what is known as rapid glacio-isostatic uplift.

This is when land formerly crushed by the weight of an icecap or glacier begins to rise again once the ice has melted. Consequently, the Kvarken archipelago is continuously rising from the sea, creating islands, expanding peninsulas and marshland and gradually becoming an extension to the World Heritage site of Sweden's High Coast on the western side of the Gulf of Bothnia.

With abundant wildlife, hiking trails and opportunities for fishing, kayaking and so on, the edge of the archipelago is no more than a 20-minute drive from Vaasa city centre and for anyone interested in the phenomenon, it is well worth visiting the *World Heritage Gateway Exhibition Hall.*

Here you can watch videos, read brochures about the area and learn about life in the archipelago in earlier times. There is an art museum, a shop selling souvenirs and World Heritage products, and a café and restaurant.

The modernistic gateway building is located by Replot Bridge, which is the longest in Finland, and is open from May-September weekdays, 10am-4pm and from 10am-6pm every day in June, July and August. Between October 1st-20th, the museum is also open on Saturdays.

Replot Bridge

Replot Bridge, which is 3,428 ft (1,045 metres long, links Replot Island with mainland Korsholm. Proposals for a bridge across the Gulf of Bothnia estimate the cost at two billion euros, which the Swedish Finance minister described as 'interesting' (i.e. too expensive!)

Back in town, the *Tikanoja Art Museum* located at Hovioikeudenpuistikko No.4, which is a prime example of why, if you don't want to swallow your tongue, you should never try to pronounce anything in Finnish!

The museum specializes in ancient paintings from Finland and has a superb collection of foreign art, especially

French 19th and 20th paintings. It also specializes in cultural history and curates both permanent and temporary exhibitions. is €9.00 (£7.75, $10.00). Seniors: €6.00 ($5.15, $6.70).

The Kunsti Museum of Modern Art is in Vaasa's inner harbour not far from the market square, is said to house one of most significant collections of modern and contemporary art in Finland.

It provides an in-depth look at contemporary themes and is well worth a visit. It is open Tuesday-Sunday from 11am-5pm. Closed Mondays. Admission is €9.00 (£7.75, $10.00). Seniors: €6.00 ($5.15, $6.70).

For anyone interested in vintage vehicles, the ***Vaasa Car and Motor museum,*** located across three storeys in an old factory at Myllykatu 18 B, specializes in vehicles and engines from the early 20th century.

These include a restored horse drawn ambulance from 1909, rally racing cars, mountain cars, motorcycles, mopeds and snowmobiles. Opening hours are 10am – 5pm daily. Admission: €8.00 (£6.90, $8.95).

The ***Brage Open Air Museum*** located at Bragenkuja No.1. on a delightful seashore just 1¼ miles (2 kms) from Vaasa city centre, is essentially an old late 29th century farmstead with a café selling mouth-watering waffles.

It comprises 24 relocated buildings, including a stable, a windmill, a smithy, a sheep barn, a piggery, a boathouse, fish sauna and seal hunting museum, as well as a fully furnished East Bothnian wedding chamber.

Opening times: June 25th-11th August, Tuesday, Thursday-Sunday, 11am-4pm. Wednesday 1pm-6pm. Closed Monday. Admission: €4 (£3.45, $4.45). Seniors: half price. Credit cards accepted.

If the weather is inclement and cold, a trip to **Tropiclandia Spa and Water Park** located at Kesäpolu No.1. (Sommarstigen No.1) may be an option. It is described as a 'bathing paradise'. Here there are water slids, waves, waterfalls, whirlpools, saunas – and the temperature is always around 90ºF (32ºC).

It is open daily from 10am-8pm. Admission is €10.00 (£8.60, $11.29) on weekdays and €17 .00 (£14,65, $19.00) at weekends. Seniors pay €12.00. (£10.35, $13.40).

Finally, birdwatching enthusiasts may wish to visit **Meteoriihi,** seven miles (11 kms) south of Vaasa. This is a site where a fragment of a giant meteorite smashed into the ground some 500 million years ago.

It left a crater four miles (7kms) across. Today, it has been filled in and there is nothing there except fields (although you can see the original impact area from the air).

There is a shed and a birdwatching tower from which you can see cranes, geese and swans, and thousands of other birds during the north-south migration.

It's safe, too. As someone once said: 'If you suffer from cosmic angst, relax – meteorites never hit in the same place again!'

* * *

Pori (Björneborg)

The Main Attractions

Like Vaasa but a little larger, Pori is a sizeable city of nearly 85,000 people that can be summed up as being situated on the estuary of, and divided by, the Kokemäenjoki river, with wonderful beaches, sand dunes, wetlands and birdlife nearby.

The influx of some 6,000 students has enlivened the city, so that it now has a buzzing nightlife and a goodly number of art galleries, museums and other cultural venues.

Each year, for five days in July, a small park with the tongue-twisting name of Kokemäenjoki becomes the venue for an annual jazz festival. This regularly attracts thousands of enthusiasts, including the President of Finland.

Held on three-stages on an island close to the city centre, the festival was first held in 1966 and has since become recognised as one of the best of its kind in Europe.

That is possibly because it is not devoted entirely to jazz, but also encompasses blues, soul, rock, hip-hop, reggae and garage music, whatever that is! In any event, it is so successful that in the past it has attracted such artists as Ray Charles, Bob Dylan, B.B. King, Miles Davis, Elton John, Stevie Wonder, Santana and the Icelandic phenomenon, Björk, all of whom in turn have enhanced the event's reputation.

That they were able to perform in the venue was down to the son of Sweden's King Gustavus, Duke John of Finland, (later King John III of Sweden), who founded Pori in 1558.

Before then, the population lived primarily in two medieval market towns, Kokemäki and Ulvila, further upriver, but as the post-glacial rebound gradually made it almost impossible to navigate the Kokemäki river, trade suffered and the town's fortunes waned.

Duke John realised that the only answer was to establish a new town with a better harbour closer to the Gulf of Bothnia. So, he ordered the population of around 300 people to move 6½ miles (10½ kms) downriver to the city's present location.

This soon proved beneficial. Shipbuilding flourished again and Pori became an important centre of trade exporting fish to the rest of Europe and importing wines and spices in return. A fair exchange, you may think!

By an extraordinary coincidence, in 1852 massive fires razed both Vaasa and Pori to the ground. Only a few buildings survived in both towns.

However, Pori rose from the ashes, this time with wide boulevards and elegant stone buildings and, once again, the town prospered. By the late 19th century, engineering plants and sawmills spread along the riverbanks and Pori was exporting timber and matches. This time, wine does not seem to be part of the deal.

History being what it is, Pori had to endure another dark period when Russian troops arrived to sack the city and seize its richest residents, most of whom were never seen again. In all likelihood, they also took the wine along with the oxen, horses and boats. The carnage lasted seven years and all foreign trade fizzled out.

Nor did the city escape the 1918 Finnish Civil War or the Second World War, when the Soviets bombed it four times in 1939 and 1940. Four years later, German forces who had occupied Pori airport, withdrew, destroying the control tower and hangers with explosives. They also used 319 Soviet prisoners of war as forced labour and starved them to death, which you may think defeated the object somewhat!.

WHAT TO DO IN PORI

Satakunta Museum located on Hallituskatu No. 11, is one of the oldest museums in Finland (established in 1888), and a delight to see with fascinating tableaux and exhibits.

The museum offers a highly visual insight into the history and culture of the Satakunta region, of which Pori is the capital. This is a museum that has been curated with imagination, tracing local traditions from birth to death. One of the fascinating exhibits illustrates how women have kept different objects in their handbags through the ages.

Open Tuesday-Sunday, 11am-6pm. Closed Mondays.
Admission €7.00 (£6.00, $7.80).   Seniors: half price.

One of the few buildings to survive the 1852 fire was Pori's *Old Town Hall,* a magnificent neo-classical edifice that served as the headquarters of the city council until 1961.

Located at Hallituskatu No. 9 the building was designed by Carl Ludvig Engel, a bricklayer's son born in 1778 in Charlottenburg, Berlin, who also designed the state buildings of Helsinki. It is now used for city offices and the Tourist Office.

The Latin inscription on the façade, *Curia Arctopolis,* means 'The Court of Pori'. *Arctopolis* is said to be a translation of Pori's Swedish name, Björneborg, which in turn means 'Bear Castle'.

If the connection seems a little diffuse, a meal in the excellent vaulted restaurant in the basement of what used to be the city jail may help clear the mind.

Pori Art Museum is in a former mid-19th century customs and weigh house on the riverfront road, Eteläranta. Unusually, it does not have a permanent exhibition but focusses instead on rotating shows by local and regional artists that tend to feature social issues such as human rights, multiculturalism and environmental appreciation.

Among these have been a strangely disturbing but compelling exhibition of giant photographs of children's toys, another consisting of photographs of derelict Stasi buildings and still another of beautifully executed flowers painted in the style of Swedish folk art.

The museum is open Tuesday-Sunday, 11am to 6pm, and on Wednesdays, from 11am-8pm. The entry fee is €7.00 (£6.00, $7.70). Seniors: half price.

On a more industrial note, the **Rosenlew Museum** in a former 1860s grain warehouse at Kuninkaanlahdenkatu No. 14, showcases the history and production of the Rosenlew company, which operated between 1853 and 1987.

Apart from the superb conversion from old warehouse to modern museum, the exhibition follows the development of Pori through the entrepreneurship of the Rosenlew family from paper and cardboard production to threshers and refrigerators, and how the advent of the 21st century ushered in the emergence of globalization.

Opening hours: Tuesday-Sunday, 11am-5pm. Closed Mondays. Admission €5.00 (£4.30, $5.60). Seniors: half price.

One of the most visited attractions and part of Pori National Urban Park is the **Jusélius Mausoleum** in the Käppärä Cemetrey at Maantiekatu No. 46. This may seem a

little macabre, but it is well worth the visit because this is a place of great beauty.

Fritz Arthur Jusélius was a local industrialist, who commissioned the Gothic Revival mausoleum for his daughter, Sigrid, who died of tuberculosis.

Designed by a well-known church architect, Josef Stenbäck, the mausoleum is adorned with a series of extraordinary frescos and bronze reliefs. These alone make the visit worthwhile.

There is a sad story, too; the sarcophagi of both Sigrid and her father are on display. Sigrid's mother and sister are buried in a family grave nearby and Fritz Arthur was a man clearly unlucky in love, for his second and third wives are also buried next to the mausoleum.

The mausoleum was inaugurated on the anniversary of F. A. Jusélius' birth, 13 June 1941. It is open from 30th April on Sundays from noon-5 p.m. and between May 1st and 31st August from 11am-4pm. From 1st-30th September, it will open for a separate fee on request. At other times, admission is free.

On a somewhat larger scale, *Pori Church (Keski-Porin Kirkko)* is the largest in the Satakunta province and also one

of the largest in Finland. Best known for its cast-iron steeple, stained glass windows, unusual art-nouveau glass paintings and its German organ, it was built in the neo-Gothic style between 1859 and 1863.

The German organ-building company, Paschen Kiel Orgelbau GmbH built the pipe organ in 2007 according to a design by the Parisian organ designer, Kurt Lueders.

The organ has 58 stops on three manuals and pedal. Consequently, the church is the main venue for the annual Pori Organ Festival.

The church is also the burial ground for more than 400 Finns who were killed during the Second World War.

Finally, for beach lovers, there is an excellent beach in Kokemäenjoki park, just opposite to Pori Art museum on Eteläranta. The prime beach, though, is *Yyteri Beach,* just over ten miles (17 kilometres) from the city centre.

Here the beach is safe, clean and well maintained, and the water is shallow and warm. It is also the longest beach in Finland, nearly four miles (six kilometres) long and backed by a range of sand dunes that attract thousands of visitors each summer.

Yyteri is also a mecca for birdwatchers who come each year to see migrating arctic bird species from early Spring until late Autumn. A 200-foot (63-metre) high observation tower gives superb views of the islands and wetlands.

Yyteri has a nudist beach and a dog beach (!) and there are restaurants, café's ,changing rooms, toilets, barbecue facilities and a hotel and spa nearby. There are also lifeguards and adequate parking.

* * *

Rauma (Raumo)

The Main Attractions

OLD Rauma
Old Town Hall
Rauma Museum
Marela Museum
Kirsti Museum
Rauma Maritime Museum
Telephone Museum
Rauma Art Museum
Church of the Holy Cross

Very few cruise ships spend a day in Rauma, but they should because this is a delightfully leafy town just 30-miles (50-kilometres) south of Pori that encompasses the largest wooden town in the Nordic region.

With more than 600 extremely well-preserved and colourful wooden houses, *Old Rauma* is home to about 700 people who must think they are living in the middle ages or in one of Hans Christian Andersen's stories.

Rauma was founded in 1442 and is the third oldest town in Finland. To wander along the cobbled streets in this UNESCO World Heritage Site, dipping into boutique shops, cafés and museums is an absolute joy.

The Old Town is just a sizeable part of a more modern Rauma, which has a population of nearly 40,000 and is best known for its lace-making tradition, paper and pulp mills, shipbuilding, marine and metal industries.

More than 600 million tonnes shipping uses the port each year. Indeed, at one time nearly 60 sailing ships were based in the port, the largest fleet in the country and the main reason for the town's prosperity.

It is a thriving town, its annual highlight being Lace Week, in mid-July when local craftspeople set out their stalls

and demonstrate their skills.

During the celebratory week, the streets of the Old Town are filled with market stalls, crowds, jugglers, acrobats, performance artists, local bands and musicians.

The festivities end with Black Lace Night when the boutiques stay open late into the evening and shows and concerts attended by people dressed in black lace bring the event to a close at midnight.

WHAT TO DO IN RAUMA

The *Old Town Hall*, a baroque building built in 1776, now houses *Rauma Museum,* which is located at

Kauppakatu No. 13, and is actually three museums – including the *Marela* and *Kirsti Museums* *(see below)*.

Rauma Museum features the history of lacemaking in the town and has several lace exhibits on display. The shop sells

lace products, artworks by local artisans and souvenirs. On the upper floor, temporary exhibitions change each year.

The opening times for all three museums are from May 5th-August 31st: Tuesday-Sunday, 10am-5pm. Closed Mondays. At other times of year, Tuesday-Friday, 12 noon-5pm, Saturday, 10am-2pm and Sunday 11am – 5pm. Mondays closed. During Lace Week, the museum is open daily from 10am-5pm.

Admission is €8.00 (£6.85, $8.95) for all three museums or 5.00 (£4.30, $5.60) for a single ticket to one museum. Seniors: €6.00 (£5.15,$8,70) for three  museums, €3.50 (£3.00, $3.90) for one museum.

Marela Museum, just along the road at Kauppakatu No. 24, is a house owned by a wealthy merchant shipowner, Gabriel Granlund, from the 1870s to 1906, and shows how he and his family lived during the halcyon days of 19th-20th century shipping.

The Marela house, which is named after Abraham Marelin, another shipping magnate of the time, comprises several buildings, including a large granary, a stables and carriage house, and a separate house for the butler. All have retained the décor, ceilings, furnishings and tiled heating stoves of the period.

The **Kirsti Museum**, located at Pohjankatu No. 3, similarly showcases life in the 18th and 19th centuries. Here, there is a main building and several outbuildings, a cowshed, stable and so on, but in this case, the same family of seamen and craftsmen occupied the main dwelling house for more than 200 years. Throughout the generations, they owned shares in ships that exported goods to Denmark and Germany. Although they prospered, they also indulged in farming for a second income and the family members owned fields and barns, and kept three cows, pigs and a couple of horses.

Meanwhile, the women of the family had a reputation for their skills in lacemaking that reached back to the early 18th century.

Although Rauma is the kind of town you just want to meander around, for its size, it is rich in museums. The **Rauma Maritime Museum**, for example, specializes in the seafaring traditions in Rauma, focusing not only on ships but also on the lives of sailors. Located at Kalliokatu No. 34, it is open every day during the summer from 11am to 5pm. Admission is €9.00 £7.75, $10.05)   Seniors: €7.00 (€6.00, $7.80)

A tiny but quirky privately-owned museum is the **Telephone Museum**, located at Eteläpitkäkatu No. 22. Here, there is a wide-ranging collection of old phones with explanations of voice communication technology that is intriguing and worth a visit whilst discovering the Old Town. It is open every day Tuesday to Friday, 12 noon-5pm, on Saturdays 10am-2pm and Sundays 11am-5pm. Admission fees are not published.

Rauma Art Museum is located at Kuninkaankatu No. 34, in Old Rauma and focusses on modern art and the history of art. The building and courtyard are among the best-preserved in the Old Town. Some artworks date to 1795 and 1827. There are different temporary exhibitions and events throughout the year, but the permanent exhibition reflects the golden era of Finnish art.

There is a shop mostly selling works by local artists, postcards, hand-printed cards, books and souvenirs.

Opening hours: Tuesday-Friday, 12noon- 5pm.00 (£5.15, $6.70). Seniors: half price.

Finally, the present-day, granite ***Church of the Holy Cross,*** located at Kirkkokatu No. 2. in the Old Town, stands on a site occupied by a church as far back as 1420, when Franciscan friars are thought to have built a wooden church to serve their monastery.

That was replaced by today's church in the early 1500s. although in 1538, it was abandoned for a century following the Swedish reformation.

Later, worshippers used the Church of the Holy Trinity nearby until it burned down in the mid-19th century (the remaining stone ruins can still be seen). They then returned to the Church of the Holy Cross, which was consecrated in 1640 by the Lutherans.

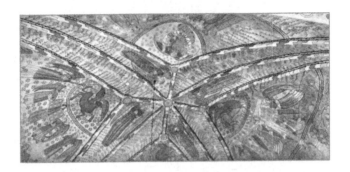

The interior of the church, which can, but doesn't often, seat some 800 people, is quite beautiful and especially noteworthy for the fresco murals depicting the story of Salvation on the walls and vaulted ceiling.

The bell tower, incidentally, was built with stones from the ruined Church of the Holy Trinity in 1640 when its white steeple began to be used by seafarers as a navigational landmark.

The Church of the Holy Cross is open daily from 9am-3pm.

To sum up, Rauma has so many museums, all worth a visit, that you almost hope it might rain!

* * *

Turku (Åbo)

The Main Attractions

Like Pori, Turku lies on the estuary of the river that divides it and, consequently, the river – the Aura River, or Plough River – is the core of the city. This is where many of the 192,000 residents come to eat, drink and people watch in the riverside restaurants and bars.

Turku is a city enlivened by festivals and summer events - open air concerts and rock festivals, street theatre, art and design exhibitions, and much else besides.

The great thing about Turku is that ship's shuttle buses tend to stop in two places, so you can opt to alight at the first stop next to the castle, wander round the castle courtyard, take some photographs and then walk 300 yards or so to the river bank where you will find old sailing ships berthed on both sides of the river.

In July 2017, nearly 600,000 visitors came to Turku to watch 101 tall ships taking part in the 'Parade of Sails' at the start of the 5th Tall Ships race to take place here.

Having wandered along the quayside, you can then re-join the shuttle bus, which will drop you off at the Tourist Information Office at Turku Market Square in the centre of town (not to be confused with the Old Great Square on Uudenmaankatu (Nylandsgatan) near the Cathedral.

Turku is the oldest town in Finland. Archaeological digs in the area revealed settlements dating back to the Stone Age. However, Turku was not mentioned in written form until publication of an Arabic travel book and 'world' map by the

Muslim scholar Al-Sharif al-Idrisi in 1154 and a Papal Bull issued by Pope Gregory IX in 1229.

As Finland's most populous and important city, it remained the country's capital through centuries of Swedish rule until 1812, by which time the country had been absorbed into the Russian Empire as an autonomous Grand Duchy.

In that year, the capital was moved to Helsinki and after the great fire of 1827, government departments also moved there.

Today, Turku is Finland's sixth largest city with 83% of the population speaking Finnish and 5.5% Swedish. The remainder speak Russian, Arabic, Kurdish, Albanian, Estonian and Somali. Finland, incidentally, does not collate statistical information about religious or ethnic minorities.

The city's economy is centred on the Port of Turku, through which some three million passengers pass each year, mostly travelling to Stockholm and Mariehamn.

The German-owned Meyer Turku shipyard has a full order book until 2024 and it was here that Meyer Turku built the *Oasis of the Seas,* formerly the largest cruise ship in the world.

Shipbuilding and shipping apart, Turku is also renowned as being a centre for high-tech companies, with some 300 firms specializing in IT and biotechnology based in the Turku Science Park. It is these areas that city councilors envisage being the future basis of the city economy.

Turku has two universities and about 35,000 students enrolled in them. Yet despite the superb educational facilities, the average unemployment rate in Turku remains high at 12.3% (2019).

In 2011, Turku and Tallinn in Estonia were designated the European Capitals of Culture not least, in Turku's case, because of the plethora of cultural venues – theatres, cinemas, art galleries and its Philharmonic Orchestra.

Each year, on Christmas Eve, a medieval market attracts thousands to the **Old Great Market Square**, where the Declaration of Christmas Peace is read in Finnish and Swedish from an old roll of parchment, a tradition that dates to 1320. Not for nothing is Turku Finland's official 'Christmas City'.

The text not only wishes the crowds gathered in the square a Merry Christmas; it is also a warning against bad behaviour!

'Tomorrow, God willin', it reads, 'is the graceful celebration of the birth of our Lord and Saviour; and thus is declared a peaceful Christmas time to all, by advising devotion and to behave otherwise quietly and peacefully, because he who breaks this peace and violates the peace of Christmas by any illegal or improper behaviour shall under aggravating circumstances be guilty and punished according to what the law and statutes prescribe for each and every offence separately.

Finally, a joyous Christmas feast is wished to all inhabitants of the city."

WHAT TO DO IN TURKU.

Given that Turku is divided by the Aura River, the attractions are similarly split into those on the east and west banks. Fortunately, there are ten bridges over the river and a small ferry transports pedestrians and cyclists across free of charge.

On the west bank, the main attractions are Turku Castle, the Forum Marinum Maritime Centre, which has its own fleet of ships, including a full-rigger *Suomen Joutsen*, the Pharmacy Museum and Quensel House, Turku Market Square and the Market Hall, and Turku Art Museum.

The Old Great Market Square, Cathedral, Sibelius Museum, Aboa Vetus and Arts Nova museum are all on the east bank, as are the Wäinö Aaltonen Museum of Art,

Museum Ett Hem A Home Museum) and Luostarinmäki Handicraft and Open-Air Museum.

WEST BANK

Turku medieval Castle, located at Linnankatu No. 80, has been a multi-purpose fortress ever since the 1280s, firstly as part of the city's defences but also as an elegant royal court, prison, granary and barracks.

As a bastion and administrative centre, it was variously ruled by the castle sheriff, commander, regent, Duke, Lord Lieutenant, or Governor-General, who also had to contend with numerous sieges, a disastrous fire which destroyed the wooden part of the castle almost completely and being bombed during the War of Continuation in 1941.

Once the home of King John III of Sweden, it is now the home of the *Turku Historical Museum*, which comprehensively presents the castle's history and is said to be one of the most visited museums in Finland.

Elegant rooms with period furniture costumes and museum artefacts are open to visitors. The banqueting hall is still used for municipal functions. There is a museum shop (with medieval costumes for children) and a café named after Duke John in which you can enjoy a coffee or lunch.

The museum is open June 3rd -1st September, Monday-Sunday, 10am-6pm and from September 2nd - 29th December, Tuesday-Sunday, 10am-6pm. Admission: €12 (£10.35, $13.30). Half price for pensioners, unemployed and conscripts!

A short walk of about 500 yards (456 metres) will take you to the *Forum Marinum Maritime Centre,* located at Linnenkatu No.72.

Apart from several exhibitions housed in two museum buildings, there are no fewer than 11 preserved ships and smaller craft moored along the riverbank, including the full rigger, Suomen *Joutsen (Swan of Finland)*, a barque, a tugboat, gunboat, motor torpedo boat, a corvette, minelayer

and the pocket liner *Bore*. The ships are open to the public during the summer months only.

The main exhibition is based on 'Work at Sea'. Other permanent displays cover the history of shipbuilding in Finland, ship engine manufacturing, the history of the *Suomen Joutsen* from 1902 to 2009 and the history of the *Bore*.

Opening times during the summer months, beginning in May, Monday-Sunday, 10am-6pm. Winter months: Tuesday-Sunday, 10am-6pm. Admission for the exhibitions is €10.00 (£8.65, $11.10). Seniors: 50% discount.

For both exhibitions and all the ships, the price is €17.00 (£14.70, $28.85) or €10 for seniors. For one ship and the exhibitions, it is €6 (£5.20, $6.65), Seniors: €4.00 (£3.45, $4.45).

The **Pharmacy Museum** is located in **Quensel House**, a

traditional bourgeoise house at Läntinen Rantakatu No.13b. It is the oldest wooden house in Turku and one of the best preserved in the Nordic countries.

Built at the dawn of the 18th century in part of the town then reserved for the nobility, the house was named after Wilhelm Johan Quensel, a Swede who came to Turku in the late 17th century to work for the Court of Appeal.

The **Pharmacy Museum**, dates back to the 19th century and has the oldest surviving pharmacy interior in Finland. Comprising two research laboratories, complete with pharmaceutical utensils of the period, a herb room and an original office, the museum offers a chance to study the history of the pharmaceutical profession and the herbs used by its members.

There is also a cafeteria in the inner courtyard serving homemade pastries made from 18th century recipes.

The museum is open from 16th Sept-2nd June, Tuesday-Sunday, 10am-6pm, 3rd June-1st Sept, Monday-Sunday, 10am-6pm and from Set 2nd-Dec 31st, Tuesday-Sunday, 10am-6pm. Admission is €6.00(£5.20, $6.65) and half price for seniors.

A couple of blocks from the Tourist Office at Aurakatu No.4. is *Turku Market Square*, which is the heart of the western city centre. Back in the 1800s, it was known as the 'New Square' to differentiate it from the Old Great Square on the East Bank. Today, Turku Market Square is the main open-air market in the town and well worth wandering around on market days. Don't miss Turku Orthodox Church

Just around the corner from the Tourist Office, is *Turku Market Hall* at Eerikinkatu (Eiriksgata) No.16. Dating to 1896, the Hall is as long as the entire block and packed with shops, delicatessens and speciality shops selling everything from reindeer meat, wonderful breads and cheeses, meat, fish and everything else you can or can't eat. There is also a coffee and cake café should you need to sit down.

Turku Art Museum, located at Aurakatu No. 6, manages one of Finland's most comprehensive art collections ranging from classical to contemporary, from early 20th century Golden Age to surrealism and pop art.

Changing exhibitions are drawn from the museum's collection of nearly 7,000 art works. There is a café serving snacks and light lunches, and a museum shop.

Open: Tuesday – Friday, 11 am - 7 pm. Saturday-Sunday, 11 am - 5 pm. Closed on Mondays. Admission: 12 € and half price for seniors.

EAST BANK

Crossing the bridge by the Tourist Office, turn left along the riverbank pathway and after 250 yards you will come to the *Aboa Vetus and Arts Nova museum* (address: Itäinen Rantakatu Nos. 4-6). This is the Museum of History and

Contemporary Art, a perfect fusion of ancient and modern in which the Aboa Vetus archaeological site and exhibitions tell the captivating story of Turku city with authentic ruins, artefacts and medieval streets. The Arts Nova section displays modern art, mostly by Finnish and Swedish artists.

The museum shop claims to be the most extensive in Turku and offers everything from jewellery to toys, cards, books and souvenirs. There is also a café where you can have lunch. The museum is open every day from 11am – 7pm. Tickets cost €10 (£8.65, $11.10). Seniors: €7.00 (£6.05, $7.75).

Adjacent to the museum is the Old Great Square, located at Vanha Suurtori No. 3.and once the political, commercial and ecclesiastical heart of the city. It was also where public executions took place and where the Christmas Declaration has been delivered on Christmas Eve since 1320.

Flanked with imperial style buildings, including **Brinkkala Mansion,** which from 1816 to 1986 served as the first police station in Finland. Today, its inner court offers video presentations, concerts, vegan food and design shops.

Approximately 350 yards metres further along, *Turku Cathedral* was consecrated in 1300 and dedicated to

Finland's first bishop, St. Henry. It is considered the most important building in the country; when its bells chime at noon, they are broadcast nationwide over the national radio.

Originally Catholic and wooden, the cathedral was extended with stone materials in the 1400s, then damaged badly by the Great Fire of 1827. After that, it was restored to its current state and taken over by the Lutheran Church of Sweden during the Reformation. Unusually, the Cathedral has three organs. There is also a Cathedral museum that explains its history.

A short, 170-yard walk along Piispankatu (Biskopsgatan) takes you to two museums, facing each other: the *Sibelius Museum* and the *Home Ett Hem Museum.*

The *Sibelius Museum* is the only museum in Finland devoted to music, but then Jean Sibelius was undoubtedly Finland's greatest composer and instrumental (in more ways than one) in developing the country's independence.

His seven symphonies, *Finlandia*, *The Swan of Tuonela*, the *Karelia Suite*, *Kalevala* and other compositions made him an international name.

What a composer! Yet he suffered terribly from stage fright, which he tried to control unsuccessfully with alcohol. But by then he was a national hero—and remains so today.

The museum was originally an historic collection of music and musical instruments belonging to the Åbo Academy University, but after an exhibition about Sibelius, some members of the media dubbed the exhibition *The Sibelius Museum.*

This resulted in a row between Professor Otto Andersson at the Department of Musicology and the rector of the Academy. Professor Andersson subsequently wrote to Sibelius asking for permission to use his name, to which Sibelius acceded gratefully.

You might think the museum's concrete exterior is hardly attractive, although it is considered by many as a pearl of modernist architecture. The interior, however, is fascinating, exhibiting not only letters and music of Sibelius, but a fabulous collection of ancient instruments from Finland and abroad.

The museum is open Tuesday to Sunday from 11am - 4pm and costs €5.00 (£4.30, $5.55). Seniors: €4.00 (£3.45, $4.45).

The **_Ett Hem (A Home) Museum,_** opposite to the Sibelius Museum on Piispankatu (Biskopsgatan), comprises art, furniture, ornaments and other objects from the elegant bourgeois home of Finnish businessman and consul, Alfred Jacobsson and his wife, Hélène. Having been a founder member of Åbo Academy University, Jacobsson and his wife then bequeathed their entire home to it.

Opening hours are Tuesday-Sunday, 11am-4pm, Mondays closed. Admission is €5.00 (£4.30, $5.55). Seniors: €4.00 (£3.45, $4.45).

Finally, the **_Luostarinmäki Handicraft and Open Air Museum,_** located at Vartiovuorenkatu No.2, a wooded area just across the bridge from the Tourist Office, and the only area of Turku that escaped the Great fire of 1827.

This is small village of wooden houses in which the city's craftspeople lived. Today, it serves as Turku's handicrafts history museum displaying not only 18th and 19th century timber houses and courtyards but also  the original workshops of goldsmiths, bookbinders, shoemakers and more, with volunteers in costume going about what would have been their daily work a couple of hundred years ago.

Opening times vary, but it is open from 10am-5pm daily from June 1st-31st August. At other times, it is closed on Mondays

Admission is €8.00 (£6.80, $8.90). Seniors: half price.

To sum up, Luostarinmäki Open Air Museum makes for a fascinating, enjoyable and educational hour at a reasonable price or so in very pleasant surroundings close to the town centre.

* * *

Helsinki (Helsingfors)

The Main Attractions

There was a time, back in the 1960s, when Helsinki was generally deemed to be a pretty boring place. Restaurants mostly had the same high fat, high calorie creamy dishes which the Finns consumed with copious quantities of alcohol, not infrequently Vodka, which had more or less been the national drink since the days of the Grand Duchy and Russian influence.

Back then, the architecture seemed dull, the austere parliament building a constant reminder of the Russian Bear. Diplomats from all countries based in Moscow came to Helsinki regularly to stock up on 'essential luxuries' (not least chocolate) at Stockman's, the main department store. If it was raining, foggy or snowing, Helsinki was miserable. If it was Sunday, it was Deadsville.

How all that has changed! The late 1960s hippy movement sent new fashions and revolutionary ideas skimming across the 300-plus islands offshore.

Waves of immigrants began arriving in 1973 after the Chilean coup d'état. Then came the Vietnamese boat people in the 1980s, refugees from the breakup of Yugoslavia, and later from Somalia, Iraq, Afghanistan and Syria.

Immigration during the dawn of the present millennium boosted the population to 621,000 and each group brought with them renewed lifestyles and exotic culinary cuisines.

Today, Helsinki fizzes like champagne on a Formula One podium. There are any number of high-quality restaurants and nightclubs. Finnish design has evolved from producing beautiful but rather staid glassware to extraordinarily vibrant and exciting artworks. One of the first things cruise passengers will see on arrival is the fabulous *Quayside Market*.

This is not a market dominated by torn jeans, fake leather

belts, T-shirts and baseball caps market; it is one of quality goods, flowers framed and pressed in resin, paintings, sculptures and ornaments to contribute to good interior design. There are plenty of stalls selling lunches, too!

It is the same with the shops. Walk along past the Presidential Palace and the City Hall to the shops lining Pohjoizesplanadi (*North Esplanade*) and Eteläesplanadi (*South Esplanade*) and you will find gloriously colourful design stores that somehow reflect the mood of what today could be described as a sunshine city, whatever the weather.

Helsinki is also a city of culture – cinema, theatre, and no fewer than 78 museums covering art, history, military events, speciality hobbies and children's interests.

Architecturally, it is influenced by Classicism, which later gave way to well-designed, functional buildings and, in the early 1900s, to the Romantic and Art Nouveau movements, for which the city is now renowned.

Wherever you go, you will find magnificent architecture. The *National Railway Station,* located on Kaivokatu, is one example. Completed in 1919 and designed by Eliel Saarinen, arguably the leader of the Finnish Romantic style, the station's facade goes largely unnoticed by the 200,000 passengers who pass through it each day, but don't miss the four statues holding large globe lamps flanking the main archway. They are especially attractive when lit in the evenings.

Perhaps the most impressive example of the National Romantic style is the *Finnish National Theatre*, located at Läntinen Teatterikuja 1, adjacent to the railway station.

Like most Finish cities, Helsinki has had to endure a turbulent history. In 1550, the Swedish king, Gustav I of Sweden, established Helsinki as a trading town.

In 1710, an outbreak of the plague wiped out most of the city's residents, who had already lived through centuries of wars and poverty. Apart from the wars fought during Swedish rule between 1249 and 1809, and those involving Russia between 1809 and 1917, it subsequently sank into the Finnish Civil War, the Winter War, the War of Continuation, the Lapland war and involvement in the war in Afghanistan.

Helsinki, in fact, didn't come into its own until the conclusion of the Finnish war, when Sweden was forced to cede Finland to the Russians and the Tsar, Alexander I, moved the capital from Turku to Helsinki.

Today, Helsinki's economy is thriving, generating about 30% of the nation's GDP. It has moved on from the days of heavy industry and now relies mostly on IT, technology and shipping for its income. At the time of writing, output and exports are growing strongly. More than 80% of Finnish companies have their headquarters here and approximately 65% of the most highly paid executives live in the Greater Helsinki area.

That said, unemployment remains high and is likely to remain so as more companies change to automated procedures. The tax burden is one of the highest among OECD countries and, worse, when the unemployed find another job, they will have to pay more than 60% in tax on their salary.

Yet, the standard of living is relatively high; according to the OECD Better Life index, Finland ranks at the top in education, skills and subjective well-being, and above average for income and wealth, health, environmental quality, personal safety, social connections, housing and work-life balance. All of which means it is not a bad place at all in which to live.

WHAT TO DO IN HELSINKI

Immediately behind the City Hall on the waterfront, **Senate Square** is surrounded by Neoclassic buildings; the Government Palace, the National Library and the University of Helsinki. The statue in the centre of Senate Square, which is often the venue for art exhibitions and street theatre, is of Tsar Alexander II.

Towering above them all is **Helsinki Cathedral,** probably the most famous and most photographed building in Finland.

Despite the genius of Finnish architects such as Alvar Aalto (Finlandia Hall) and Eliel Saarinen (Central Station),

it is Carl Ludvig Engel's Lutheran Cathedral that has been adopted as the world-renowned symbol of the city.

Completed in 1852, the cathedral is redolent of the Sacre Coer Basilica in Montmartre, Paris. In fact, Engel based his design on St. Isaac's Cathedral in St. Petersburg and named it after Tsar Nicholas I. When Finland gained independence in 1919, the St. Nicholas name was dropped.

Now, it is just the Lutheran Cathedral and, consequently, its white interior is devoid of much ornamentation, the Lutherans not being great fans of the ornate. The Cathedral is open from 9am until 6pm.

Uspenski Cathedral, located not far away at Pormestarinrinne No.1, is said to be the largest Orthodox church in western Europe and one of the remaining symbols of Russian influence on Finnish history. There is a plaque commemorating Tsar Alexander II at the rear of the cathedral.

More than half a million tourists visit the church each year. In 2007, while hundreds of people were milling about inside, someone stole an icon of St. Nicolas ('The Wonder Worker'). It was one of the most valuable icons in the Cathedral's possession and was supposed to have magical

powers. Clearly, they are not powerful enough because, at the time of writing, the icon has still not been found.

The Cathedral is open Tuesday-Friday from 9.30am-4pm, Saturday 10am-3pm and Sunday 12noon-3pm. In July and August, the hours are 9.30am-6pm on weekdays.

From the Market Square, the ***Esplanadin Puisto,*** one of the city's most elegant and popular parks, stretches for four

blocks, flanked by the North and South Esplanades. The statue in the centre of the park is a statue of Johan Ludvig Runeberg, Finland's national poet and composer of the national anthem.

Equally popular as a sunbathing, picnicking and people-watching venue is ***Kaivopuisto Park*** on the headland of the western bank of South Harbour. Here you will find extensive

lawns, meandering pathways, a small observatory, sculptures, stunning views if you walk to the top and not infrequently, rock, pop and classical concerts.

A 15-minute ferry ride from the east side of the Market Square, opposite the Presidential Palace, takes you to the interlinked islands of ***Suomenlinna,*** a large offshore park and fortress with ocean views, and lots of its own attractions.

The islands offer an escape from the hustle and bustle of the city with walking and jogging paths, picnic areas, cafés and restaurants, not to mention museums. UNESCO designated Suomenlinna a World Heritage Site in 1991.

Depending on the time of year, between one and four ferries run every hour. You can purchase tickets in advance from service points, many kiosks and shops as well as from ticket machines. The crossing costs €2.80 (£2.40, $3.10). The last ferry is at 2.am – but remember, your ship probably leaves at 5pm or 6pm.

Suomenlinna was the main naval base for the Finnish fleet when Finland was subject to Swedish rule, so there is much to see – barracks, old buildings, cannons, old artillery pieces, a shipyard, in which sailmakers, carpenters and other craftspeople have built ships since the 1750s.

The prime attraction, though, is **Suomenlinna Fortress.**

Built in the mid-18th century, it comprises four bastions, the oldest of which is Bastion Zander. It is open to visitors and riddled with tunnels that call for caution; they are not lit, so a torch is required to explore them and the ground in some of them is rough and uneven.

Suomenlinna Church is also worth a visit because it is only one of three churches in Finland that also serve as a lighthouse and as a beacon for air traffic.

One the most interesting and popular attractions at Suomenlinna is the **Submarine 'Vesikko'** from the Second World War.

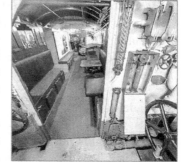

Here you can experience the cramped interior the 20-strong crew lived and worked in during the Winter and Continuation Wars.

Vesikko, based in Suomenlinna, operated in the Gulf of Finland on convoy, safety and patrol duties.

However, in accordance with the Paris Peace Treaty of 1947, Finland was obliged to scrap all its submarines. The exception was *Vesikko*, which was converted into a museum and opened to the public in 1973.

The ***Ehrensvärd-Museo*** is housed in an attractive 18th century house, once the home of Augustin Ehrensvärd, who designed the fortress. Paintings, prints and models give a good idea of what it was like to live on the island in the mid-1700s. Ehrensvärd's tomb is located in the square outside. After his death, the house became the official residence of the fort's commanders.

Another fun museum is the ***Suomenlinna Toy Museum***, which exhibits old toys, the oldest of which go back to the beginning of the 19th century. Here you can see a multitude of old dolls, teddy bears and other toys that give an insight into how children played, not least during wartime.

As mentioned earlier, at the time of writing, there are 78 museums in Helsinki, far more than can be described here. Here are some of the most important ones.

The National Museum of Finland located at Manerheimintie No. 34, describes Finnish history through its permanent exhibitions from the first settlers 10,000 years ago to the 19th century. It also curates temporary exhibitions, which have included how 140,000 'forgotten' Finns from Ingria, an area near Saint Petersburg, faced ethnic cleansing by Stalin via deportation, execution or Gulag prison camps.

Opening times are Tuesday-Sunday, 11am-6pm. Admission is €12.00 (£10.35, $13.30)

Helsinki City Museum (Helsingin Kaupunginmuseo) at Aleksanterinkatu No. 16. Just off the Senate Square, this is the main building of the Helsinki City Museum's five buildings. For anyone with an interest in history, this is a 'must see' exhibition that explores the history of Helsinki and its transition from Swedish to Russian rule and Independence . It tells the story through film, video, 450,000 artefacts, models and a selection taken from the one million photographs in its possession. The museum also highlights the personal experiences and everyday life of Helsinki residents.

The museum incorporates four other museums at different locations: the Hakasalmi Villa, the Burgher's House Museum, the Worker Housing Museum, which shows how industrial workers lived in the early 1900s and the Tram Museum, which displays vintage trams and depicts daily life in Helsinki's streets during past decades.

All these museums are open Monday-Friday 11am-7pm, Saturday-Sunday 11am-5pm and entry is free for all of them.

The Ateneum Art Museum (Finnish National Gallery) located in a palatial 1887 Neo-Rennaissance building at Kaivokatu No. 2, is the main and most important art gallery in Finland.

It covers Finnish art from the Gustavian period of the mid-18th century to the modernist movements of the 1950s as well as a handsome collection of international art, including van Gogh, Gauguin, Cézanne, Léger, Chagall and Edvard Munch.

Open: varying times but always 10am-5pm, Mondays closed. Admission: €17.00 (£14.75, $18.90). Seniors €15.00 (£12.95, $16.65).

Kiasma, a curvaceous contemporary building located at Mannerheiminaukio No.2, picks up from where the Ateneum National Gallery left off, namely from about 1960.

The enormously popular well-stocked museum features Finnish and international contemporary art, including digital art. There is a theatre a café, terrace and shop.

Open: Tuesday- Saturday 10am-6pm. Sunday closed at 5pm. Monday closed. Tickets: €15.00 £(£12.95, $16.65). Seniors €13.00 (£11.20, $14.45). Guided tours in English, lasting 45 minutes, take place at 2pm on the first Saturday of the month (included in admission).

The Design Museum at Korkeavuorenkatu No 23, is specialist museum that explores the integral role of design in the evolution of the nation's evolution. Changing exhibitions focus on contemporary design – everything from clothing to household furniture. Open: Monday closed. Tuesday-Sunday 11am-6pm. Admission: €12.00   Seniors: €10.00

From June to August, 30-minute tours in English take place at 2pm on Saturday and are included in admission. Combination tickets with the Museum of Finnish Architecture nearby are a great-value way to see the two museums.

Finland's premier historical museum is the The *National Museum of Finland (Kansallismuseo)* at Mannerheimintie No. 34. Its website describes it as 'an oasis of culture and Finnish history'. It covers 10,000 years from the Stone Age to the present day. Having recently undergone a major renovation, its highlights include an exceptional pre-history exhibition. There is a wonderful section called Vinti for children, who can learn their history by grinding coffee, trying a conveyor belt, building a house and other hands-on experiences. This section is just as fascinating for adults!

Built in 1916 in the National Romantic style, the museum building looks remarkably like a Gothic church. If it is raining, this is a great day out!

Open: 11am-6pm daily. Admission: €12 (£10.35, $13.40). Seniors: €9.00 (£7.80, $10.05). In July and August, 30-minute guided tours in English at 11.30am from Tuesday-Friday are included.

The exhibition programme at the *Amos Rex Museum,* also on Mannerheimintie, extends from ancient cultures to experimental, contemporary art and 20th century modernism.

The museum is closed on Tuesdays. The opening hours vary but it is always open from 11am-5pm on all other days of the week. Admission is €15.00 (£12.95, $16.75). Seniors:

€12.00 (£10.35, $13.40). Please note bags larger than 12 x 12 inches (30x30 cms), liquids, umbrellas, camera tripods, selfie sticks and outer wear must be placed in the guarded cloakroom and storage lockers. There is a museum shop and half a dozen restaurants adjacent to the museum.

Seurasaaren Ulkomuseo (Open Air Museum of the Society Island) is a lovely wooded island museum with a collection of 87 historic wooden houses and buildings relocated from all parts of Finland, including haylofts, a windmill, mansion, vicarage and church. You can also see the huge 70-foot (21-metre) rowing boats used to ferry churchgoing communities to the church. Guides in traditional costumes demonstrate various crafts and local folk dances. There are several cafés on the island and it is also a great place for a day out in the fresh air and a picnic on the beach or in the woods.

The museum is approximately 6/10ths of a mile (5.5kms) northwest of the city centre and reached via Bus No. 24 from central Helsinki. Opening times vary according to the time of year but it is always open between 11am-5pm. Admission: €10.00(£8.60, $11.15). Seniors €7.00 ($6.100, $7.80).

Another thoroughly enjoyable way of spending time is to take a 90-minute boat trip along Helsinki's beautiful canal and see the sights along the shorelines, including the city highlights and Suomenlinna Maritime Fortress, the Helsinki zoo and a fleet of icebreakers.

Whatever you do in Helsinki, have a fabulous day!

* * *

Kotka

The Main Attractions

Kotka lies 82 miles (133 kms) or an hour-and-a-half's drive east of Helsinki, where the Kymijoki (Kymi River)

rushes down to meet the Gulf of Finland and the Baltic Sea, offering rapids to kayakers and the best salmon fishing in southern Finland. Anglers regularly catch 33-pound (15-kilo) fish, the record being 77-pounds (35- kilos) more than 100 years ago.

Surrounded by wooded countryside, Kotka is a picturesque town (look out for the four magnificent mural paintings) with green, seafront parks overlooking the archipelago. Its population is a little fewer than 55,000, a number that is steadily decreasing due to people moving to the capital.

Kotka's port is the second largest in Finland, serving not only the foreign exports of Finland but also of Russia. It is also the biggest transit port in Finland.

Until 1902, the official language was Swedish but then the town briefly became bilingual for four years. From 1906 onwards, the Swedish speaking population gradually diminished and today represents only about one per cent of the population, with just one Swedish speaking school.

The town's history is not well documented outside Kotka itself. However, its location only 125 nautical miles (231 kilometres) from St. Petersburg, meant that since receiving its charter in 1878, it became enmeshed in many naval battles between Sweden and Russia throughout the centuries. The city was also bombed heavily during the Second World War. The effects of these conflicts, however, seems mostly to have been on shipping trying to enter and leave the port.

Technical advances in the forest and metal industries meant that Kotka was among the first towns in Finland to become industrialised. More than 40% of Finnish sawn timber exports are shipped through its port and the local paper and pulp mill produces around 375,000 tons of pulp used for the printing paper and soft paper industries annually.

Today, Kotka's economy is primarily dependent on timber, pulp, cellulose and phosphate exports, but the city also relies on sugar refining and flour milling, shipping, tourism and the game industry, which provides games for high-end mobile devices such as the iPhone, iPad and Android mobile phones.

WHAT TO DO IN KOTKA

The Maritime Museum of Finland (Maritime Centre Vellamo) at Tornatorintie 99 is housed in a state- of-the-art, metal and glass building shaped like a giant wave.

The museum features numerous exhibitions relating to Finland's seafaring traditions with displays of ship models, navigation, shipwrecks, fishing, logging and so on. Among several ships moored at the museum's quayside is the icebreaker, *Tarmo,* which dates to 1908 and is the third oldest icebreaker in the world.

Tarmo churned up the ice, creating shipping channels through the Gulf of Finland and the Baltic like a farmer's plough in a frozen field until she was retired in 1970.

Here, too, you can find the coast guard ship, *Telkkä,* and, in the boat hall, the boat that belonged to Tove Jansson, the Finnish author of the Moomin books.

The museum has a 100-seat restaurant and a shop well stocked with books, posters, old sea charts, quality gifts, cards, jewellery and a wide variety of products made from recycled materials.

The museum is also where you will find its associate Coastguard Museum, Kymenlaakso Museum and the Vellomon Information Centre.

Open: Tuesday-Sunday 10am-5pm. Admission: €10.00 (£8.60), $11.15). Seniors: €6.00 (£5.15, $6.70).

The **Kymi River (Kymijoki**– *joki* means 'river') located at Keisarinmajantie No. 118 is one of the biggest rivers in Finland. It is renowned for having the best salmon fishing in southern Finland, but pike, perch, whitefish and walleye are also on offer.

The river's rapids are a major attraction for canoeists and visitors who wish to speed through them on rafts.

Further upstream **the Langinkoski (Old Imperial Fishing Lodge),** which once belonged to Tsar Alexander III of Russia, The Tsar first visited Langinkoski when he was Crown Prince in 1880. He was so taken with the location that he decided to have a rustic wooden fishing lodge built close to the rapids. He moved in nine years later and was a frequent summer visitor thereafter.

Today, the lodge is a museum that annually attracts some 15,000 visitors. Set in a riverside forest nature reserve with walking trails, it contains original furniture and the rooms are more or less identical to how the Tsar left them.

Opening times are from May2nd-31st, daily from 10am-4pm. June 1st-31st August, from 11am-6pm. At other times by appointment. Tel: +358 295 33 6991. Email: langinkoski@kansallismuseo.fi. Admission is €8.00 (£6.90, $8.95). Seniors: €6.00(£5.20, $6.70).

The **Maretarium Aquarium**, located at Sapokankatu No. 2, comprises 22 giant water tanks containing different types of water from rivers, lakes and the sea, and approximately 60 species of fish native to Finland's rivers and lakes.

The Baltic Tank, which is the largest, contains more than half a million litres of water, pumped in directly from the sea

and thus continually preserving the fishes' natural life cycle.

In the Maretarium, the fish, frogs and water creatures live in harmony with the seasons. Consequently, salmon and trout spawn in the Autumn; Burbot do so in February, pike, bream, perch and other fish spawn in the Spring, and gudgeon, walleye and ray-finned fish in the Summer.

Divers feed the Baltic Sea fish daily in the summer at 3pm, and two to three times a week during the rest of the year. There are also video shows and a changing exhibition of nature photographs, as well as a coffee shop offering lunch and refreshments and a Sea Shop selling souvenirs and World Wildlife Fund products.

Opened in 2002, the Maretarium is the result of close cooperation between Kotka City Council, Helsinki University and the Finnish Game and Fisheries Research Institute.

Open: June 3rd-25th August 10am-7pm every day. At other times: Monday-Sunday, 10am-5pm except Wednesday, 12 noon-7pm. Admission: €14.50 (£12.50. $16.20). Seniors €12.00 (£10.35, $13.40).

The Orthodox Church of St Nicholas towers above Isopuisto Park on Papinkatu, in Kotka city centre. Built between 1799 and 1801, it is the oldest building in Kotka, having survived the bombing during the Second World War.

The church, with its Neo-classical façade, bell tower and dome is a shrine for St. Nicholas, who was said to be the original Father Christmas.

He was also the patron saint of sailors, helper of the poor and patron saint of the island of Kotka.

Inside, the ceiling above the altar is painted with gold stars on a blue background and the icons are adorned with gemstones and precious metals. At Easter, priests clad in gold parade round the church seven times.

Open Tuesday-Friday, 10am-3pm, Saturday-Sunday 12 noon-5pm. Monday closed. There is no admission fee but donations are appreciated.

Kotka Church at Kirkkokatu No. 26 is easily identifiable by its distinctive steeple, which can be seen from almost

every part of the town. Consecrated in 1898, the Neo-

Gothic church's interior is impressive for its rose windows, ornamental pillars, wood carvings and baroque organ.

Kotka Sculpture Promenade is a defined walk lined with statues and carvings of exceptional and consistent high quality, although most of them are contemporary and not necessarily to everybody's taste.

Check the Tourist Information Office for details. Address: Kauppakatu No.2. Open: June 1st-August 19th, Monday-Friday, 10am-6pm. Saturday: 10am-3pm. Email: info@kotkahamina.fi. Tel: +358 40 135 65 88.

The ***Haukkavuori Lookout Tower*** at Keskuskatu No. 51,

is the highest point of Kotka and the tower rises 236 feet (72 metres) above sea level.

For visitors able to climb the 139 steps to the top, the views over the city and archipelago are stunning. Otherwise there are changing exhibitions at the Uusikuva art gallery inside.

During the Winter War , the tower was used as an air surveillance outpost staffed almost entirely by women.

Open: June 4th-31st August, Tuesday-Saturday 12- noon-6pm. Groups by appointment at other dates. Tel +358 40 6433 591. Email: minni.kuisma@kotka.fi.

Sapokka Water Garden located at Tallinnankatu No 12 about 7/10ths of a mile (1.25 kms) from the city centre is one of the top and most enjoyable attractions in Kotka. Situated on a small headland jutting into a natural inlet used as a small boat marina, it is a wooded park with ponds, brooks, and a

60 ft (20 metre) waterfall surrounded by a multitude of native plants and flowers, and animal sculptures.

The water garden has been lauded as no other park in the country, winning multiple awards for environmental, lighting and stone structures. The designers also had a sense of humour, commissioning bronze sculptures of rabbits, cats, ducks and pheasants, which are scattered about in a variety of surprise locations.

Colourful flowers burgeon though Spring and Summer then gradually give way to the fabulous, award-winning lighting during the darker evenings of Autumn.

Surrounded by seaside coffee chops and a fan of jetties in the small boat marina, the park is open 24 hours a day and, best of all, it is free.

* * *

Mariehamn, Åland Islands.

The Main Attractions

Translated, Mariehamn means Maria's harbour, a reference to the fact that that the city is named after the Russian Empress Maria Alexandrovna. It is the capital of Åland, an autonomous region of Finland that comprises some 6,200 islands and skerries between Sweden and Finland, where the Baltic Sea narrows to become the Gulf of Bothnia.

Mariehamn is 100% Swedish-speaking and home to roughly 11,000 people or 40% of the 29,000 population of Åland. This means that the rest of the archipelago is either devoid of people or very sparsely populated. On average, there are only 2.8 people per island (excluding Mariehamn).

For instance, the island of Märket (*pronounced Mare-ket' and translated as 'The Mark'*) is essentially unpopulated. This is where the Swedish-Finnish border splits the skerry as if with a zig-zag lightning strike, half-way between the east coast of Sweden and the western limit of the Åland archipelago.

Märket has just two buildings and a lighthouse. Uniquely, the border that runs through the island means that it has two different time zones.

The Åland islands are non-military and to gain the right to live in the archipelago, you must be a Finnish citizen and have the Ålandic Right of Domicile.

For some young Finnish men, this is an attractive proposition because it means they don't have to do National Service. However, they can still vote in Finnish parliamentary elections, run for parliament, set up a business and buy real estate there.

That said, the Right of Domicile is not that easy to acquire. It demands that Finnish citizens live on the islands for five years and that they can speak fluent Swedish. Similarly, if they vacate the islands for five years, they lose the right.

Non-Finns may also obtain the right, provided they fulfil all the necessary requirements.

The islanders are self-governing, with their own flag, police force, national airline, postage, license plates and internet domain codes (.ax).

Founded in 1861, Mariehamn is today a thoroughly modern city with all the amenities and customs of similar towns and cities on the Swedish mainland. Happily, it still retains some of the wooden houses from the 1800s in one of the oldest streets, Södragatan (South Street).

WHAT TO SEE IN MARIEHAMN

One of the first sights cruise passengers will see is the *Museum Ship Pommern,* an iron-hulled, four-masted barque and windjammer built in Glasgow, Scotland, in 1903. She is berthed next to the cruise terminal and *Åland's Maritime Museum* at Västerhamn, Mariehan's western harbour.

Pommern was one of the famous German sailing ships known as the Flying P-Liners, later purchased by a

Mariehamn shipowner, Gustaf Erikson, who was known for buying sailing ships at shipbreakers' prices at a time when shipping companies were turning to steam ships.

Launched in 1903 in Glasgow, Scotland, Erikson used **Pommern** as a grain ship sailing between Australia, Britain and Ireland between the two great wars.

She had a crew of 26 and twice won the grain race from Spencer Gulf in Australia to the Lizard in Cornwall, England. She completed the voyage in fewer than 100 days on at least four occasions and once sailed for 15 weeks and four days at a stretch.

The *Åland Maritime Museum,* adjacent to her berth regarded as one of the best commercial sailing ship museums in the world. Indeed, this is a truly wonderful museum – a

real gem for anyone remotely interested in ships and life at sea or the history of the Åland Islands.

Mariehamn was the home port for the last fleet of tall ships in the world and the museum has a superb collection of models, figureheads, recreated ship's interiors with original furnishings and equipment and a host of nautical curiosities collected by seafarers the world over.

However, it is the stories that make this museum so interesting, beginning with tales of 13th century peasants sailing up and down the Baltic coastlines to sell firewood, fish and agricultural products, or trading them for such products that they could not manufacture or produce themselves – salt, spices, coffee and iron.

Later, they would load timber onto their ships, but it was not until the late 1800s that vessels from Åland became commercial enterprises.

In the early 20th century, larger iron and steel ships sailed from the archipelago to all points of the planet. By the 1920s, Åland was almost the only place in the word that had a fleet of sailing ships. These continued to circumnavigate the earth carrying wheat and other grains until 1950.

One of the most emotive exhibits in the museum is the captain's saloon of the sailing ship *Herzogin Cecilies*, which had repeatedly won the grain race. But when she lost her bearings and ran aground off the coast of Devon in the English Channel, her keel split and, despite the efforts of the crew over several months, she was finally and formally declared a wreck.

Gustav Eriksson, the owner, ordered all that could be saved of her to be transported back to Åland, where the captain's cabin was reconstructed as a major exhibit in the museum, which tells the story of shipbuilding in Mariehamn and on other islands. All told, some 300 ships were built, mostly for Finnish investors.

The islands bustled with carpenters, blacksmiths, sawyers, labourers and caulkers while the women cleaned and filleted fish, and cooked while sailors worked on sails and rigging.

The museum also looks at various shipping disasters in the Baltic, not least the loss of the cruise ferry *m.s. Estonia* which sank in September,1994. That disaster cost 852 people their lives – the worst sinking of a European ship in peacetime since the *RMS Titanic*.

Another fascinating exhibit is the light of the original 1885 lighthouse on the island of Märket, marking the border of Finland and Sweden. It was the first lighthouse in Finland to have a flashing light – ten white per minute.

Ships could see the kerosene-fueled light from more than eight nautical miles away. Later, it was replaced with an electric light, which operated until 1976, when all Finnish lighthouses were automated.

Cruise passengers may also be interested in the section on the Plimsoll Line. It is named after Samuel Plimsoll, who devoted most of his life to safety issues at sea and who stood up to shipowners who deliberately overloaded ships, thus risking the lives of their crews. He died in 1898.

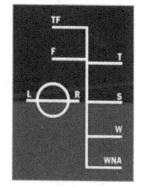

The Plimsoll Line shows how much cargo can be loaded onto a ship in various types of water and temperature.

Vital to the stability and buoyancy of a ship, it is a horizontal line showing the lowest level to which a ship can displace the water. Other lines are marked with the letter S for summer temperate seawater, TF, for tropical fresh water, T for tropical seawater, W for winter temperate seawater and WNA for winter in the North Atlantic. Today, the Plimsoll Line is obligatory on all ships.

Finally, the Cape Horn Room in the museum tells the story of the three and four-masters that sailed through ferocious storms off the South America's eastern coast.

These ships often carried extraordinary cargos – steam tractors to Punta Arenas in Chile, massive heavy mahogany furniture for German clubs and so on. That they survived the howling winds, mountainous waves and icebergs, often with tattered sails and sailors clinging for dear life to the yardarms was an ongoing miracle.

An excellent 14-minute documentary film, *We rounded the Horn,* runs continuously with sailors recounting their time on such ships and what it was like in those conditions.

The Åland Maritime Museum is an absolute 'must' for anyone with the slightest interest in seafaring. It is open daily from June to August from 10am-5pm. Between September and May, the hours are from 11am until 4pm daily. *Pommern* is closed from October to April. Admission €14.00 (£12.00, $15.45). Seniors: €8.00 (£6.85, $8.85). This fee covers both the museum and *Pommern.*

In the eastern harbour of Mariehamn, *The Maritime Quarter (Sjökvarteret)* is a 'living' marine centre with boat building activity, a smithy and other handicrafts, as well as a marina for traditional ships and wooden boats.

This is a delightful area in which to stroll. There is a Ship and Boat building museum, a museum of historical marine engines, a shop and five workshops selling high quality products and souvenirs, and further out on the breakwater, a Seafarer's chapel.

Several workshops continue to build wooden boats, giving the area a real sense of what life was like in the harbour in former times.

If maritime history is not of interest, Mariehamn has much else to offer – attractive parks, boardwalks along the island coastline and a busy shopping centre lined with restaurants, cafés and bars.

The main shopping street in Mariehamn

The Åland Museum incorporates the *Cultural History Museum* and the *Åland Art Museum* under the same roof at Torggatan No. 1.

In the recently renewed permanent exhibition, visitors can follow the history of Mariehamn from the first sailors who stepped ashore to the global and multicultural society of today. Arranged in chronological displays from pre-history and medieval times to the 18th and 19th centuries, the museum covers some 7,500 years of Åland's dramatic history and everyday life in the different periods.

The *Art Museum* showcases a broad spectrum of art on the Åland Islands from sculptures and paintings to modern video installations, and stages regular temporary exhibitions by mostly Scandinavian artists. As with most museums, there is a café and museum shop.

The museums are open daily from 10am to 5pm from May to August. At other times of year, they are closed on Mondays, and open from 11am-5pm with an extension to 8pm on Thursdays. Entrance is free on the first Thursday of each month. Otherwise the admission fee is €8.00 (£6.85, $8.85). Seniors: €5.00 (£4.30, $5.50).

St Goran's (St. George's) Evangelical Lutheran church at Östra Esplanadgatan No.6, is also well worth a visit. Built in 1926-7, it is the most modern church in Mariehamn and is conceived in an art-nouveau style with Gothic and national romantic characteristics.

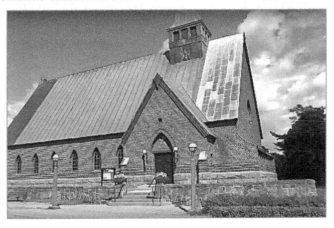

It was designed by the architect Lars Sonk, who was born in Finland but grew up in Åland to become one of the best-known architects in Finland.

The church, with its copper roof, was commissioned by a wealthy shipowner, August Troberg and his wife Johanna, who donated it to Mariehamn.

Of especial interest are the ceiling paintings and brilliant stained-glass windows, and a scintillating mosaic altarpiece. Outside, is a statue of Anadyomene (another name for Aphrodite), the goddess of love and sexuality.

The church is open from 10am-6pm, Monday-Friday, and 9am-3pm on Saturday from Mid-June to August.

To sum up, Mariehamn is a perfect antidote to the frenetic city life of other Baltic Sea capitals. With leafy parks and coastal boardwalks, it is not only a picturesque town but one in which it is a delight just to wander around.

* * *

St. Petersburg, Russia

The Main Attractions

Everything about St. Petersburg is daunting. It is a huge city with a population of more than five million, the second largest in Russia after Moscow. It is treasure trove of global culture, stuffed with fabulous palaces, theatres, concert halls, cathedrals and churches, and countless museums.

It is one of the largest cultural, economic and scientific centres in the world. For cruise passengers visiting for only one or two days, it invokes a quandary of monumental proportions. Even by whittling down the main attractions to a 'Top Ten', you would need a week to see them all, so it is not so much a question of *what* to do, but what to *choose* to do!

Indeed, the UNESCO World Heritage list cites St. Petersburg as having 36 historical architectural complexes and some 4,000 outstanding individual monuments of architecture, history and culture.

According to Wikipedia, the city has 221 museums, (other sources say 250), 2,000 libraries, more than 80 theatres, 100 concert organizations, 45 galleries and exhibition halls, 62 cinemas and around 80 other cultural establishments. Squeezing that lot into two days would be like trying to put a ton of coal into a paper bag.

St. Petersburg is a relatively modern city, founded by the Tsar, Peter the Great in 1703.

He was keen to increase Russia's foreign trade, which was hampered by the port of Archangel on the northern coast freezing over in winter. Flowing into the Gulf of Finland and the Baltic, the River Neva estuary was the perfect location for a new port.

Ten years after construction of the city began, St. Petersburg had evolved into the capital of Russia and the Russian Empire. Apart from a two-year period between 1728 and 1730 when Moscow was temporarily designated the capital, St. Petersburg remained Russia's capital city until the Bolsheviks moved their revolutionary government to Moscow in 1918.

Even so, several national institutions, including the Supreme Court and the National Library, remain in St. Petersburg, which today is regarded as the 'northern capital of culture'.

Originally named after the Apostle St. Peter, the city has been called by many names: Saint Petersburg, Petri and

Petrograd, which Alexander Pushkin used in a poem in the 1830s. Later, Tsar Nicholas II confirmed Petrograd as the official name and, as the prefix 'Saint' had been dropped, the city's patron was also changed from St. Peter to Peter the Great.

Later, in 1924, the Bolsheviks renamed the city Leningrad after their revolutionary leader, Lenin. This lasted until 1991, when a referendum with a 65% turnout resulted in nearly 55% of the voters electing to restore the name to Saint Petersburg.

Of course, the city is known under many other names, such as the 'Cradle of the October Revolution', the 'City of Three Revolutions', 'The City of Culture', 'Venice of the North' (which Stockholm in Sweden also claims).

Sadly, St. Petersburg is also known as 'The Capital of Crime'. After *Perestroika, Glasnost* and the collapse of the Soviet Union in the late 1980s and early 1990s, crime in Russia spiked.

Organized criminal gangs took control of the city. Racketeering, extortion, prostitution, corruption and gang warfare flourished. So, too, did a spate of murders. Those killed were mostly government officials, businessmen, foreign students, homosexuals and investigative journalists probing too deeply into the gangs' affairs. Gang warfare also took its toll.

As Vladimir Putin commented: "Whoever does not miss the Soviet Union has no heart. Whoever wants it back has no brain". That said, he is not infrequently accused of corruption himself.

Fortunately, by 2011 crimes against tourists had fallen by more than half. Today, St. Petersburg is relatively safe. Homosexuality is legal in Russia, but care should be taken to avoid flamboyance or any public display of sexuality as there are still white supremacists and others who disapprove, sometimes violently. Cruise passengers and crew on organized tours are not likely to be affected if the follow the usual advice.

St. Petersburg is better remembered for its stunning

 architecture, wide boulevards, rivers cruises along canals bustling with tourist boats, superbly crafted wrought iron bridges, leafy embankments and peaceful parks.

Passengers taking a river tour may well find themselves accompanied by a young man running along the embankments, waving, laughing and giving thumbs up signs. They may then notice that he waves to them from each of the many bridges along the canal route.

He will be there, too, when they arrive at their destination. His stamina, fitness, joyfulness and intelligence make him

one of the most inspiring sights to see in the entire city. He is well worth a generous donation!

In the evenings, the sun slips lower in the sky to bathe the cathedral domes and mansion facades in golden light. This, too, is a sight not to be missed. In short, St. Petersburg is a photographer's dream and a city that provides memories to last a lifetime.

Incidentally, just over 50% of the population belong to the Russian Orthodox Church. Five and a half per cent are Christian or Muslim, and 36% are described as 'spiritual but not religious' or atheist.

Approximately seven million tourists visit St. Petersburg each year. The city's cruise port, *Marine Façade,* handles nearly 600,000 cruise passengers, arriving on 250-odd cruise ships annually. Passengers represent 180 nationalities, with Germans, Americans and British passengers comprising the bulk of them. The numbers of Japanese and Chinese passengers are also said to be growing rapidly.

The port has seven berths capable of serving cruise ships up to 340 metres long, including MSC Fantasia which arrived for the first time in 2017. Carnival ships made 43% of all the cruise ship calls, Royal Caribbean and Celebrity 16%, MSC 11% and Norwegian 7%.

WHAT TO DO IN ST. PETERSBURG.

As anyone planning to visit St. Petersburg independently must be in possession of a visa, almost all cruise passengers sign up to the ships' excursions. For those who do go independently, I strongly advise that they hire a driver; it is well worth the cost. Whichever you choose and wherever you go, remember that seven million tourists visit St. Petersburg each year, so expect large crowds.

Four million of them annually visit the ***Winter Palace and Hermitage Museum,*** which is St. Petersburg's prime attraction. For many of them, the Winter Palace is the *reason* they come to the city.

It is certainly the most famous building in St. Petersburg, dominating both the Palace Square and the southeastern bank of the Neva River. It also played a central political, symbolic and cultural role in the three-century history of the city.

Back in 1708, a wooden house built for Peter the Great and his family stood in this prime location. Later, it was replaced by a stone building, the foundations of which are now those of the Hermitage Theatre.

The Empresses Anna Ionannovna and Elizaveta Petrovna both ordered extensions. In the latter case, the architect, Francesco Rastrelli decided to tear the palace down and rebuild it from scratch. He finished it in 1762 for Catherine the Great and it is his baroque design that we see almost unaltered today. However, the interior underwent numerous restorations and improvements in the late 1700s and early 1800s.

For nearly 200 years, until the assassination of Tsar Alexander II in 1881, this magnificent palace was the official residence of the Russian Tsars.

The Winter Palace has seen more than its fair share of history, not least in the Palace Square, which was the scene of the 'Bloody Sunday' or 'Red Sunday' massacre in January 1905. That was when soldiers of the Imperial Guard fired indiscriminately on thousands of striking workers, led by a priest, who had come to present a petition to Tsar Nicholas II.

The numbers of dead and wounded in various clashes around the city are still debatable. Tsar Nicholas's officials documented 96 dead and 333 injured. Government sources maintained more than 4,000 were killed. Today, the accepted estimate is an average of 1,000 killed or wounded.

Tsar Nicholas neither gave the order to fire nor was he to blame for the shootings, which he described as 'painful and sad', but the killings were much more than that; they were a match to the kindling of resentment and revolution.

As a direct result of the massacre, strikes involving more than 400,000 workers spread like wildfire across the country and as far afield as Warsaw and the Baltic region.

Public bitterness was intense. People railed against Tsar Nicholas, whom they had hitherto regarded as a father figure to whom, in desperate times, they could traditionally appeal by handing in petitions.

Tsar Nicholas agreed to set up a Duma (parliament) to mollify them, but this was not enough. He was castigated for being out of the city at the time, for his lack of empathy and most of all for his imperious and monocratic rule.

With the strikes spreading out of control, the autocracy cracked down mercilessly. According to Wikipedia, in the six months after October 1905, the authorities shot or hanged approximately 15,000 workers and peasants. Another 20,000 were injured and 45,000 were sent into exile.

Public anger was such that the blame fell not just on the bureaucracy but on the shoulders of Tsar Nicholas himself. He was no longer considered fit to rule. The seeds of the 1917 revolution had been sown.

In 1914, the Winter Palace was ransacked and transformed into a hospital for wounded soldiers.

Three years later, Nichola II abdicated and the palace became the headquarters of the Provisional Government under Alexander Kerensky, the leading political figure after the February Revolution.

His government, however, failed to end food and fuel shortages in St. Petersburg (then Petrograd), mainly because Kerensky opted to continue the war, which was causing the shortages.

Eventually, in October 1917, the Bolsheviks surrounded the palace. The Russian cruiser, *Aurora,* bombarded the Neva façade and the Bolsheviks attacked the palace with light artillery and machine gun fire.

On gaining entry, they then rampaged through the Palace, ripping priceless paintings from their frames with bayonets, smashing exquisite crystal, china and dinner services, ransacking the library and, not least, the extensive Imperial wine cellars.

These were arguably the largest and best stocked with fabulous vintages in the world. The revolutionaries syphoned off hundreds of these fine wines into the Neva River. Not surprisingly, hordes of people swarmed around the palace drains, drinking whatever they could.

Eventually, the Bosheviks declared martial law and restored order, but it was often said later that Petrograd had suffered the biggest hangover in history.

The revolutionaries arrested Kerensky's government. and imprisoned them in the Peter and Paul Fortress across the river. Kerensky managed to escape and subsequently formed a small army which unsuccessfully failed to recapture the city.

Later that year, the Winter Palace was declared part of the Stage Hermitage Museum, which became a museum of the Revolution. The palace building suffered further extensive damage during the Siege of Leningrad during the Second World War but was restored in the 1950s and gradually returned to the Imperial splendor that we see today.

The palace is also the main building of the Hermitage Museum and is the most popular of all the attractions in St. Petersburg.

The Winter Palace is open Tuesday, Thursday, Saturday and Sunday from 10.30am-6pm and on Wednesday and Friday until 9pm. Closed Monday. Entry to the main museum, General Staff building (permanent exhibition of the

Hermitage), Winter Palace, Menshikov Palace, and Museum of Imperial Porcelain is 700 rubles ((£840, $11.00, €9.95).

Entry to the Winter Palace, and just one of the Hermitage buildings (Menshikov Palace or the Museum of Imperial Porcelain) is 300 rubles (£3.60, $4.70, €4.25).

Entrance is free on the first Thursday of each month.

Peterhof – The Russian Versailles, lies approximately 18.6 miles (30 kilometres) west of St. Petersburg and is a series of palaces and gardens designed by Peter the Great. They were the summer residence of the Tsars until the 1917 Revolution. Today they are a UNESCO World Heritage site.

The three-storey baroque Grand Palace is the centre of the Peterhof complex, overlooking the Grand Cascade and situated on a ridge that separates the upper and lower parks. Many people consider the latter to be more spectacular than the Grand Palace.

The *Upper Park* was originally a vegetable garden with ponds stocked with fish. Later it evolved into a formal garden adorned with a variety of statues. There is no charge to visit the upper garden.

The *Lower Park* is the main attraction in the Peterhof ensemble, which is accessible by hydrofoil from St. Petersburg. Visitors arriving in this way will walk along the side of sea channel to the Grand Cascade, which in turn leads to the lower garden and Grand Palace.

The cascade and sea channel looking north to the hydrofoil landing stage on the Gulf of Finland.

The sea channel divides the lower gardens into two sections – east and west. The eastern side contains **Alexandria Park**, one of Tsar Nicholas II's favourite places. It was created in 1826 with a small palace and neo-Gothic church.

On the western side is the *Marly Palace*, which is only open on Saturday and Sunday. It contains fine examples of antique furniture, each room guarded by old ladies.

The lower garden is best remembered for the cascades and numerous fountains, all of which have been given names.

During the Second World War, the Germans caused serious damage to both the palace, gardens and fountains, several of which were destroyed completely. One was the central *Orangery Fountain,* which depicts Triton fighting a sea monster. Together with the *Pyramid Fountain*, which requires 505 jets to create the large geyser-like fountain and was similarly wrecked, it was recreated in the 1950s.

German damage to the *Grand Palace* was so extensive that the lavish interiors also had to be recreated. Here, the opulence of the ornate Ceremonial Staircase, the gilded Ballroom, the Throne Room with its stunningly beautiful parquet floor are reminders of why the 1917 Revolution took place.

Although many visitors regard the gardens as more impressive, the palace interiors – especially the Throne Room, the Western Chinese Study and the Drawing Room with its fabulous silk wall hangings would be well worth a visit even without the gardens.

The palace is open daily from 10.30am until 7pm (Last admission at 5.45pm). On Thursday, it is open until 9pm (last entry at 8pm). Admission is 550 rubles (£6.60, $8.65, €7.80).

As St. Petersburg is graced with so many opulent palaces and lavishly decorated churches, what in other circumstances would be 'must see' attractions sometimes have to take a back seat. Sadly, cruise passengers with no more than a couple of days in the city must make some hard choices. (Of course, a second visit is always possible!)

For obvious reasons, The Winter Palace and Peterhof take precedence over the Baroque *Tsarskoye Selo* (which means 'The Tsar's Village and is otherwise known as *The Catherine Palace)*. This is a pity because for two centuries this was a sumptuous imperial summer residence for the Empresses Elizabeth and Catherine II.

Located in the town of Pushkin, about 15 miles (25 kms) south of St. Petersburg, Catherine Palace is best known for its Great Hall, known as the Hall of Light, The series of golden state rooms, not least the world-renowned Amber Room are wonderful to behold.

Peter the Great commissioned the palace for his wife, Catherine I, who ruled Russia for two years after his death. In those days, it was a modest two-storey building.

Their daughter, the Empress Elizabeth, later chose Tsarskoe Selo for her main summer residence. She commissioned Bartholomeo Rastrelli, the Imperial Court's chief architect, to redesign the building; The brief? To rival Versailles.

Rastrelli, who also designed the Winter Palace, surpassed himself, designing the current palace which is more than half a mile (one kilometre) in circumference. Even more impressive; the design called for more than 220 pounds (100 kilos) of gold to decorate the palace exteriors. When Catherine the Great found out that Elizabeth had used state and private funds on the building, she was not best pleased!

Tsarskoe Selo is also home to the lesser known neo-classical *Alexander Palace,* where following the Bloody Sunday massacre, Tsar Nicholas II and the last of the Romanov family spent their final days under house arrest.

Here, they were confined to just a few rooms of the palace, but were allowed to walk around the extensive, 300-

acre gardens, accompanied by armed guards with bayonets drawn.

There were two gardens, a formal garden designed by Dutch landscape artists in 1720 and the free-flowing English garden with its pavilions, ponds, bridges, monuments and imitation Turkish and Chinese pavilions.

It was in these gardens that Rasputin was buried, temporarily, in the 300-acre gardens at Tsarskoye Selo Park.

The murder of Grigori Efimovich Rasputin on December 16th, 1916 has become legend, or at last the accepted version of it has. This version is based on the diaries of the principal conspirator, Prince Felix Yusopov, who belonged to one of the richest families in Russia at the time.

Rasputin had gained fame not only as a debauched drunkard but also as a deeply religious man renowned for his ability to heal people.

Alexandra, the wife of Tsar Nicholas II, had called him in to see if he could help her son, Alexei, who suffered from haemophilia. This is a condition in which the blood is unable to coagulate. Instead, it wells up to create pressure on the bones, muscles and joints, and causes excruciating pain. Incredibly, Rasputin did manage to prevent the bleeding, at least temporarily.

Gradually, Alexandra's faith in Rasputin's healing abilities burgeoned, as did Rasputin's influence on her. As a pacifist, he tried to persuade Tsar Nicholas – through Alexandra - to end what he called 'the senseless slaughter' of Russian soldiers fighting pitched battles along the entire eastern front in 1916.

The Russians were suffering serious setbacks and Tsar Nicholas decided the situation was so critical that he needed to take control of his armies personally. That took him away from St. Petersburg and left Rasputin alone with Alexandra. Such was his influence over her and his subsequent political power that an outspoken member of the Duma, Vladimir Pureshkevich, and Prince Nicolay Yusopov plotted to murder him.

The plan was to feed him cyanide in cakes and Madeira wine at Yuspov's palace. When Yuspov discovered that the cyanide was having no effect, he shot Rasputin with his pistol. However, the bullet wound was not fatal.

Yuspoov was horrified – and terrified - and called on Pureshkevich to help. Pureshkevich was then believed to have shot him, as well. Later, Yusolpov, Pureshkevich and other conspirators all claimed only to have shot a dog, although no dog carcass was ever found.

A BBC documentary later proved that this was only half the story. In fact, after Rasputin had supposedly been given cyanide, been shot and beaten with a 'bladed weapon', he was shot in the centre of his forehead by a third killer and dumped into the freezing River Neva.

Photographic and other evidence later showed that the 'third man' was a British spy, Oswald Rayner, who committed the crime on the orders of the British government who were concerned that if Russian troops were withdrawn from the eastern front, hundreds of thousands of German troops would be released to fight on the western front.

As the situation in St. Petersburg in 1916 and 1917 became increasingly dangerous, Bolshevik revolutionaries called for the Tsar's family to be imprisoned in the St. Peter and St Paul Fortress in St. Petersburg. Alexander Kerensky, the leader of the Provisional Government, decided instead to spirit them away to exile in Siberia. Armed guards forced the Romanovs onto a train and once it had left the station, they were never seen again. They were all murdered at

Katerinaburg. Nobody was ever convicted of the murders, either of the Romanovs or Rasputin.

After the 1917 Revolution, the Bolsheviks exhumed Rasputin's body and burnt it. It was as if they wanted to be absolutely sure he was dead.

Prince Yusopov's family was one of the richest in St. Petersburg. *Yusopov Palace* on the Moika River, the scene of the conspiracy and murder, is located at Naberezhnaya Reki Moiki No.94. After the October Revolution, in 1917 it was handed over to the revolutionary education authorities, who wisely decided to preserve the interiors.

Tours to the palace focus not only on the rooms where the conspirators met and Yusupov first shot Rasputin, but also

give guests a chance to see the opulent living quarters on the ground floor.

Especially impressive are the picture gallery, the fabulous chandeliers and Yusupov's bath.

Even more impressive is the palace's extraordinary private theatre. Today, it is still used for classical concerts, operas and operettas, Russian ballet and theatrical performances.

Many wealthy families hosted musical and theatrical performances, but Prince Yusupov's theatre was very special. During the 1800s, it attracted such luminaries as Franz Litzt, Anna Pavlova and soloists from the Mariinsky and Mikhailovsky theatres.

Yusupov Palace is open daily from 11am until 5pm. Admission to state rooms 700 rubles (£8.35, $11.00, €9.95). Rasputin exhibit 400 rubles (£4.80, $6.30), €5.70). The Rasputin exhibit is not wheelchair accessible.

Apart from the excessive grandeur for which the

Romanov's and other wealthy families were renowned, St. Petersburg is not short of ornate churches, the most high-spirited of which is undoubtedly *The Church of the Saviour on Spilled Blood,* located at No. 2, Naberezhnaya, Kanala Griboedova.

This is a church that stuns the senses both outside and inside. With its five onion-shaped domes, each covered with jeweller's enamel, the entire church is exuberantly decorated and arguably the most spectacular building in St. Petersburg. It contains more than 75,000 square feet (7,000 square metres) of exquisite mosaics.

St. Petersburg is crammed with palaces and churches, each one worthy of a visit: The Church of the Saviour on Spilled Blood outstrips them all.

Construction of the church began in 1883. It marks the spot where political nihilists belonging to a terrorist group known as the 'People's Will' fatally wounded Tsar Alexander II two years earlier.

Immediately afterwards, his heir, Alexander III, announced that he would build a church on the site in his father's memory. It would, he added, be built in the style of traditional 16th and 17th century Russian Orthodox churches, as opposed to what he felt was the tainted influence of western architecture on the city.

Inspired by St. Basil's Cathedral in Moscow and Vladimir Cathedral in Kiev, Alexander III designed the church himself. Today, it and rises confidently above the city in unambiguous contrast to the Baroque, Classical and Modernist architecture elsewhere in St. Petersburg.

In 1970, after decades of deterioration, church authorities declared the church a sub-division of St. Isaac's Cathedral museum and funded its dramatic interior restoration. When it re-opened in 1997, thousands of Russians and tourists who swamped the church were amazed to see the extravagant use of mosaics linking Alexander II's murder with the crucifixion.

A shrine dedicated to him marks the exact spot where Alexander II was fatally wounded.

The Church is open daily from 10.30am to 6pm (last admission 5.30pm). From May until September, it is open in the evenings until 10.30pm. Closed Wednesday.

Admission is 250 rubles (£3.00, $ 3.90, €3.55). The audio guide costs 100 rubles (£1.20, $1.60, €1.45). There are ramps at the entrance and exit for wheelchairs.

The gilded dome of *St. Isaac's Cathedral,* located at **No.** 4, Isaakievskaya Square, towers above the rest of the city and the church which was originally the largest cathedral in Russia. Visitors with a head for heights may climb the 262 steps to the Colonnade, the 'drum' of the

dome from which there are probably the best views of the city.

Beneath the dome, red granite columns and sculptures dominate the impressive façade, whilst the inside of the dome is adorned lavishly with frescos and gilded statues of the saints.

Built between 1818 and 1858, St. Isaac's can accommodate 14,000 standing worshippers. That would be a rare occasion today because in the 1930s, the church fathers converted the church into a museum. Now, services are held only the more important religious occasions.

The church interior is embellished with columns of lapis lazuli and dark green malachite, scores of paintings and exquisite mosaic icons. The altar is similarly  aggrandized with a colourful stained glass image of Christ Resurrected.

St. Isaac's Cathedral is open daily from 10.30am to 6pm (Last admission 5.30pm). Evenings from May1-September

30 until 1030pm. Night openings of the Colonnade in the 'White nights' – June 1-August 20) 10.30pm until 4.30am. Photography is permitted but visitors should turn off flashlights

Admission to the cathedral is 250 rubles (£3.00, $ 3.90, €3.55). The audio guide costs 100 rubles (£1.20, $1.60, €1.45). Admission to the Colonnade is 150 rubles (£1.90, $2.35, €2.15).

Evening opening times of the Cathedral is 400 rubles (£4.80, $6.30, €5.70). Colonnade 300 rubles (summer only) is (£3.60, $4.70, €4.25). Night admission to the Colonnade is 400 rubles.

The Cathedral of Our Lady of Kazan located at Nevsky Prospekt No. 2, Kazanskaya Square, is another impressive cathedral, partly inspired by the Basilica of St. Peter in Rome and intended to be the premier Orthodox Church in Russia. It was built between 1801 and 1811. In keeping with just about everything in St. Petersburg, this Russian Orthodox cathedral was built to enormous scale with a huge stone colonnade shaped like a horseshoe wrapped around a large grassy frontage.

The huge bronze doors, incidentally, are a copy of the Baptistery in Florence, Italy

After the Napoleonic invasion of Russia in 1812, the cathedral was regarded mainly as a memorial to their victory over Napoleon. A year later, Field Marshal Mikhail Kutuzov, who won the most crucial campaign of the war, was interred here. In 1815, the victorious Russian army brought enemy banners and the keys to 17 cities and eight fortresses to the cathedral's sacristy.

Later, the 1917 revolutionary authorities closed the cathedral, then re-opened it as the pro-Marxist 'Museum of the History of Religion and Atheism'. One writer put it more bluntly, describing it as 'Leningrad's largest anti-religious museum', the inclusion of Spanish inquisition waxworks more than likely to have prompted that description.

The Orthodox Church recently resumed religious services in the cathedral, part of which remains the museum, although now, the authorities have dropped the word 'atheism' from its title.

The cathedral is open from 8.30am until 8pm daily. Entrance is free.

Kazan Cathedral is about as central as you can get in St. Petersburg, positioned as it is on *Nevsky Prospekt,* the main street.

Originally designed by Tsar Peter 1 as the beginning of the road leading to Moscow and the ancient city of Novgorod, Nevsky Prospekt is now a bustling, two-and-a-half mile (four kilometre) long avenue lined with top line stores and restaurants, beautiful architecture, elegant bridges and palaces, and half a dozen churches of varying denominations (Alexander Dumas described it as 'the street of religious tolerance'). It is also the hub of the city's nightlife.

The Prospekt (which means Avenue) is St. Petersburg's main thoroughfare and is named after the Alexander Nevsky Lavra monastery at its eastern end. Apart from Kazan Cathedral, other landmarks are the **Stroganov Rastrelliesque Palace** that once was the home of the **Stroganov** family, after whom the famous beef stew was named. It is now a Fine Arts Museum with each room decorated according to the period of the paintings.

Singer House (The House of Books)

Don't miss the wonderful view down the Kanal Griboedova to the Church of Our Savior on Stained Blood.

For shopaholics, pop into the enchanting **Eliseyev Emporium** at No. 56 and glory in its Art-deco interiors. A cross between Harrods and Fortnum and Mason in London, the Emporium consists of three retail halls on the ground floor, where you can have coffee and fabulous pastries – or just settle for champagne, caviar and blinis followed by some Russian chocolates. It is expensive, but what the heck – the atmosphere alone is worth it, not least listening to the piano that plays itself continually. The first floor also houses a restaurant and a theatre.

If you can't find what you want here, try **Gostiny Dvor,** at No. 35. This is St. Petersburg's oldest and largest department store in the city and one of Nevsky Prospekt's most famous landmarks. It has been trading for 250 years.

Severely damaged during the Second World War, it was restored and partially reconstructed during the ten years after the war. Today, the store comprises 161,458 square feet (15,000 square metres) of retail space and boasts no fewer than 122 different departments offering just about anything you can think of for sale.

On a more cultural note, the **State Russian Museum** is an extensive museum complex located in several buildings, including the Marble Palace of Count Orlov, St. Michael's Castle of Emperor Paul, the Rastrelliesque Stroganov Palace and the Summer Palace of Peter.

Together they comprise the largest collection of Russian Fine Art in the world. The main exhibition is in the **Mikhailovsky Palace**, former residence of Grand Duke Michael Pavlovich at Inzhenernaya St, 4, in Arts Square, just off Nevsky Prospekt,

Cruise passengers will likely have limited time, so it is best to concentrate on the main exhibition.

After the Revolution, the Bolsheviks confiscated huge numbers of privately-owned artworks that were then handed over to the museum. Such was their number, that the

permanent exhibition had to be expanded to include the palace's Rossi and Benois Wings.

Today, the collection includes more than 400,000 paintings and other works of art covering everything from 11th century icons to present day video performance art.

The museum is open 10am-8pm Friday to Monday. Wednesday 10am-6pm, Thursday 1pm-9pm. Admission to the permanent exhibition and the Benois Wing is 800 rubles (£9.55, $12.55, €11.33). The Benois Wing only is 500 rubles (£5.95, $7.85, €7.10), the same fee as for exhibitions in the Marble Palace, the Stroganov Palace and St. Michael's Castle.

Another way to spend a fascinating hour or so is at the *Faberge Museum* located in the Shuvalov Palace on the Fontanka River Embankment (No. 21).

It contains more than 4,000 exhibits, including fine arts, gold and silver items, paintings, porcelain and bronze, as well as the nine Imperial Easter eggs that

Fabergé created for the Romanov Tsars, Alexander III and Nicolas II.

As mentioned earlier, there are any number of museums in St. Petersburg, not least the Street Art Museum, the Museum of Russian vodka, the National Pushkin Museum, Dostoevsky Museum, the Universe of Water Museum complex, the Museum of Theatre and Music and many, many more.

On the other side of the Neva River, the ***Cruiser Aurora*** and the ***St Peter and St. Paul Fortress*** beckon. This is part of a delightful river trip that also affords spectacular views of the Winter Palace and takes you back into history.

Built between 1897 and 1900 , the ***Aurora*** was one of three cruisers built for Russian Navy service in the Pacific. The three cruisers all survived the decisive Battle of Tsushima in the Russo-Japanese war of 1904-05. This was later described as the most important naval event since Trafalgar.

Only one-third of the Russian fleet survived the war. *Aurora* was interned in the Philippines under US protection. After the Russian defeat and the peace treaty that ended the war, *Aurora* returned to Russia to become a cadet training ship in the Baltic and later a museum ship crewed by the Russian navy in St. Petersburg.

In 1917, most of her crew joined the Bolsheviks in October Revolution and fired a blank shot to signal the start of the attack on the Winter Palace.

The museum ship is open from 11am – 6pm but is closed Monday and Friday. Admission is 600 rubles (£7.20, $9.45, €8.50). There is no wheelchair access to the ship.

The star-shaped **Peter and Paul Fortress** marks the birthplace of St. Petersburg. It was the original citadel to be constructed in the city, founded by Peter the Great in 1740. Its occupants, however, never fired a shot in anger and the fortress never served its defensive purpose.

Nonetheless, during its checkered history it served as a base for the military, various government departments and the St. Petersburg Mint, one of the largest in the world.

During the October Revolution, the 8000-strong garrison joined the Bolsheviks, who used the fortress and the grim Trubetskoy Prison to incarcerate hundreds of Tsarist officials. They also used the fortress as an execution site.

The fortress also contains the **St. Peter and St. Paul Cathedral**, which is easily identified by its gilded cupola and 402-foot (122.5-metre) bell tower, the tallest in the city. The cathedral is the oldest church in St. Petersburg and the city cathedral for more than 150 years. Although named after the saints, the word 'Saint' is usually dropped when referring to the fortress and cathedral, which is where all the Russian Tsars are buried, except for Peter II and Ivan VI.

The remains of Nicholas II and his Romanov family, who were murdered at Katerinaburg after the 1917 Revolution, were finally laid to rest in St. Catherine's Chapel 80 years later

Today, the fortress and its various buildings comprise the premier part of the State Museum of St. Petersburg History.

The fortress is open daily from 9.30am-9pm (last entry at 8pm). Opening times for the Cathedral and the Trubetskoy Bastion Prison are open from 10am – 6pm. Other museums open an hour later. The museums and exhibitions are closed on Wednesday. The fortress closes at 9pm. The cathedral and grounds are wheelchair accessible. Elsewhere there are stairs, cobblestones and deep curbs.

Admission for the Cathedral and Grand Ducal burial vault is 350 rubles (£4.20, $5.50, €5.00). No charge for photography. Visitors can a single ticket valid for all exhibitions over a two-day period or separate tickets for individual exhibitions. The ticket offices are in the Boathouse and Ioannovskiy Ravelin.

The Mariinsky Theatre, is a monumental pastel green and white building that almost looks as if it is a separate wing of the Winter Palace.

Located at Teatralnaya Ploshchad (Theatre Square) No.1. it is home arguably to Russia's finest ballet and opera companies.

Built on the site of a former circus, the theatre opened in 1862 to herald a new golden age for the Russian Opera Company under the principal conductor Eduard Napravnik, who remained with the theatre for some 50 years. Many of Tchaikovsky and Rimsky-Korsakov performances premiered under his baton.

In 1886, when the Imperial Ballet' dilapidated wooden headquarters were condemned, the company moved from to the Mariinsky Theatre under the legendary ballet master, Marius Petipa, who choreographed the first performances of Tchaikovsky's Sleeping Beauty in 1890 and The Nutcracker in 1892.

Julius Reisinger had choreographed Swan Lake's premier in 1877, but it was Petipa (and Lev Ivanov) who made it famous in 1895.

After fire damage in 1880, the theatre underwent a major reconstruction for a period of 13 years, during which time the present-day auditorium was created. The famous stage curtain designed by Alexander Golovin was installed in 1914.

The new, seven-storey Mariinsky II Theatre, which straddles the Kryukov canal and is connected to the old Mariinsky Theatre by a glass gangway, is one of the largest theatres and concert venues in the world, occupying some 860,110 square feet (80,000) square metres.

The auditorium alone can accommodate as many as 2,000 people. Backstage, stages, workshops and rehearsal rooms can accommodate the entire Marinsky staff of 2,500 people. They can work on five productions simultaneously and with the most modern acoustic and technical equipment available, move huge sets onstage with the click of a mouse.

Almost all cruise ships run evening excursions to the theatre and whether or not you are a fan of ballet, it is an experience not to be missed, not least because of the stunning interior and famous Mariinsky curtain. If you are travelling independently, check with the Theatre or ticket agencies for times and prices.

Although the *St. Petersburg Metro* is not strictly a tourist attraction, it is certainly worth a visit because all eight stations along the original metro line, constructed in 1955, are renowned for their beauty and architectural ingenuity, and listed as places of cultural significance.

Finally, given that St. Petersburg is almost overflowing with prime attractions, it is likely that few cruise passengers will have time to visit the city's parks, primarily because there are more than 150 of them covering some 2,400 acres (1,010 hectares) of parkland.

However, the three main ones are the Moskovsky Victory Park at Kuznetskovskaya Ulitsa No 25 in the Moskovsky District, the Marititime Victory at Krestovskiy Prospekt No 23A on Krestovskiy Island, and the Alexander Garden at Admiralteyskiy Prospekt No. 12 running parallel to the Neva River and Admiralty Quay and extending from Palace Square to St. Isaac's Cathedral. The Alexander Garden is the closest to the city centre – the others are some way out of town.

One final tip: if you are on a tour of the city, you will inevitably be taken to the main tourist shop just off Nevsky Prospekt. Here, you will be given 45 minutes or so to look around. Even if you do not have a visa, it is an easy matter to wander off to explore Nevsky Prospekt, which is just around the corner, provided you get back to the shop on time for your tour bus departure.

So, whatever you do in St. Petersburg, you are bound to return home with some great memories.

* * *

The Baltic States

The Singing Revelation

How the Baltic States battled heroically against oppression and, with song alone, inspired the collapse of the Soviet Union.

Remarkably, nowhere in *The Traveller's Dictionary of Quotations* is there a single mention of either the Baltic States collectively or even of Estonia, Latvia or Lithuania individually. This is a 1,000-page book that lists tens of thousands of remarks and observations by countless travellers about almost every country in the world, including Tonga, Lesotho, Easter Island, Lapland and Vanuatu!

Yet, it was in the Baltic States that one of the most remarkable events in recent history took place and remains of intense interest given Vladimir Putin's provocative policies in the region.

He is once again massing armaments, nuclear weapons and Russian troops, who for years occupied Estonia, Latvia and Lithuania, along their respective borders and in Kaliningrad, the Russian annexe between Lithuania and Poland. In so doing, he has forced NATO to react and step up its presence in the region. It's a very dangerous game.

Sadly, the people of the Baltic States have been through all of this, and worse, before. Over the years, they have shown remarkable fortitude for theirs is a story of incredible courage and triumph over oppression and adversity.

Wedged between the Baltic Sea and Russia, the three Baltic states of Estonia, Latvia and Lithuania are bordered by Russia, Belarus, Poland and Kaliningrad. These flat, thickly forested lands are unspoilt, rural and sparsely populated.

Only a little bigger than Denmark, Estonia has a population of only 1.4 million and about 40% of the country is forested with pine, spruce and junipers, and dotted with around 1,500 inland lakes.

Also heavily forested, Latvia's principal natural asset is its long, sandy beaches. One, at Jurmala, is nearly 20 miles long and Latvia's answer to the French Riviera.

Lithuania, a little smaller than Ireland, is the largest of the three countries with a population of 3.4 million. Like its neighbours, it is mostly flat, its highest point a somewhat underwhelming 964 feet (294 metres) above sea level.

Forests cover roughly one third of the country, which also has an abundance of rivers and some 3,000 lakes and wetlands.

Lithuania's greatest natural asset, though, is the Curonian Spit, a line of sand dunes and pine forests that run from Klaipeda in the north to Kaliningrad in the  south, thus forming the Curonian Lagoon.

Here, the sand dunes hide a deeper treasure. Forty to 65 million years ago, these dunes were primaeval pine forests until rising sea levels and sand buried them. As the pines gradually fossilized, the resin became a seam of amber, two to three feet thick beneath the surface.

Today, whenever there has been a storm, treasure hunters comb the coast in search of the glowing chunks of amber scattered like pebbles along the beaches. In their raw state, buffeted by tides and storms, these are dull compared with the amber that is excavated by some 150 different companies, particularly in Kaliningrad.

Amber's peculiarity is that when the pine resin was still sticky, insects attracted to it became solidified inside it. This caused scientists to wonder whether it would be possible to extract the DNA of a dinosaur from a blood-sucking insect that was 65,000 years old. It was this idea that inspired Stephen Spielberg to film Jurassic Park.

(A word of warning. You need to be extremely careful if you plan to buy amber as there is a huge amount of fake amber around. If you plan to buy, be sure to have it tested by experts before you commit to the purchase).

Unfortunately, storms are eroding the sand banks along the Curonian Spit and it is eventually expected either to break up into a chain of islands – or to fill the lagoon with sediment. In the early 19th century, the Lithuanians planted tens of thousands of pine trees along the spit in a bid to protect it. More trees were planted in the 1960s and they have behaved in very strange way, growing into deformed shapes and

becoming a major tourist attraction known as the ***Dancing Forest***.

Like the Swedes and Finns, people in the Baltics have an especially close relationship with Nature. Many have a summer house and get away to the countryside as often as they possibly can, especially in summer. That is a time for sailing, jogging, cycling alone or with friends, walking, canoeing or just heading out to sea for some fishing.

They yearn for a more basic, rural lifestyle, picking berries or, best or all, barbecuing or smoking fish, freshly caught from the rivers and streams.

Whereas we tend to romanticize Nature, the Balts enjoy it in a refreshingly hands-on, non-sentimental way. They are perfectly at ease working in an office in the city one day and chopping firewood out in the sticks the next.

Together, Estonia, Latvia and Lithuania boast no fewer than 14 national parks between them, all of which means that these countries are just teeming with wildlife, everything from brown bears, lynx and wolves to eagles, and both white and black storks.

The first humans to arrive in Estonia were Finno-Ugric people from southeast Europe around 6000 BC. Today, the language spoken by Estonians is closely related to Finnish and Hungarian, which means that to most people they are incomprehensible. That's because there are 14 different cases of any noun. Verb conjugation is a nightmare and a verb's meaning can change according to how its root is pronounced, if, indeed, that is possible for a non-Balt.

What's more, there are no definite or indefinite articles, or even gender, in Estonian. Needless to say, that translates to when they are speaking English, as well.

These people were among the first tribes to drift across Europe from Asia, leaving the lower slopes of the Urals, following the river courses, subsisting mostly on fish and clothing themselves in animal skins.

They had long since reached the Baltic coast when Tacitus mentioned them in the 1st century AD.

"Strangely beast-like and squalidly poor," he wrote, "neither arms nor homes have they. Their food is herbs, their clothing skin, their bed, the earth.

"They trust wholly to their arrows, which, for want of iron, are pointed with bone. Heedless of men, heedless of gods, they have attained that hardest of results, the non-needing of so much as a wish."

So, it seems they were contented, possibly because at that time, they probably just grunted and didn't have to speak Finno-Ugric. Eventually, the Latvian and Lithuanian languages did evolve and today they are the last two languages of the Indo-European language group to survive.

Indeed, Latvian, which is remotely related to the Slavic languages (Russian, Polish and Ukrainian) is now endangered. This is sad, but probably just as well because it is no more comprehensible than the others and has no fewer than twelve vowels and 10 diphthongs. And people say English is difficult to learn!

Although the Estonians, Latvians and Lithuanians have a shared history, they are as different from each other as the French are from the Italians or the Belgians from the Irish.

Lithuanians, for example, are outgoing and the most nationalistic, but remarkably disinterested in their northern neighbours. The Estonian character is more closely related to the austere nature of the Scandinavians, while the Latvians are more exuberant.

However, a common trait amongst all three nationalities is their intense desire to be left alone, especially by the Russians.

The borders of the three countries are dominated by Russia and Belarus (Mr. Putin's close ally) which is heavily militarized. For some 800 years, the Baltic countries were all occupied at some time or another by the Danes, the Germans, the Swedes, Poles and Russians.

Between 1700 and 1721, the Great Northern War between Charles the 12th of Sweden and Peter the Great of Russia resulted in a Russian victory and the Russian occupation of Estonia and Latvia.

Lithuania gradually became part of the Russian Empire between 1772 and 1795, although Klaipeda and Kaliningrad fell to the Prussians. Eventually, all three countries ended up as subjects of the Tsars and were absorbed into the Russian Empire

In 1915, the Germans, irritated that they had been excluded from the Baltic by the Russians, attacked Vilnius in Lithuania, taking 22,000 Russian prisoners of war. Once the Germans had conquered Lithuania, they then subjected its people to intense Germanization of their country.

They declared martial law. They banned all public meetings. They censored newspapers. Courts had German judges and schools, German teachers. All classes were taught only in German.

Following the defeat of the Germans in 1918, all three Baltic states became independent and for a brief 22 years they all flourished.

Sadly, their independence was cut short in brutal fashion when the Hitler-Stalin Pact of 1939 put the Baltic States under Soviet influence once again. Stalin invaded in June 1940 and the Red Army again went on the rampage. Thousands were deported or shot. In Estonia and Lithuania, some 80,000 people simply went missing. They had been forcibly conscripted into the Soviet Army, deported to labour camps or executed. In Latvia, 15,000 bodies were discovered and re-buried.

The depleted populations were replaced by more than 150,000 Russians, who arrived carrying banners prepared by fifth columnists. These people were sent ostensibly to man heavy industry, but equally to implement a massive Russification programme originally begun by the Tsars.

Then, in 1941, the Nazi-Soviet pact collapsed, German forces again invaded the Baltics, forcing the Russians back into the Soviet Union.

Under Hitler and the Nazis, some 90,000 Jews in Latvia were murdered and another 10,000 disappeared. It was a fate similarly shared with 150,000 Jews in Lithuania.

In August 1944, the German occupation of the Baltic States succumbed to a fresh Soviet onslaught followed by intensified Russification, the aims of which, amongst others, were to subdue religion.

The Soviets nationalized all church properties and holdings. They converted churches into concert halls or museums. Others were simply abandoned.

St. Casimir's in Vilnius became a Museum of Atheism. Riga's Orthodox cathedral became a planetarium. Anyone who attended church found their careers threatened and their children banned from higher education. Many priests, evangelists and activists were imprisoned. Estonia lost two-thirds of its clergy. Despite the repression, the Soviets soon discovered that whereas you can close churches, arrest and execute priests, you cannot stamp out the inner fires of Faith.

That is perhaps no more evident than at the Hill of Crosses in Lithuania. The tradition of leaving crosses there began in 1831 to commemorate the fallen who had rebelled against Russia.

The Soviets bulldozed the hill three times, but each time the crosses and statues were re-erected and today, the Hill has become a site of pilgrimage and a symbol of faith for Christians everywhere.

Today, religion is alive and well in all three countries: Lithuania is solidly Catholic. Latvians and Estonians are either Lutheran, Roman Catholic, Russian or Estonian Orthodox. Religion, like music, dancing and particularly singing, has always been a part of Baltic folklore.

After 50 years of continuous German and Soviet occupation, traditional song festivals attended by tens of thousands of people gradually became political events. The songs they sang reflected a burning and innate sense of nationalism, and a desperate desire to shake off the Russian yoke.

Inspired by the singing, about two million people from all three Baltic states joined hands at seven o' clock in the evening on August 23rd, 1989 in a peaceful but extraordinarily powerful anti-Soviet protest.

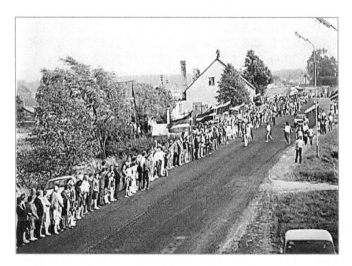

The human chain stretched some 400 miles (nearly 650 kilometres) from   Tallinn on the northern coast of Estonia through Latvia to Vilnius in Lithuania. Its purpose? To demand the restoration of their independence.

It became known as the 'Baltic Way" and it became an example to the rest of the world, demonstrating that non-violent political action can be a mighty weapon. In time, it would eventually help to pave the way for the disintegration of the Soviet Union itself.

The people sang songs that the Soviets had banned for 50 years. They attracted worldwide attention and support. Suddenly, the Baltic was no longer just a local issue at the top of Europe. The story was headlined in newspapers and television all over the world.

Demonstrations of solidarity took place in Berlin, Bonn, Melbourne, Stockholm, Toronto and, notably, in Moscow.

Indeed, the 'Singing Revolution' had become for oppressed peoples everywhere a 'Singing Revelation'. Vigils in the Soviet Union, where authorities had cracked down on demonstrations, eventually led to the independence of Georgia, Ukraine and Moldova.

Then, on March 11th, 1990, the Lithuanian Soviet Socialist Republic adopted a motion signed by all 120 members of the Supreme Council to restore the country's independence. It was the first time that a Soviet Republic had ever done so and it was the beginning of the end for the Soviet Union.

Michael Gorbachev immediately declared the vote illegal and soon afterwards ordered Soviet forces to attack the country once more. Troops stormed Vilnius Television tower. Unarmed Lithuanians confronted the Soviet soldiers, who opened fire. They killed 14 people and wounded 700 others, but the Lithuanians would not be defeated. Once again, they took to singing.

Russian tank units also rolled into Tallinn and Riga in the autumn of 1991, but, like the Lithuanians, the Estonians and Latvians also formally declared their independence.

People began to tear down the ubiquitous statues of Lenin. They were tense moments. Worse, the Soviet economy was now in dire straits and the Soviet Union itself was breaking up as yet more states declared independence.

Gorbachev, head in hands, admitted: "We cannot beat this". On August 21st, 1991, Soviet troops began to withdraw from Estonia and Latvia. A month later, in September 1991, all three Baltic countries became members of the United Nations. Even the Soviet Union finally recognized their independence.

After one singing concert, Kaie Tanner. an Estonian choral conductor, commented:

"When we had Singing Revolution, I remember feeling that we have 80,000 people here and that you can't arrest, and you can't kill all of them. I think that it made Estonian people think that music can make a difference and that's why we continue with this tradition. We are singing ourselves free. Showing what we are!"

Sten Weidebaum, from the Song and Dance Festival Foundation, added:

"In Estonia, we love to say that we sang us free. In a way, it's true because of song celebration tradition. We survived as nation through those Soviet years. That made us to believe that, yes, we are still here, we are still speaking Estonian, we are still singing in Estonia and we even have new composers who are making *wonderful* and uncensored music of love to country and to each other."

It is hardly surprising, somehow, that soon afterwards, Estonia and Latvia won the dubious honour of winning the

Eurovison Song contest. In a sense, the exuberance, the optimism and pure joy in the winning songs permeated the immediate post-Soviet era in all three Baltic states.

They each forged close ties to the United States. They became members of the European Union, NATO, the World Trade Organization and the OECD (the Organization for Economic Cooperation and Development).

They each boast free and fair elections, a free press, civic pride, lively political competition and debate, and a respect for civil liberties and human rights.

That is something that cannot be said about their occupiers. Indeed, the Baltic States are the only former Soviet republics that are currently rated by Freedom House as truly 'free' countries.

Once they had shaken off the Soviet yoke, their economies rebounded and, at the time, recorded the fastest rate of growth in the world.

The Estonian economy, in particular, increased by nearly 10% a year. Latvia and Lithuania were not far behind. Indeed, their economies were so robust, they became known as the 'Baltic Tigers'.

Sadly, that status ended abruptly in 2008, thanks to housing bubbles, a large build-up of debt and the global economic crisis in 2008-2009.

The impact in Latvia was so jarring that it sparked off violent protests at the imposed austerity measures. It also precipitated the collapse of the government and led to an emergency bailout of £7.5 billion pounds from the IMF (in 2009).

A year later, both Estonia and Lithuania had returned to economic growth and by 2011, Estonia was back to a brisk 8.1% growth, the highest in the EU. Lithuania nudged 10% and Latvia, a healthy 5.5 per cent. Today, the economies of all three countries are not only stable. They are thriving.

After the Russian troops left, each of the three countries made huge advances in health and education. There are no problems with medical supplies. Scandinavians book into Estonia for cosmetic surgery and all three countries offer inexpensive medical tourism.

In 2012, an OECD yardstick test found that Estonia, always the most go-ahead of the three countries, had the 11th highest quality of education in the world.

Most people speak at least two and usually three languages. Almost everybody is reasonably fluent in English, which is taught in schools from an early age.

All three countries have a minimum wage and a statutory 28 days holiday. The work forces are highly educated.

Estonia, particularly, is highly wired in the digital age. It was in Tallinn that Estonian whizz kids invented Skype. It was also where the Estonians first introduced the world's first 'paperless' parliament. That's an advance that European bureaucrats in Brussels should perhaps take note of, given that they print thousands of documents in three languages every day, and must transport them to Strasbourg in convoys of taxis and vans!

Of course, all the Baltic States face challenges, the principal ones being a 15-20% decline in their populations, mostly because of low birth rates, emigration to the United States and ageing populations. That, by all accounts, is likely to continue.

The future economy is likely to be driven by domestic sales, the Baltic export markets having declined partly because of the Russian embargo on American and European food and agricultural products. This was imposed in 2014 as a response to the West's sanctions over Soviet actions in the Ukraine. Russian jets buzzing NATO and Baltic navy ships has massively increased tension in the region and it is the main risk to the outlook for growth in the Baltic States.

The armed forces of all three Baltic States are on high alert and, although nobody knows Mr. Putin's intentions, extensive Russian military manoeuvres on their borders have created a much increased and an ever-present fear that Russia might once again pour its troops over their borders.

That fear is exacerbated by the fact that Russia could probably overrun the three countries in 48 to 72 hours despite their membership of NATO. That means that if one country is attacked, the others would be duty bound to come to their aid.

Russian hints that it might use nuclear force. Diplomatic scaremongering or not, the rhetoric persuaded NATO that a presence was urgently needed in the Baltic region.

Portuguese, British, Swedish and Finnish jets have been scrambled on many occasions. Lithuania re-introduced compulsory military service and keeps a close eye on any incursions into their air space.

Another invasion would be easy enough because the Baltic states are sparsely populated and are weak militarily.

Would Putin risk a war that could easily escalate into a Third World War? It seems extremely doubtful, but if an aggressive, expansionist and totalitarian regime is in power in Moscow – and one with massive military power – the danger will always exist. That means that the western powers, equally, must remain on high alert.

As for the Balts, they hide their fears and carry on as normal. They work hard. They play hard and above all, they love their country, their countryside and their traditions. It is these that give them the most joy.

In the early 1800s, a young poet called Kristan Jaak Peterson from Riga, wrote four lines that epitomize the deepest feelings that the Estonians, Latvians and Lithuanians have for their countries.

"Why should not my country's tongue", he wrote,
Soaring through the gale of song
Rising to the heights of Heaven
Find its own eternity?

If the story of the Baltic states is one of 800 years of war, occupation, horror and the worst that humankind can do, then it is also a story about the passion and the courage of ordinary people brought together by an extraordinary tradition.

Singing and dancing here goes back centuries. They were instrumental in forging the respective national identities and bringing together people of all walks of life.

That is why UNESCO has recognized the Latvian Nationwide Song and Dance Festival as a masterpiece of the heritage of humanity.

***

Tallinn, Estonia.

The Main Attractions

A photographer's dream, Tallinn Old Town is a glorious mix of old and new, architecture and culture, of Baltic, Nordic, Teutonic and Russian influences. It is a city of ancient churches, medieval cobbled streets and merchants' houses with fabulous food and great local beers in first rate restaurants and bars on every corner.

In short, it is an outrageously photogenic, 1,000-year old walled city with a Hanseatic centre that is said to be one of the best preserved in the world. It is a fairy tale city that you will love to bits. No wonder it is listed as a UNESCO.World Heritage Site.

Most cruise passengers will never leave the Old Town, although outside the walls, the city is both charming and modern with brightly painted wooden houses, sophisticated business districts, an efficient tram and bus system (free for residents) and recently renovated docks, as well as beaches, parks and outlying forests.

Tallinn receives about 4.5 million visitors a year, mostly from Europe but increasingly from Russia, China and Japan. It is a figure that has grown steadily over the past decade. Nearly 650,000 cruise passengers arrive annually on some 340 cruise ships and approximately 10 million passenger movements, mostly from Swedish and Finnish ferries, make the Port of Tallinn one of the busiest in the Baltic region.

For all its old-worldliness, Tallinn, with a population of 434,562 (2019), is Estonia's capital as well as its financial, industrial, educational and scientific research centre.

Located just 50 miles (80 kms) south of Helsinki and 200 miles (321 kms) west of St. Petersburg, it has the highest number of business start-ups per person in Europe. It is also a city of whizz kids immersed in information technology. Not for nothing is this the European Union's IT Headquarters and NATO's Cyber Defence Centre. Indeed, Tallinn is said to be one of the top ten digital cities in the world.

People have lived on the site for some 5,000 years and possibly as long as 11,000 years. From the hill *Toompea*

(Cathedral Hill), the 11th century fortress still overlooks the city, which was well defended with city walls and 66 defence towers.

Formerly known by its Hanseatic name, Reval, the city has been occupied or controlled by Vikings, Teutonic knights, Danes, Swedes, Finns, Hanseatic Germans and Russians.

Like most of Denmark, southern Norway, Sweden and Finland, Estonia and Livonia (now Latvia) were consumed by the Plague. In the early 1700's, they succumbed to Imperial Russia during the Great Northern War, although they managed to maintain control of their cultural and economic affairs with Russia acting as the governorate.

The late 1800s brought more intense Russification and the 20th century evolved into German occupation and, when the Germans retreated at the end of the Second World War, invasion and re-occupation by the Soviets. In 1991, the Estonians re-established their democratic independence.

Happily, Tallinn, unlike other towns, escaped serious damage throughout history and despite extensive Soviet Air Force bombing during the Second World War, the medieval Hanseatic town survived more or less untouched.

Today, as we have seen, Tallinn is a lively, bustling city of great charm populated increasingly by non-Estonians. In fact, Estonians make up less than 50% of the city's population. Russians account for 34% and the rest are Ukrainian, Belarusian, Finnish, Jewish, Lithuanians, Armenians, Latvians, Germans, Poles and others.

Sometimes referred to as the Silicon Valley of the Baltic, Tallinn thrives largely because of its focus on information technology and tourism, which have been so successful that the city now accounts for more than half the Estonian GDP.

The city is also the financial and economic hub of Estonia and has strong links with Sweden and Finland. Major industries include shipbuilding, metal processing, electronics and textiles.

Cruise passengers may also be delighted to know that Tallinn has more shopping floor space per head of population than Sweden. In fact, it has more than anywhere in Europe apart from Norway and Luxembourg.

Cruise shuttle busses will drop off passengers just outside

the main port gates into **Tallinn Old Town**, once home to wealthy merchants from Germany, Denmark and elsewhere.

With millions of tourists arriving each year, it may be crowded and parts of it will unquestionably be 'touristy'. That said, this is most definitely the absolute 'must-see' venue with its Gothic spires and cupolas, colourful gabled houses and half-hidden courtyards. The winding cobblestone streets and architecture are beguiling and there is plenty to see, do and try from art galleries, museums and quaint shops to countless bars and restaurants.

This is a place in which to wander, to get lost, to discover and, of course, to photograph.

Raekoja Plats & Tallinn Town Hall

The ***Town Hall Square (Raekola Plats)*** has been the hub of the Old Town for 800 years and remains its social centre to this day. Ringed by medieval merchant houses, in winter it is the venue for the town's Christmas tree and lively Christmas market, which has taken place here since the

Brotherhood of Blackheads, a military organization that evolved into an association of merchants, ship owners and foreigners. The fraternity is thought to have raised the first tree in 1441.

In summer, café owners set up their outdoor tables and serve lunches and beers to thousands of tourists, not all of them aware that once an argument over a bad omelette resulted in an execution in the centre of the square.

On market days the square is packed with so many people that you can barely see the cobblestones, but if you stand on the small compass stone in the centre the square on other days, you can just about spot the five spires of the Old Town's churches and cathedral over the rooftops.

Aside from the market, the square is also a venue for the 'Old Town Days' festival, when local people don medieval costumes and keep alive the old traditions.

On the southern side of the square, the 600-year-old Town Hall, the oldest in the entire Baltic region and Scandinavia, was built on the ruins of a stone building first erected around 1250. With its 210-foot (65-metre) high tower, it was later rebuilt and reconstructed several times. In 1530, a weathervane in the shape of a warrior called Old Thomas, was added to the roof.

Much loved, the figure eventually became a popular symbol of the city. Today, a more modern version of the vane graces the roof; the metal original is kept in the basement of the Town Hall.

Cathedral (Toompea) Hill is a 10th century Estonian stronghold standing on a limestone plateau on which some archaeological evidence found there points to 11th century

Viking settlers. In 1219, Valdemar II of Denmark attacked the hill fort and replaced it with a sturdier castle.

Eight years later, the Brothers of the Sword, a Catholic military order dating back to 1202, re-fortified the hill, dividing it into three sections: the Small Castle, the Great Castle and an outer ward. However, a devastating fire in 1684 destroyed most of the Great Castle which then fell into a period of general neglect.

In the late 18th century, however, Tsarina Catherine II ordered it to be completely rebuilt. The moat was filled in and the outer ward was re-designed as a public square which eventually housed the administrative building of the Estonian Governate.

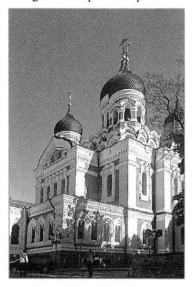

Between 1894 and 1900, during the period of Russification, the Russians built the *Orthodox Alexander Nevsky Cathedral*, the towers of which contain 11 bells, the largest of which weighs 16 tonnes.

Local people, including the city authorities, regarded the

cathedral, with its five onion domes, gilded crosses and ornate interior, as a badge of Russian oppression and hated it so much that in 1924, they planned to demolish it. However, the plans failed to come to fruition because its destruction was considered too difficult and costly.

Like many churches in the USSR, which was officially non-religious, the Cathedral was neglected and gradually fell into serious disrepair.

As time passed, the old hatred of the church dissipated and when Estonia became independent in 1991, the cathedral was restored meticulously. Today, it is a major tourist attraction.

Arguably the best views of the city are from *the Kohtuotsa Viewing Platform* on the northern side of Toompea Hill. Here you can look over the red roofs and church spires right across to the port and Gulf of Finland.

Look out for the pastel pink wall with the catchy phrase "The Times we Had". Nobody knows who painted it there but over the years it has almost become a landmark itself.

The **Patkuli Viewing Platform** offers fairy-tale views and there is much discussion about which is the better. The answer is that Kohtuotsa is more crowded, but it is sometimes difficult to take photographs there because other tourists hog the front row taking selfies.

Patkuli is higher, arguably offers slightly better views and is less crowded. The downside is that it is further away and involves climbing 157 steps to get there. Sometimes, the morning sun can also make photography a challenge.

Back in town , the city's largest medieval structure, **St. Olaf's Church,** located at Lai No. 50, is thought to have been built on the site of an earlier, 12th century church dedicated to the Norwegian Viking King, Olav II, who brought Christianity to Scandinavia in the 11th century.

The original Catholic church was later rebuilt and during the early 16th century Reformation was converted for Lutheran beliefs.

At the end of the Second World War, Soviet agents from the KGB set up radio detectors in the 407 foot ((124 metre) spire, which they used as a base to maintain surveillance of the Tallinn population until 1991. Lightning has struck the steeple on at least ten occasions and, on three occasions in 1625, 1820 and 1931, resulted in serious fires.

In 1950, St. Olav's became a Baptist church and remains so today. Cruise passengers who are physically fit (if there are any) may climb the 232 steps to the observation platform, which also offers excellent views of the city. However, the tower is closed during the winter months.

The church is open every day from 10am until 6pm from April 1st – 30th June and until 8pm from July 1st - 31st August. Admission costs €3.00 (£2.50, $3.35).

Views from Kohtuotsu, Patkuki and St. Olaf's Church, however, pale into insignificance compared with **Tallinn TV Tower**, which at 1,030 feet (314 metres) is the tallest building in Estonia.

Here you can take one of two high-speed elevators to the futuristic viewing platform on the 21st floor, which offers 360-degree views of the city. You can also enjoy an adrenalin-pumping walk round the outdoor terrace if you have a head for heights. Some people even base jump from it. However, this is not recommended for cruise passengers over 70. (Actually, it's not recommended at all!)

If you insist on having a vertiginous view, you can always peer through a glass hole in the platform floor and see the ground below.

For those who are uncomfortable even inside the viewing platform, there are interactive screens linked to cameras at the top of the tower which provide less nerve-racking views of the surroundings. You can also zoom in and see more clearly what you would not be able to see from the outer walkway.

There is a cinema, a restaurant, a mini-TV studio and gift shop as well as a 'Gene-ius' exhibition that explores our inner spaces and DNA.

Aside from that, there is a completely new virtual reality experience which starts with the walk round the edge of the tower and continues by sitting in a flying machine and taking a 'flight' around it. The virtual reality experience is viewed with a VR headset and can be experience by two people at the same time. The experience takes approximately 10 minutes. Safety instructions are given on site.

A short journey on the 34A, 38 or 49 buses will take you to the tower, which is approximately six miles (10 kilometres) from the city centre and is open daily throughout the year from 10am until 6pm. Admission starts at €13.00 (£10.85, $14.45). Seniors: €7.00 (£5.85, $7.80).

The ticket price for the VR experience is an extra €5.00 (£4.20, $5.60).

Passengers who prefer the real thing can sign up for the harnessed walk around the outside of the viewing platform, which costs a further 10 euros ($8.35, $11.10) and demands a considerable degree of bravery or a mental health check, whichever way you look at it.

Adjacent to the Tower, the extensive and beautifully designed *Tallinn Botanic Gardens* offer tranquility from the urban bustle with thousands of plant species and greenhouses with wide-ranging tropical plants and cactus displays.

The gardens are open from 10am - 8pm daily from May 1st-30th September, and from 11am-4pm from October 1st to 30th April. Admission is €5.50 (£4.60, $6.10). Seniors: €3.00 (£2.50, $3.35). Audio guides are available to guide you round the gardens.

Kadriorg Art Museum is located in Kadriorg Park at A. Weizenbergi No. 37 in the north of Tallin. (Take tram No. 1 or 3 to their final stops). The museum is housed in a Baroque palace built by Tsar Peter the Great as a summer residence. (It is just a few minutes' walk past the Swan Pond on the right; you can then see the palace on the other side of the street).

The museum is the only museum in Estonia to collect and preserve early foreign art, primarily west European and Russian paintings, graphic arts, sculpture and applied arts. It contains approximately 9,000 artworks from the 16th to 20th centuries.

Opening times are Tuesday, Thursday-Sunday 10am-6pm, Wednesday 10am-8pm. Closed Mondays and Public holidays. Admission: €6.50, (£5.40, $7.25). Seniors: €4.50 (£3.75, $5.00).

Kumu Art Museum is similarly located on A. Weizenbergi street at No.34. (Take the same trams. The museum is a 10-minute walk through the park). This is the headquarters of the Art Museum of Estonia, which comprises five separate museums). Winner of the 2008 European Museum of the Year Award, the museum was originally planned to be a national gallery but evolved into a museum that both collects Estonian art from the early 18th century to art pre-dating World War II, art from the Soviet occupation and modern art.

Apart from the permanent exhibition, it curates 11-12 larger exhibitions in four exhibition halls. There is also a 245-seat auditorium with film programmes, performances, concerts, seminars and conferences, and a library with the widest selection of art literature in Estonia.

The museum is open daily from 10am-6pm except for public holidays. Admission is €8.00 (£6.65, $8.90). Seniors: € 6.00 (5.00, $6.70).

The ***Estonian Maritime Museum*** located at Pikk No. 70 in the 500-year-old ***Fat Margaret Tower*** in the Old Town, was founded on the initiative of former captains and sailors in 1935 and covers all things nautical relating to Estonia and beyond. The roof of the building also offers great views of the port and the Old Town. There is a small coffee corner and a museum shop.

In 2012, the museum opened a new exhibition the Seaplane Hanger of the **Seaplane Harbour,** which is located at Vesilennuki No. 6. Spread across three levels (underwater, surface and air) it contains a submarine, a Short 184 seaplane and a shipwreck as well as ice boats, an icebreaker, various other vessels, naval mines and equipment.

Opening times May-September: Monday-Friday 10am-7pm. October-April: Tuesday-Sunday, 10am-6pm. On most public holidays it closes at 5pm. Admission to Fat Margaret Museum: €10.00 (£8.35, $11.15). Seniors: half price. Combined ticket Fat Margaret and Seaplane Harbour: double the above prices.

***

Kuressaare, Saaremaa Island
Estonia

The Main Attractions

Saaremaa Island is the largest island in the West Estonian archipelago measuring a little more than 1,000 square miles (about 2,675 square kilometres) and is home to nearly 31,400 residents.

The first settlers arrived around 5,000 BC and there are reports of many local battles with Vikings from east Sweden. The island was also home to pirates who, according to one account, numbered about 500 operating with 16 ships that continuously plied the entire east coast of Sweden and west and southern coasts of Finland.

As in Finland, Saaremaa Island continues to grow as a result of the post glacial rebound at a rate of 0.790 inches (two millimetres) a year. Nott surprisingly perhaps, the island is a limestone plain no higher than about 50 feet (15 metres).

The island also had the misfortune to be struck by the fragments of a meteorite that struck earth between 1,000-4,000 years ago. The largest fragment left a crater 360 feet (110 metres) in diameter and a depth of 72 feet (22 metres).

Saaremaa Island also lies on the main migration path of waterfowl flying to and from the Arctic each Spring and Autumn.

Its 'capital' is the fortress town of Kuressaare, originally named Arensburg, which dates back at least to the 12th century and which today has a population of 13,276.

Across the centuries, the town was badly damaged during numerous wars and invasions, but several impressive historical buildings have survived

Kuressaara Castle located at Lossihoov No.1 is one of the most impressive and well-preserved fortresses in Estonia. The original fortress was probably built of wood in the 13th century by Catholic crusaders of the Teutonic Order. Their mission, sanctioned by the Pope was to conquer today's Estonia, Latvia and Lithuania, and suppress the inhabitants' stiff resistance to being Christianized.

The fortress eventually became the stronghold of the Bishop of Saare-Laane but fell to Denmark in 1559. The Danes modernized it, but during the Swedish-Danish war of 1643-45, it fell to the Swedes. They continued updating the fortifications, then lost the castle to the Russians.

In the 1800s, the Episcopal castle was used as a workhouse (poorhouse). Today, it is the only medieval fortress in Estonia  that remains completely intact.

There is a history museum there that explores both the distant past and recent history of Saaremaa and its population through the permanent and temporary exhibitions. There are also activities for both children and adults – from treasure hunts to archery!

Opening times: June 1st-September 1st, 10am-6pm daily. September 2nd-30th April, Wednesday-Sunday 11am-5pm. Closed Monday and Tuesday. Admission is €8.00 (£6.79, $8.90).

Saaremaa Museum, founded in 1865 and one of the oldest and largest museums in Estonia, lies in the castle grounds. Indeed, the castle is a part of the museum, which is visited by some 70-80,000 people each year.

The museum tells the story of Saaremaa as a region, focusing on its culture, natural environment, and history, particularly on the castle. The bastions house exhibits of everything from cannon, weaponry and handcuffs to wrought iron souvenirs, a pottery and a glass furnace where visitors can try their hand at glassblowing. They can also witness the art of dolomite and stonecutting.

During the summer months, there is an exhibition dedicated to the Communist terror of 1941.

Opening times: May 1st-31st August, Mon–Sun 10am-9pm. September 1st-April 30th, Wed–Sun 11am-6pm. Admission is €8.00 (£6.75, $8.90). Seniors: €6.00 (£5.05, $6.70).

Kuressaare Town Hall at Tallinna Street, No.2 was designed by the Swedish nobleman Count Magnus Gabriel de la Gardie and built between 1654-1670 in a strict but distinguished Northern Baroque style.

Badly damaged in a fire in 1710, it was subsequently rebuilt on several occasions. The Latin text above the portal translates as 'Always asking advice from people, it obeys its

duty in favour of society. AD 1670'. The Town Hall underwent a major restoration between 1961-1973.

Today, it houses the Town Hall Art Gallery (Raegallerii), Tourist Information Centre and Registry Office. What once was the wine cellar has been converted into the Raekelder restaurant.

Opening times: 15th May-31st May and 1st-15th September: Monday-Friday 9am-5pm. Weekends 10am-4pm. June 1st-31st August: 9am-6pm, weekends 10am-4pm. 16th September-30th April: Monday-Friday 9am-5pm, Saturday10am-3pm. Sunday closed. There is no entry fee.

St. Nicholas Church at Lossi tänav No. 8 is the oldest Orthodox church on Saaremaa Island, built with three naves in 1790 on the orders of Catherine the Great.

The church lacks the grandeur of Orthodox Churches in St. Petersburg and Helsinki, but its white pillars, pale green arches and several ancient paintings and icons, give it an intimacy that is lacking in the larger churches.

Well worth a quick visit and do look out for the frescos on the external walls. The gates and surrounding wall were built with dolomite rock.

An amusing sculpture is that of ***Suur Toll and Piret***

which is situated in front of the SPA Hotel Meri at Pargi tänav No 16. Created in 2002 by an Estonian sculptor, Tauno Kangro, it depicts a mythical hero of Saaremaa, and his wife Piret.

According to the 'Visit Estonia' website, the 'Sõrve peninsula was important to Tõll, as from there he reached the shortest way to the island Ruhnu, where he had his cabbage field. When his wife Piret started to make a fire under the cauldron, then Tõll went through the sea to his cabbage field and came back in half an hour, so that he could hand Piret the cabbages when the water had just started to boil.'

Kuressaare Town Park, located in a former cemetery at Lossipark No. 1, was developed in the late 1800s when some local people realised that the sea mud around the town was curative. Not long afterwards, they erected bathing houses in the sea just behind the castle. A park committee was formed in 1861 and residents donated seedlings and money to buy workhorses and vehicles.

In 1930, the park authorities ordered several specimens of rare trees from Tartu University and today there are some 80 different species of trees and bushes there.

Kuressaare is not exactly a hive of activity at the best of times, which makes it an extremely pleasant town to visit and but an hour or two spent in the park is restful and peaceful. There is also a café (Zurra Murra) converted from an old train

station which, according to some reports, 'serves the best cheesecake ever'.

For a more substantial meal, **Saaremaa Windmill (Kuursaal)** located at Pärna tn No.19 is the oldest working restaurant in Kuressaare. The management offer simple, fresh and seasonal locally sourced food, make their own wine and 'shots', barbecue the meat and smoke the fish.

Built in 1899, the windmill replaced the first Eastern Orthodox Church in Kuressaare (after it burned down in the early 1780s).

Mindful that during the First World War the French used the sails to send messages about the numbers of enemy troops the Estonians opted to saw off the sails during the Second World War.

The windmill continued to operate until 1941, after which it was used for storage. In 1974, it opened as a café and quickly became one of the most popular eateries in town. The current Restaurant Veski opened in 1997 and two years later, the windmill celebrated its 100th anniversary.

The restaurant is open Sunday-Thursday 12 noon-9pm and until midnight on Friday and Saturday.

Cruise passengers with a passion for bird watching may wish to visit the ***Roomassaare bird-watching tower*** just west of the airport runway, about five miles (8 kms) south of Kuressaare town. A total of 384 bird species have been recorded here, of which 210 are 'regulars', the rest mostly migrants or winter visitors. It is estimated that about 115 arrived here by mistake and are therefore rare in Estonia.

Lying on the migration route for millions of passerines and some 50 million waterfowl and shorebirds, even in summer there are plenty of birds to see ranging from Steller's Eider, broad-billed sandpipers to Black storks and pygmy owls.

***

Riga, Latvia

The Main Attractions

Riga is the largest of the three Baltic capitals with a population 632,614, which equates to one third of Latvia's population. It is a city of superlatives – fabulous Art Nouveau architecture, the largest medieval church in the Baltics, the most stunning views from the highest church, the largest market in Europe and the narrowest alleyway in which you can touch opposite walls simultaneously.

The city's Gothic spires and more than 500 Gothic, Baroque, Modernist and Art Nouveau buildings all packed into a cobblestoned centre jointly contributed to Riga's listing as a UNESCO World Heritage Site. Old-worldly, yes – but it has plenty of contemporary art centres, thriving pavement cafés, discos, bars, and restaurants with cutting-edge cuisine, as well.

It is a bustling, colourful city with an abundance of wonderful architectural treasures and something for everybody.

Riga Old Town - Art Nouveau

More than one-third of all the buildings in Riga's Old Town are recognized as comprising the finest collection of art nouveau buildings in Europe.

Check out the mansion houses along Alberta iela (street0 with their colourful facades, sculptures and gargoyles in the designated Art Nouveau district.

The *Art Nouveau Museum* at Alberta street (iela) No. 12 is the only museum in any of the Baltic States to focus exclusively on Art Nouveau architecture and interior decoration.

Built in 1903, it was originally a private mansion owned by a Latvian architect.

Ornamental reliefs of native Latvian flowers, plants and animals adorn the exterior.

Inside, the museum features an authentic Art Nouveau apartment, complete with furniture, paintings, tableware, and ornaments, including clocks and clothing. The central spiral staircase is considered to be one of the greatest masterpieces of its kind in Europe.

A digital exhibit also explains how Rigans lived in the early 1900s. There is even a special studio in which visitors can have their photograph taken against an Art Nouveau backdrop.

Opening hours 10am-6pm. Admission in summer months €9.00 (£7.65, $10.00). Seniors: €5.00 (£4.25, $5.55). In winter months: €5.00. Seniors €3.00 (£2.55, $3.35).

The Cat House - situated at Meistaru iela No. 10 opposite to the Great Guild Hall in the centre of the Old Town, dates to 1909. It is a mix of architectural styles with medieval turrets and an Art Nouveau portal. It is best known, however, for the two black copper cats perched on its turrets.

There are several versions of the origin of the cats, but the essence of them all is the same – that the owner, a wealthy Latvian businessman, fell out with members of the Great (Tradesmen's) Guild nearby because the nationalistic German occupants rejected his application for membership.

In response, he placed the cats with arched backs and erect tails with their backsides facing the Guild as a mark of his disapproval. When he finally gained admittance much later, he reversed the direction in which they were facing.

Another version is that The Town Council refused him permission to build the house but that he built it anyway and placed the cats in the offensive position as an insult to the Council members until he eventually won a court order sanctioning the build.

All this was 100 years ago. Today, the cats face nowhere in particular, but have become a symbol of the city and are much appreciated by tourists with long lens cameras.

Arguably the most dramatic building in Riga is the ***House of the Blackheads*** at Rātslaukums No.7, a stone's throw from St. Peter's Church.

Originally built in 1344 for the Brotherhood of Blackheads, a fraternity of young, unmarried and wealthy German merchants, the current building's incredibly opulent facade reflects the various architectural styles and artistic trends of the past.

The Brotherhood was so named because in the 1300s, it adopted St. Maurice as its patron saint. He was usually depicted as a black soldier in knight's armour – hence the name, Blackheads,. (No organization would get away with that today!).

The fraternity was powerful and extremely influential. Its members used the building as a venue for lavish receptions, conferences and concerts. If its members  subsequently married, they were automatically received into the city's elite circles and became councilors and members of the Great Guild.

Unfortunately, the Germans bombed the House in 1941 and the Soviets levelled it to the ground in 1948. Thankfully, the original plans for the design survived, so some 50 years later, the city fathers decided that it should be rebuilt. The was completed in 2001, just in time for the city's 200th anniversary.

The replica building is testimony to the extraordinary prowess of Riga's artisans, craftspeople and antique restorers. The interior is equally spectacular with crystal chandeliers, painted ceilings and exact replicas of 19th century furniture and stained glass.

The cellars are filled with ancient weaponry and elsewhere you can see the silverware, paintings, pottery and snuffboxes that once belonged to the Brotherhood members.

Opening times: 10am-6pm daily. Admission: €6.00. Seniors: half price.

The Three Brothers at   Maza Pils Nos.17, 19 & 21 comprise three houses that form the oldest complex of residential houses in Riga. They were built in the 15th, 16th and 17th centuries respectively, some say by three members of the same family, although that is not proven.

The Oldest Brother, No. 17 (to the right of the photograph) **is** the oldest masonry dwelling house in Riga

and was built around 1490. With its gabled roof and Gothic niches in the façade, it originally had just one room with a 'chimney kitchen' in which Rigan and Dutch merchants could conduct their business. There was also an attic for storing merchandise and other goods. About two hundred years later, in 1697, the house was converted into a bakery and extended into the yard at the back. The extension was later demolished, and the reconstructed building later underwent a major restoration between 1955 and 1957.

The Middle Brother, No. 19, was built in the first half of the 17th century and gained its present façade in 1646. Painted a pale-yellow ochre colour, this house was constructed according to the architecturally conventional style of the period and was one of the finest buildings in Riga during the 17th century. Unlike its brother to the left of the photograph, it had a capacious hallway, a spacious room on the first floor similar to the layout of the Older Brother and living quarters above and to the rear of the house. Above the rather grand stone portal, which was added in 1746, the Latin inscription 'Soli deo gloria' means 'Glory only to God'.

The Youngest Brother, No. 21 (the house to the left of the photograph) was built in the second half of the 17th century. It gained its present look during the mid-late 1600s. A wooden staircase from the hall leads to small office rooms, which may have doubled up as apartments on each floor. This is the narrowest and smallest of the three brothers. Above the arched entrance, there is a mask, which, according to the owners of the building, protected its inhabitants from evil spirits.

Today, the State Inspection for Heritage protection and the Latvian Museum of Architecture are housed in the Three Brothers ensemble. One of the museum's exhibits is a reconstructed room from the 15th-18th century and a renovated fireplace with a chimney from the 15th-16th century. Otherwise it is comprised of more than 1,000 original outlines, sketches and drawings of architects

Open: Monday 9am-6pm, Tuesday-Thursday closes at 5pm. Friday closes at 4pm/; closed at weekends. Admission is free.

Riga Cathedral located at Herdera laukums No. 6, is one of the oldest sacred buildings of the medieval period in Latvia. The foundation stone was laid in 1211 and a monastery and Cathedral school were added shortly afterwards.

The church was transformed into a basilica in the 14th-15th centuries, during which time the tower was raised to 460 feet (140 metres), making it the tallest tower in Riga at the time.

Built in an eclectic mix of Romanesque, Early Gothic, Baroque and Art Nouveau styles, the Cathedral also comprises the *Museum of the History of Riga and Navigation,* which contains more than half a million items with exhibits covering 800 years of history displayed in 16 halls.

The 13th century cloister, which once linked the Cathedral with the monastery, is part of the museum where it displays ancient cannons, tomb plates, coats of arms, a plaster replica statue of Tsar Peter I and several artefacts unearthed during archaeological digs nearby.

Although the interior of the Cathedral is unremarkable, the German E.F.Walker organ is one of the few of its kind in Europe and magnificent to behold. It has 6,768 pipes, most of which are hidden. They are grouped in 124 stops arranged in rows on the main console. These produce a rich sound that has variously been described by *afficionados* attending the regular organ concerts as 'bright and softened, tender and harsh, silvery and velvety'.

Opening times: May 1st-30th September, Saturday-Tuesday 9am-6pm. Wednesday-Friday, 9am-5pm. All other times 10am-5pm. Admission €3.00 (£2.*55, $3.35)*.

The Orthodox Nativity of Christ Cathedral at Brīvības bulvāris No. 23, is the largest Orthodox church in Riga.

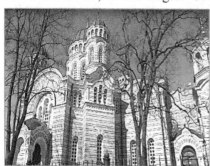

Construction began in 1876 and took eight years to build. It opened for services eight years later, in 1884.

To begin with, there was no belfry, but then Tsar Alexander II donated

12 bells to the Cathedral, so an additional dome was added to accommodate them.

Renowned for its fabulous collection of ancient and valuable icons and paintings, the Cathedral survived both World Wars. Later, in the 1960s, the Soviets closed it down, dismantled crucifixes, melted the bells down and converted it into a planetarium. As if to emphasis the desecration and underline their ignorance, they then named the church 'The Republic House of Knowledge'.

Not until the 1990s, after the collapse of the Soviet Union and the fall of the Berlin Wall, did church authorities authorize the restoration of the cathedral, which was consecrated by Archbishop Alexander in May 2000. The restoration work continues.

St. Peter's Church at Reformācijas laukums No. 1 is the tallest church in Riga with great views of the Old Town, Riga Bay and the Daugava River. The original church, built in 1209, was just a small hall with a separate bell tower. It's tower, completed in the late 1400s, was 426 feet (130 metres tall but collapsed in 1666.

Twenty-four years later, a second, wooden Baroque tower

replaced it, but that one was struck by lightning and burned down. Tsar Peter I ordered it to be renovated but disaster would strike again during the Second World War, when the church was demolished.

In 1967, craftsmen built a metal tower with an elevator, which today transports visitors to a height of 236 feet (72 metres) – although the tower is actually 403 feet (123 metres) high. The tower clock, which traditionally has only one hand, rings the bells on the hour and chimes a Latvian folk song five times a day.

In 1970, workers erected a gilded rooster wind vane on the roof. Its six predecessors were either damaged or blown down during storms between the 15th century and 1941. It is now listed as a UNESCO World Heritage site.

The church is open from May 1st-31st August from 10am to 7pm Tuesday-Saturday, from 12 noon-7pm on Sunday. Closed Monday. At other times of year, it closes at 6pm. Admission is €9.00 (£7.65, $10.00)

One of the most popular attractions in Riga is the vast **Central Market** at Nēģu iela 7, Latgales priekšpilsēta, on the banks of the river Daugava, next to the International Bus Terminal and Central Railway station. Housed in and outside what once were Zeppelin-style airship hangers, it is officially the largest market in Europe with more than 3,000 stalls.

Stalls are located in separate hangars depending on whether they are selling, meat, fish, vegetables or dairy products. There is also a huge outdoor market, a night market and a 'Round the Clock Farmers' market, which together are designated as a  UNESCO World Heritage site.

Each day, between 80,000 and 100,000 people shop here, which also means it is a prime site for pickpockets, so do leave the jewels and Rolex watches on the ship and keep handbags and wallets well secured.

In a new section of the market there are more than 20 different restaurants, cafés and bars selling everything from oysters, pizzas, gastro hot dogs, Thai soup, Falafel and every other kind of food imaginable, all to be washed down with Prosecco, wines or craft beers.

The market is open daily from 10am-6pm, (5pm on Sundays).

The Swedish Gate located at Atgriežu iela is the oldest remaining portion of the Old Town wall, in 1698 to celebrate

the Swedish occupation of the city.

It was subsequently restored during the Soviet occupation. Apparently, the apartment above the gate was the home of the city executioner, who used to place a red rose on the window ledge on the morning before carrying out a ***death sentence.***

The Latvian National Museum of Art located at Jaņa Rozentāla laukums No. 1 has the largest collection of art in Latvia, comprising more than 52,000 works by Baltic and Russian painters and sculptors from the 19th and 20th centuries. With its majestic Baroque and Classic façade, it is considered a national monument.

There is also a roof terrace with excellent views of the city. Opening times: Tuesday-Thursday 10am-6pm, Friday open until 8pm, Weekends 10am-5pm. Closed Monday. Admission €6.00.(£5.10, $6.65).

The Museum of the Occupation of Latvia at Raiņa bulvāris No. 7 covers the period between 1940 and 1991, when Latvia was successively occupied by the Soviet Union in 1940-1941, by Nazi Germany in 1941-1944, and again by the USSR from 1944 until 1991.

With graphic first-hand accounts and photographs of the atrocities perpetrated on the Jewish population, this is not for the faint-hearted. Equally, it is almost required viewing, especially as the museum's stated mission is to remind the world of the crimes committed by foreign powers against the state and people of Latvia.

The museum contains some 60,000 items, including video testimonials of those who were deported or persecuted.

The museum shop stocks books, films, postcards and souvenirs reflecting the theme of the museum.

Opening times: 11am-8pm daily. Closed on public holidays. Admission €5.00 (£4.25, $5.55).

The Freedom Monument located at Brivibas laukums, stands proudly 145 feet (44 metres) tall above the city as a symbol of the Latvian struggle for independence.

Paid for entirely by public donations and popularly known as 'Milda', a common Latvian name for girls, the monument was erected in 1935 and has special meaning for all Latvians and especially for Riga residents, who were forbidden during the Soviet occupation to gather near it or lay flowers upon its base.

In fact, it is regarded as a miracle that the Soviets didn't tear it down.

At the base of the monument, 56 sculptures represent the Latvian people's spiritual stamina and work ethic. Look out for the half man-half bear figure who symbolizes their struggle against the oppression inflicted by the Russian bear.

Other friezes on the granite base portray Latvians fighting – and singing – for their freedom. At the top of the monument, a female Liberty (fashioned from copper) triumphantly holds up three golden stars that represent the unity of the country's three historically cultural regions.

After what became known as the Re-awakening, Latvians one again gathered here to honour those who had fallen during the War of Independence or endured the occupation and repression that only came to an end in 1991 with the disintegration of the Soviet Union. From that moment on, two soldiers have always stood as an honour guard at the base of the monument.

For Latvians and especially Rigans, just to see them there stirs their emotions and memories of the hard times and evokes both a deep sense of gratitude for the freedom they have today and a concern for the future given the provocative policies of Vladimir Putin.

* * *

Klaipėda, Lithuania

The Main Attractions

Klaipėda is the third largest city in Lithuania and its only port, which means that the population tend to look to the sea rather than inland, hosting Tall Ships regattas and annual sea festivals, a maritime museum and numerous beaches.

In some ways, it is a tale of two cities: The Old Town is where tourists and cruise passengers go. Beyond it is a jungle of cranes and shipyards and the unprepossessing sprawl of the 'New Town. It is here and in the rest of Klaipėda County that the majority of the 233,311 permanent residents live, 87% of whom are Lithuanian. Nearly 10% are Russian, Ukrainian or Belarusian.

Despite the Russian influence, Klaipėda has a markedly German feeling about it. There are still a few old buildings with half-timbered facades that were constructed in the German *fachwerk* style so popular in the 19th century. Unfortunately, after the end of the Second World War, the Russians tore down most of the churches and *fachwerk* buildings in a bid to eradicate all things German.

That is a shame because Klaipėda was under the thumb of German rulers from the mid-13th century until 1918, so much of the city's history was destroyed.

Teutonic Knights tasked with converting or conquering pagan Baltic tribes built a fort on the shoreline in 1252 and called it Memelburg, thus founding the town. The name was later shortened to Memel and did not assume its current Lithuanian name until the mid-16th century.

According to some accounts, Klaipeda originally meant 'bread eaters', a disparaging definition applied because the people ate bread made from crops outside the city. Wikipedia, however, suggests that the name refers to the boggy terrain around the town and most likely is of Curonian origin meaning 'even ground' ('Klais/klait') (flat, open, free) and 'ped' (sole of the foot).

In any event, the city was ruled by successive German states until the 1919 Treaty of Versailles, under which the whole Klaipėda region became a protectorate of the First World War allies (the Entente States) and was governed by French administrators.

This clearly didn't suit the Lithuanians, who rebelled and took the region by force. Although the allies and League of Nations all protested, in 1923 they eventually accepted the *fait accompli* and a year later formally signed the Klaipėda Convention.

This granted the Lithuanians extensive legislative, judicial, administrative and financial autonomy with its own democratically elected parliament.

However, in 1939, just five days after the Nazi occupation of Czechoslovakia, Germany's foreign minister, Joachim von Ribbentrop gave the Lithuanians an ultimatum: cede the entire Klaipėda Region or Germany would invade. In a single moment, the Klaipėda Convention was dead in the water.

Just before the outbreak of the Second World War in 1939, German nationals accounted for 70% of Klaipėda's population. The ethnic Lithuanians had moved out of the city and comprised 70% of the population of Klaipėda County.

At the end of the war in 1945, the Soviet army entered the city to find only 20 local people still living there. Given the Soviet's history of occupation in the Baltic States, it was not surprising that the Russians re-populated the city. Eventually, they comprised a quarter of its population.

After that, Lithuania remained under the Soviet yoke until the peoples of all three Baltic States, 'sang themselves free' and finally won their independence.

Sadly, most visitors to Klaipėda tend to skip the town and instead take the ferry to the Curonian Spit, the slither of wooded sand dunes that stretch from the city to the border with Kaliningrad, thus forming the Curonian Lagoon.

Whilst this is undoubtedly fascinating and there is always a chance you might find some pieces of genuine amber along the beach, a day in Klaipėda is equally, if not more, rewarding. Whether your interest is historic architecture, museums, sculptures, street art or just meandering and sipping a beer or glass of wine in one of the many bars along the riverbanks, it all makes for a laid-back, relaxing and enjoyable day.

For cruise passengers who opt to see the city, one of the first sights they will see is the **Swing Bridge** that links the cruise terminal to the Old Town and its castle. Built in 1855 and still working, this is the only swing bridge in Lithuania. It was originally known as the Kettenbrücke or Chain Bridge because it was built with riveted iron and adorned with chains. The German name was dropped at the end of the Second World War.

Two people are required to rotate the bridge manually, so that boats can sail into the castle's former moat, now a marina. (N.B. Be sure to check the opening and closing times on the information board and allow plenty of time to get back to your ship).

Next to the bridge, a strange 7ft 8ins (2.4 metre) high bronze sculpture known as *The Black Ghost* appears to be climbing from the water onto the edge of the quay. This weird figure is based on a 16th century legend about a castle guard

who claimed to have seen just such a ghostly, hooded figure. Apparently, the 'ghost' asked the guard whether there were enough grain supplies in the town. The guard replied that there was indeed a plentiful supply, to which the black figure warned him that the stocks would not last – and then vanished.

Also next to the swing bridge is the *Old Mill Hotel,* arguably one of the most spectacular buildings in Klaipėda. In the 18th century, it was the first and largest rice mill in Lithuania. In 2008, however, it was converted into a 31-room, 3-star hotel with spectacular panoramic views of the Dane river embankment, the Curonian Lagoon and the site of the old castle.

If a catchphrase were to be attached to Klaipėda, it would surely have to be *'City of Sculptures'*. Apart from the Black Ghost, the streets are dotted with small, often humorous sculptures.

One of the delights of wandering around Klaipėda and diving spontaneously down the side streets is to keep an eye out for these little gems. See if you can spot the bag of money, the dragon climbing up a wall and the little mouse that local people say makes your wishes come true.

In the process, you are almost certain to stumble on some stunning examples of street art.

There are even more sculptures – 116 created by 67 sculptors to be exact - in The *Martynas Mazvydas Sculpture Park* located on the site of an old cemetery at K. Donelaičio g. 6B. The cemetery functioned between 1820 until 1959, after which it fell into disuse. In 1975, the Soviet Executive Committee decreed that there should be a change of use and announced that anyone who wanted to rebury their relatives in a newer cemetery could do so. Any fenced tombs or graves that remained would be demolished, the committee said.

The park was created in 1977 and, as one historian observed: 'Here, as nowhere else, reflects the vandalism act of the Soviet Union based on good intentions.'

The first sculptures tended to be historical, reflecting Klaipėda's history during the 19th and early 20th century. Examples include the monument commemorating the Lithuanian annexation of the Klaipėda region in 1923, the Memorial to Second World War victims and the Monument to Lithuanians lost at sea. Later additions gradually assumed a more mischievous character.

The Senasis Turgus Market located at Turgaus a.5, has been held regularly since the mid-1800s and is the oldest marketplace in Klaipėda. It is not much different from any other market in that it focuses almost entirely on local produce – meat, fish, vegetables, fruit and dairy products.

Danė's Quay & Meridinas Ship. The banks of the River Danė are perfect for passengers who just want to enjoy a peaceful walk around the town. The main attraction here is the barquentine *Meridianas*, which was built in Turku, Finland in 1947. She was handed over to the Soviet Union on her completion along with 48 other ships in accordance with the 1944 Finnish-Soviet peace treaty. This specified that

Finland should pay the Soviet Union reparations for war damages totaling 300 million gold dollars.

Meridianas became an educational training ship and joined the Baltic training ships fleet in 1954. For many future captains and helmsmen, she was their first ship. After an accident in 1968 she was decommissioned, sold off and in 1971 became a restaurant.

However, the owner who bought her lost interest and allowed the ship to fall into serious disrepair. Eventually, a local lawyer bought her for just one Litas (the Lithuanian currency until it was replaced by the euro in 2015). Later, the owners made an application to the government to sink the ship on the grounds that the necessary repairs would cost too much money that they could not afford.

At this juncture, new owners took over and by 2014, *Meridianas* had been successfully restored with repairs to the body, deck superstructures, masts, internal installations and ornamentation.

Today, the ship is once again a restaurant with a small marine exhibition that explains the history of *Meridianas,* her journeys at sea, the structure of the ship and displays various maritime artefacts.

Klaipėda Castle & Museum located just across the swing bridge has a rich history reflecting the city's turbulent past, although today little remains of it apart from the ramparts, brick bastions and the moat, that was transformed into an impressive marina.

Originally built in the 13th century by Teutonic knights, the castle was frequently laid waste and then rebuilt, not least in the 1800s when it was almost destroyed. After the Russians occupied Lithuania between 1756 and 1762, the castle was no longer deemed of much importance and gradually fell into disuse. However, archaeologists

excavating the ruins in the mid- 1900s revived intertest in the castle, which is now a museum with four separate exhibitions, two of which highlight the history of the castle and the importance of the port of Klaipėda, and which are housed in the castle's impressive 16th-18th century brick tunnels.

Here, you can see archaeological finds, documents, city stamps and recreated 17th costumes, the originals of which archaeologists found in the old town and castle grounds. There is also an impressive model of the castle and city in the late 1600s.

A third exhibition focusses on contemporary art and the fourth is a state-of-the-art display describing the effects of the Second World War on the city and its people.

The castle grounds are also used for an annual international jazz festival and other events.

The castle museum is open from 10am until 6pm Monday-Saturday. Closed Sunday, Monday. Admission is a modest €1.75 (£1.50, $1.95) and half price for seniors. All-in-one tickets for the Castle Museum, Blacksmith's Museum and History Museum of Lithuania Minor are cheaper at €2.90 (£2.48, $3.20).

The **Blacksmith's Museum (Kalvystes Muziejus)** located at Klaipėda Šaltkalvių g. 26-3 is housed in a what used to be the workplace of the renowned blacksmith Gustav Katze, who won several awards for his creations. The forge functioned until 1944, when he returned to Germany.

The museum comprises two floors and a garden of artefacts ranging from authentic bellows and forges, wrought iron weathervanes, street lanterns and wooden clog-style horseshoes to the metal crosses and ornate fences used to enclose tombs and graves in the now defunct cemetery (now the Sculpture Park).

Open: Tuesday-Saturday 10am-6pm. Closed Sunday and Monday. Admission is €1.45 (£1.25, $1.60) and half price for seniors.

The *History Museum of Lithuania Minor* is housed in one of the oldest buildings in the Old Town, at Didžioji Vandens g. 2, and covers the genesis of the coastal region known as Lithuania Minor and its history as a part of East Prussia. It tells the story through cartography, numismatics, photography, postcards, and various artefacts of the Teutonic Order as well as wooden furniture, folk art, looms and an explanation of how beehives are made from straw.

Open: Tuesday-Saturday 10am-6pm, Closed Sunday & Monday. Admission €1.45 (1.25, $1.60). Half price for seniors.

The *Museum of Clocks* at Liepų str. 12 contains a vast array of some 1,700 rare 16th-20th century clocks and watches from both Lithuania and the rest of Europe. A branch of the Lithuanian Art Museum in Vilnius, it covers the evolution of clock and watchmaking on the first floor with examples of ancient sundials, hour glasses and calendars as well as clocks using water, sand, sun and fire as their driving force.

The second-floor focusses on the shape and design of mechanical clocks from the 16th century Renaissance to the electro-mechanical, electro-magnetic and quartz clocks and watches of the present day.

The museum also celebrates the equinoxes and solstices and gives carillon concerts on Saturdays and Sundays between 12 noon and 12.30pm.

Opening times: March-October, 10am-5pm, November-February, 11am-5pm. Admission €1.80 (£1.40, $2.00). Half price for seniors.

The *Lithuanian Sea Museum* is in a former 19th century German fort at the northernmost point of the Curonian Spit (at Smiltynės g. 3). To get there, you have to take a ferry to Smiltyne from the Old Ferry Terminal at Danės g. 1. From there it is a well signposted walk of just over a mile (1.7 kilometres).

If marine life is your interest, the walk is well worth it because this is a huge museum with more than 88,000 exhibits, mostly shellfish, coral, crustaceans, seabirds, fish and mammals.

Twenty-four aquariums are divided into freshwater, Baltic, Nordic and tropical marine ecosystems and, as with other state-of-the-art maritime museums, there is an acrylic tunnel that enables visitors to see sharks, rays and other marine life in close-up.

There is a 1,000-seat dolphinarium with regular shows and each year a dolphin therapy programme admits 60 children suffering from autism, Downs syndrome, cerebral palsy and other serious disabilities. There is also a Baltic Sea Animal Rehabilitation centre for injured animals.

Outdoor pools are used to house penguins, Baltic seals and North Sea sealions. There is also a maritime exhibition hall in an underground corridor beneath the fortress rampart which focusses on Lithuanian shipping history. Above ground, on the rampart there is a collection of antique and modern anchors

The building is suitable for wheelchair access and there is a café in the Dolphinarium.

Open: June-August, Tuesday-Sunday 10.30am-6.30pm. Closing times vary thereafter but the museum is always open until 5pm.

Opening days at other times of year: September Wednesday-Sunday, October-March Friday-Sunday, April - May Wednesday-Sunday.

Admission to Aquarium, Dolphinarium and Museum exhibition, June-August €10.00 (£8.55, $11.10). At other times, €7.00 (£6.00, $7.75). EU seniors with a pensionary certificate half price. Adults with mild disability free.

For all that the Curonian Spit has its attractions, it poses a dilemma for cruise passengers with only one day in which to see everything. The Sea Museum is certainly one of the best in Europe and its location places it close to the Spit's beaches, but there is much to see and do in Klaipėda, too. It would be a pity to miss it!

* * *

Gdańsk, Poland

The Main Attractions

Undeniably touristy and deservedly so, this gem of a city is one of the absolute highlights on any Baltic cruise. Quite different from any other city in Poland, its historical centre is stunning. That seems even more remarkable when you consider that German bombers almost totally destroyed it during the Second World War and that, after it, a defeated population rose from the ashes to reconstruct every elegant building you can see to the last meticulous detail.

Gdańsk Town Hall in 1945 and today

With 1,000 years of history and maritime trading, Gdańsk's population of some 470,000 people has evolved into an historic mix of nationalities, cultures and religious denominations. Aside from the beauty of its reconstructed Old Town, it has some of the best museums in Poland, a plethora of restaurants, bars and cafés, a fascinating waterfront and great shopping, not least for amber. (If you buy, make sure you get it certified). What is more, the city is also ranked highly for its living standards, quality of life and safety.

As the capital and largest city of the Pomeranian Province in northwest Poland, Gdańsk developed from humble beginnings first mentioned in writing at the end of the 10th century. That was when the fortified port began to expand into an urban township which, thanks to increased maritime trade, fisheries and craft guilds, soon became the largest and most important city in Pomerania.

The city's history is convoluted. It became part of Poland, Prussia and Germany at various stages whilst also enjoying interludes as a free, semi-autonomous city state.

Teutonic knights were the first to take over the city in the early 14th century and by the 1360s, it had become a member of the Hanseatic League of German merchants, which controlled trade throughout Scandinavia.

In the mid-15th century, when the Polish-Lithuanian army defeated the Teutonic knights, the city's population voted to be part of the Polish crown under King Jagiellon. In return, he bestowed many privileges on them and, as a result Gdańsk thrived and became one of the wealthiest and most important cities in the region for the next three centuries.

Its affluence was enhanced further after the 16th century Reformation as Catholicism was spurned, and more and more merchants of varying nationalities and religious faiths settled in the city.

The Swedish wars during the 18th century led to the partition of Poland, which had ruled Gdańsk until 1793. Then, after the Napoleonic wars, the Prussians seized the city, renamed it Danzig and triggered more than 100 miserable years of debility and austerity.

After the Allies defeated Germany in the First World War, the Treaty of Versailles established Gdańsk as a free city, and Gdańsk thrived once again.

Sadly, that period of prosperity was halted in 1933, when the Nazis came to power. Fascism became rampant. Six years later, on September 1st, 1939, the guns of the Battleship Schleswig-Holstein fired shots onto the city, and in so doing initiated the Second World War.

On that same day, German police and SS units besieged the Post Office in Gdańsk. Inside, 50 workers put up an extraordinarily brave defence for 17 hours. Eventually, after 20 of them had been killed and the building was collapsing around their ears, the Germans attacked them with flame-throwers. The survivors were sentenced to death and shot, although their bodies were not discovered until 1991.

The Second World War left Gdańsk in ruins and Poland was divided and occupied by German troops in the west, and the Red Army in the east. The country also became the focal point of Hitler's so-called 'final solution'. Polish Jews were among the first to be carted off to Germany's notorious concentration camps and murdered in their millions.

In June 1941, Hitler's armies attacked the Russian zone and pushed northeast almost to the borders of Moscow. Stalin's forces retaliated and forced the Germans back, re-took all of Poland, and despite valiant attempts by incredibly brave Polish partisans, imposed a communist regime that lasted until 1989.

By that time, Poland was in a desperate state; the economy

was failing, prices rose to ridiculous heights sparking a wave of strikes, and the country was forced to take on huge loans from the west. Meanwhile, the strikes led to the foundation of the independent trade union, Solidarnosc (Solidarity) led by an electrician called Lech Walęsa in Gdańsk, As opposition to the communist regime strengthened, in 1981, the government declared martial law, but was unable to contain the union's momentum.

Then, a combination of Mikhail Gorbachev's reforms in the Soviet Union and a faltering Polish economy with runaway inflation and long queues for food outside shops with little to offer, combined with pressure from the West resulted in Solidarity taking part in Round Table talks with the government. These, in turn, led to an agreement for a general election in 1989.

The Poles voted for a Solidarity-Opposition Communist coalition and Lech Walęsa was elected president, thus giving impetus to the collapse of the European communist bloc, the rise of Freedom movements in the Baltic States, the 'Singing Revolution, the fall of the Berlin Wall and, ultimately, to the collapse of the Soviet Union itself.

Since then, Poland has enjoyed an ever-expanding economy; between 1992 and 2019, it recorded uninterrupted growth averaging 4.2% a year and is the seventh largest economy in the European Union.

Gdańsk is once again a pulsating, thriving city The Port of Gdańsk handles nearly 40 million tons of cargo and nearly 70 cruise ships annually. All told, Gdańsk attracts more than two million visitors each year.

Smaller cruise ships sometimes dock at Oliwskie Pier in the New Port about four miles from the town centre. Close to the cruise quay, there is a pier from which pleasure boats offer 15-minute trips to the Old Town of Gdańsk.

Larger ships tend to dock in Gydnia, about a 45-minute shuttle bus ride to Gdańsk Old town.

Shuttle buses usually drop passengers of at Pszenna Street, a five-minute walk from the Green Gate, which is the waterfront gateway to *The Old Town.*

The Green Gate was built in 1568 from bricks imported from the Netherlands and decorated by a bevy of master sculptors. It was once the official residence of Polish Kings, although in the event no Polish King ever stayed there.

However, Lech Wałęsa had his office there before he moved to the European Solidarity Centre.

Once you have passed through the four arches, you will find yourself in what is arguably the most attractive pedestrian area in the world. This is *Dlugi Targ (Long Market) Square,* lined with

exquisitely reconstructed mansions, once the home of the most prominent and wealthy citizens.

As you approach the Town Hall Tower you will see the Neptune Fountain in front of Artus Court, a vaulted Gothic Hall three buildings from the Town Hall.

The Neptune Fountain was first conceived in the early

17th century when the Gdańsk Mayor wanted to replace a small wrought-iron fence round a now defunct well with a sculpture that would make a statement about the city's prosperity and maritime trading links.

The 1,433-pound (0.64-ton or 650-kilo) sculpture was cast in bronze in 1615.

The Mayor decreed that Neptune's head should face the townhouses, with the head bowed in deference to the Polish kings and the city's most prominent and wealthy citizens who lived in the townhouses opposite.

Thanks to long delays due to building work on the Artus House backdrop, the dilapidated plumbing system and the Thirty Years' War, the fountain was not inaugurated until 1633. During the centuries that followed, the fountain underwent numerous repairs and renovations. It was partially damaged during a German bombing raid during the Second World War, after which it was moved to a safer location with many of the city's other treasures. It was only returned in 1954 after restorers removed more than half a century's pigeon droppings.

A local story tells how Neptune became fed up with people throwing gold coins into the fountain that, one day, he lost his temper and smashed them into tiny fragments with his trident. Local people collected these and with them concocted the renowned but lethal Gdańsk Goldwasser liqueur. This is made with 40% proof vodka and up to 20 or 30 different types of herb, which give the drink a rich, fiery and syrupy taste.

In 1988, after yet another renovation, local bureaucratic prudes decreed that Neptune's genitals should be covered with a fig leaf. Who knows, perhaps they had drunk too much Goldwasser? Or maybe they were just envious?

Behind the fountain are two of the great buildings of Gdańsk – the Artus Court and its near neighbour , the Golden House, which is located three buildings back towards the Green Gate. *Artus Court* served as the merchants' exchange and meeting hall for the members of various guilds. Named after King Arthur, Artus Court's history goes back to the 14th century, although it was rebuilt and renovated many times thereafter.

The interior consists of one large Gothic hall, its walls covered with oak paneling, tapestries, coats of arms, and paintings depicting the Siege of Marienburg, Orpheus

among animals and the Last Judgement. The hall is further enhanced by wonderfully rich furniture and model ships hanging from the ceilings.

The centerpiece, though, is a magnificent 36-foot (11-metre) high tiled stove, the highest of its kind in Europe. Built in 1546, its six tiers are adorned with 540 tiles portraying European kings and queens, coats of arms, allegorical figures and such virtues as Honour, Loyalty, Dignity and Faith.

Today, Artus Court is a major attraction with a small museum. Opening times vary but are usually Monday-Tuesday 10am-1pm, Wednesday, Friday & Saturday 10am-4pm,

Sunday 11am-4pm. Ticket prices change annually, but are approximately 10 zlotys (£2.00, $2.65, €2.35). Seniors half price.

The Golden House was formerly the home of several city mayors and, as a result, sometimes referred to by British people as the Number Ten Downing Street of Danzig. It took nine years to build and was completed in 1618.

The façade comprises gilded stone base-reliefs describing battle scenes and a statue of Mercy above the entrance.

An inscription reads: "Act Justly, Have No Fear", a phrase said to be whispered in the halls by the ghost of Judyta Speymann, whose family once lived there. Other statues on the façade represent prudence, justice, strength and temperance. At the top of the building, the four figures waving are Cleopatra, Oedipus, Achilles and Antigone – and above them, the figure of Fortune.

The Golden House is open 24 hours a day except Sundays. Prices are not published which suggests entrance is free.

The Town Hall, constructed between 1327 and 1346, is also home to the ***Gdańsk History Museum***. For a small fee, you can also climb to the top of the 267 foot (81.5 metre) high clock tower, which as the tallest building in Gdańsk offers superb views of the city. The tower also contains a 37 carillon bells.

The interior is lavishly decorated with colourful frescoes and painted ceilings, a remarkable achievement given that the building was so badly damaged during the Second World War. It was carefully reconstructed just seven years after the war's end.

The Red Room is decorated in the Dutch Mannerist style of the late 1500s. Other exhibitions focus on Gdańsk's history and replica interiors from different periods.

Opening hours: Monday, Tuesday, 10am-5pm; Wednesday, 10am-4pm; Thursday-Saturday, 10am-5pm, Sunday 11am-5pm. From June-August: closed Monday, open Tuesday, Thursday, Saturday, 11am-6pm, Wednesday, 10am-4pm, Friday, 10am-5pm, Sunday, 11am-5pm. Admission is 12 zlotys with half price for seniors (£2.40, $3.15, €2.80).

The Town Hall marks the point where Dluga Targ (Long Market) continues into ***Ul. Dluga (Long Lane)*** which, like the Long Market, is lined with buildings reminiscent of Amsterdam canal houses.

Each building tells its own story, from the seemingly 'medieval' facade close to the Golden Gate (which was painted by Soviet authorities), to the statues atop buildings rebuilt after the Second World War.

It is a street not to be missed, although you are likely to be accosted by restaurant workers insisting that theirs is the only establishment worthy of your presence. This does become a little annoying after a while.

At the end of Dluga Street is the **Golden Gate** and, as you pass through it, Fore Gate complex, a former prison and torture chamber usually described simple as the **Prison Tower,** just across the street. Here children can 'hang' themselves in shackles once used for the less fortunate residents incarcerated in the tower. This is also the location of the **Amber Museum**, which documents the city's history as a major trading and design centre for amber since medieval times.

The museum sets out the origins, history, features and different kinds of amber, also known as Baltic gold. There is a workshop on the ground floor where you can watch craftspeople polishing and shaping amber jewellery. There are also some extremely realistic displays of torture chambers here, so you get two for the price of one!

Opening times are October - April: Tuesday 10 a.m. - 1 p.m., Wednesday 10 a.m. - 4 p.m, Thursday 10 a.m. - 6 p.m, Friday - Saturday 10 a.m. - 4 p.m., Sunday 11 a.m. - 4 p.m.; closed on Monday.

May - September: Monday 10 a.m. - 1 p.m., Tuesday - Saturday 10 a.m. - 6 p.m., Sunday 11 a.m. - 6 p.m.

Admission is 12 zlotys (£2.40, $3.15, €2.80). with half price for seniors. Admission is free on Mondays (May-September) and on Tuesdays (October -April).

The Great Armoury, a pastel pink Renaissance building located at Targ Weglowy 6 in the heart of the town, functioned as an arsenal until the 19th century.

The façade is stunning, especially when the sun shines on the golden lions. The one immediately to the right of the entrance appears to be particularly rampant.

The protuberant structure at the centre of the top floor was used to haul up kegs of gunpowder and cannon balls for storage.

As with so many other buildings in Gdańsk, the Great Armoury was damaged badly in the Second World War and had to be completely reconstructed after it.

For a while, it functioned as a supermarket and, later, as a furniture shop, but has since been restored to its former glory and now houses an art gallery curated by the Gdańsk Academy of Fine Arts. There is an excellent wine bar on the ground floor which gives you an excuse to see the interior of the building if you not an enthusiast of contemporary art.

A commentator on TripAdvisor noted that one exhibit 'consisted of three electrical multi-sockets each with a plug in. Another was a film showing a woman walking down the middle of a busy road carrying a dog', which may explain the need for a wine bar!

Open: Exhibition 11am-6pm daily. January 12 noon-6pm; December 10am-8pm; Entry to Main Hall 10am-6pm. No entry fee published. Probably as for other museums in the area.

Here visitors have a choice – either walk up the road facing the Great Armoury (Piwna) to the massive Basilica of St Mary of the Assumption of the Blessed Virgin Mary or continue along Weglarska Street until you reach the Covered Market (Hala Targowa at Plac Dominikański).

If you choose former and still want to see the market, just retrace your steps to the Grand Armoury, turn right and keep going.

The ***Basilica of St. Mar of the Assumption of the Blessed Virgin Mary*** is arguably the most impressive monument in Gdańsk and is frequently considered either as the largest or third largest brick church in the world with a 256 foot (78 metre) high tower that dominates the skyline. It was first constructed in the mid-1200s on the site of an old timber chapel.

The church was extended several times and only reached its current size by 1502. The Reformation occurred a dozen or so years later and the Protestant Lutherans took over the Catholic Basilica. Again, the Second World War was disastrous. The roof burned and some of the vaults collapsed. Bells melted and it was years before the Basilica was

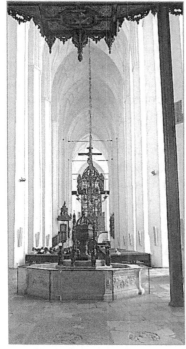

reconstructed.

The interior is equally spectacular and can apparently accommodate 24,000 worshippers. It is, however, sparse and less opulent than many similar churches, although many visitors say the basilica's simplicity increases its sense of spirituality, not least because the vaulted ceilings seem to be rising to the heavens.

The Basilica is open year-round, Monday to Saturday: from October to the end of April from 8.30am-5pm and from May to the end of September from 8.30a.-

6.30pm. The viewing platform at the top of the tower is open on 24 March until the end of November.

The Neo-Gothic *Covered Market (Hala Targowa)* was built in 1896 on the foundations of a 12th century church, although those were not discovered until the market was renovated recently. Surprisingly, the exterior frontage could easily be mistaken for a 19th century railway station.

The market not only boasts vast array of shops selling all kinds of food and Polish delicacies, it also boasts a mini museum around the church's foundations, which have been left as they were found. On display are various artefacts discovered during the excavations, and photographs and drawings of how the original church might have looked.

From the market, you could retrace your steps until you arrive at the first crossroads. Turn left into Szeroka Street and you will see a brick building at the far end. This is *The Old Crane, a* hulking mass of a building that is reminiscent of an old castle. It was once one of some 200 granaries that lined the River Motawa and used to load and unload cargoes of grain and timber at the river's edge.

Once you arrive at the Old Crane, you are just minutes away from lunch, for this is the **Long Wharf,** where scores of restaurants squashed side by side vie for your custom. The quality is high, too, unlike the prices which are very reasonable.

Replete after lunch, you may well feel it is time to return to the ship. If so, continue to walk along the Long Wharf until you arrive back at the Green Gate and the bridge that leads across the river to your shuttle bus.

For passengers with enviable stamina or a compulsive interest in other attractions, there are four museums that rank high for your attention.

The first is the **Museum of the Second World War** located in a striking example of modern architecture at Władysław Bartoszewski Square 1. It traces the causes of war and the way in which the Second World War affected both soldiers and civilians in Poland.

The building itself is a stark contrast to 'medieval' Gdańsk. Its tilted, box-like structure has been described as narrating the tragedy of the past, the vitality of the present and opening the horizons of the future.

Focusing on the politics, ideology and human suffering of conflict, the exhibition is split into three parts – the Road to

War, The Horror of War and the Long Shadow of War, each combining with the other to create a powerful statement that leaves few unmoved.

Exhibits range from Nazi propaganda posters to the Holocaust exhibit in which a maze of racks containing hundreds of photographic portraits of Jews rise to the ceiling and an entire wall is stacked with old suitcases. A replica of a bomb shattered courtyard and Russian tank casts you right back into wartime life in Warsaw.

Documents, photographs, traumatic film clips and artefacts collected not just in Poland but from the Siege of Leningrad, the Katyń massacre and Czechoslovakia bombard the senses, evoking evoke powerful emotions.

Many of these artefacts are personal effects donated by private individuals. Often, it is the little things that shout the loudest. A single, isolated and framed strand of barbed wire seems devastatingly poignant. Christmas decorations adorned with swastikas and wireless sets warning that the penalty for listening to the BBC is execution send shivers down your spine. This is a museum not to be missed and should be seen by everyone, such is the power of its message.

It is recommended that visitors spend three hours in the museum and, if possible, to book tickets in advance online.

Opening times: Closed Mondays and public holidays. September-June, Tuesday-Sunday 10am-6pm (last entry 5pm). July-August, 10am-8pm. is 23 zlotys (£4.60, $6.05,€5.40). Seniors 16 zlotys (£3.20, €4.20, €3.75).

Approximately 200 metres from the Museum of the Second World War, the *Polish Post Office Museum* concentrates on the story of the 50 Polish post office workers who resisted a savage German attack at the beginning of the Second World War.

As mentioned earlier, they held out for 17 hours until the building began collapsing around them, by which time 20 workers were dead. The Germans finally assaulted them with flame-throwers forcing them to surrender.

The workers' stand soon became legendary. Not until years later did anyone ask why the Post Office workers were so well armed. It turned out, in fact, that they were members of the Polish intelligence services and that the Germans attacked them in a bid to suppress attempts to form a resistance movement.

The European Solidarity Centre (ESC) located at Plac Solidarności No. 1 focusses on the post-war fight for freedom by workers striking in the former Lenin shipyards during the 1970s. This culminated in communist troops firing on the workers, killing 45 of them in the resultant riots. This, in turn, led to the formation of the Solidarnosc (Solidarity), the Polish Trade Union Resistance Movement led by Lech Wałęsa in the 1980s.

(The Monument to the Fallen Shipyard Workers of 1970, a 105 foot (42 metre) steel sculpture weighing 137 tons is nearby).

The ESC is open May-September, Monday-Friday from 10am to 6pm, and to 7pm at weekends except for public holidays. October-April closes one hour earlier and all day Tuesday. Entrance to the building is free. The exhibition costs 25 zlotys (£5.00. $6.60, €5.85). 20 zlotys f(££4.00, $5.30, €4.70).or seniors.

National Museum (Muzeum Narodowe w Gdańsku) is located at ul. Toruńska No.1 in a former early 15th century Franciscan monastery. This section of the National Museum specializes in older art , mostly from the areas of Gdańsk and Pomerania, but it also exhibits Polish paintings representing the romantic to inter-war movements. (modern art, ethnography, photography etc. are housed in different branches around the city).

There is also a collection of 12th to 16th century Pomeranian and west European religious sculpture, including two altars from the early 15th century. Additionally, there are Dutch, Flemish and Pomeranian paintings, drawings and prints, Baroque and pewter artworks by blacksmiths and goldsmiths, and a fabulous collection of ceramics, especially tiled stoves, Dresden china and so on.

The museum is open Tuesday to Sunday from 10am until 5pm. No admission prices are published.

The *National Maritime Museum,* the headquarters of which are located at Ołowianka 9-13, comprises several exhibitions at different locations, including the granaries, the museum ship *SS. Sołdek,* the Old Crane, the Maritime Culture Centre, the museum sailing ship *Dar Pomorza* and the Motlawa ferry which runs between the Old Crane and the Granaries on the island of Olowianka every 15 minutes.

Opening times for the main permanent museum are Tuesday-Frfiday 10am-3pm, Saturday-Sunday 10am-4pm. Admission is 10 zlotys (£2.00, $2.65, €2.35). Seniors 6 zlotys (£1.20, $1.60, €1.40). Free on Wednesday.

Passengers who have visited Gdańsk previously may like to wander around the Zaspa district which is renowned for its monumental *Zaspa Murals* painted on the sides of buildings by artists from all over the world. Some of these are 118 feet (36 metres) high.

You can see nearly 60 murals in different styles, techniques and themes by taking a free tour with a local guide from Pilotow No 10. For further information, you can visit the Cultural Information Point at Dlugi Targ 39-40, next to the Neptune Fountain.

Alternatively, take the No. 6 tram from the city centre or a 20-minute Uber taxi ride costing approximately 140 zlotys (£8.00, $10.55, €9.40) to *Oliwa Park* and the adjacent *Oliwska Archikatedra (Cathedral).* This trip makes for a very pleasant day away from the bustle of the city. The Cathedral, located at Biskupa Edmunda Nowickiego 5, is

renowned for its organ, which has a variety of moving parts, including angels playing trumpets, moving suns, moons and stars, etc. The Cathedral acoustics are superb and there are frequent organ concerts with free entrance (and a collection plate).

Oliwa Park, which surrounds the Cathedral and the Abbot's Palace, is a pure delight. Streams babble, paved pathways wind beneath a canopy of trees, flower beds blaze with colour, and duck ponds, and a Japanese garden, offer ultimate tranquility.

Finally, a reminder of where it all began: *Westerplatte*, the

main cruise quay on the tip of land that the Nazi battleship Schleswig-Holstein shelled at the start of the Second World War. The quay is but a five-minute walk to the Vistula Mouth Fortress and the Memorial to the Westerplatte defenders. The Memorial stands on 72 foot (22 metre) high hill created from debris removed by dredgers clearing the entrance to the port. The memorial itself towers another 82 feet (25 metres) above the hill and consists of 236 granite blocks weighing a total 1,150 tons. Passengers fortunate enough to dock at the Westerplatte Quay will easily be able to see the Memorial from their ship.

To sum up, Gdańsk is a fascinating city with so much to see and do that it would be impossible to visit all the places mentioned above. On the other hand, it is the kind of city that you will want to return to – either on another cruise or a three or four-day city break. Often, return visits become even more memorable!

* * *

Gdynia, Poland

The Main Attractions

The main reason cruise ships dock in Gdynia is that the port can handle larger ships than in Gdansk, which is only a 10 mile (16 kilometre) shuttle bus ride away. The difference between the two cities could not be greater.

Whereas Gdansk (Danzig) has 1,000 years of history, Gdynia is a relatively new city created after the First World War. At the time, Poland was immersed in the Polish-Soviet War and Gdansk was controlled by the Germans, who made up 80% of its population.

German dockworkers were aggrieved because they felt the city's finances were being inappropriately hived off to finance the war, so they went on strike nd refused to unload military supplies that the Allies had sent to help the Polish Army.

The Poles then recognized that they urgently needed a major port that they, and they alone, could control

In 1920, the Treaty of Versailles in which the Allies re-established Poland as an independent state, came into effect. This designated Danzig as the Free City of Gdansk and created a narrow corridor, thus splitting Germany down the middle.

At that time, Gdynia was little more than a small fishing village and seaside resort at the northern end of the corridor. It was also the perfect place in which to construct a major port, a project the Poles achieved within five years.

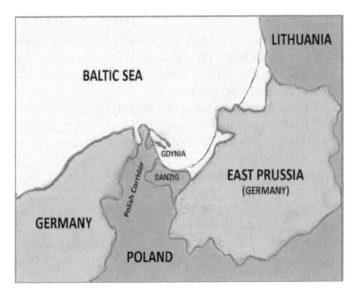

Once the port was completed, the Poles began work on the city itself. By 1926, the population had grown to around 12,000 . By 1939, it had grown ten-fold and was the sixth largest city in Poland.

At that juncture, Germany troops invaded Poland, sparking the Second World War. They occupied Gdynia, absorbed it into the Reich and renamed it *Gotenhafen (lit: Goth's Harbour.*

Despite Allied bombing raids, the city escaped relatively undamaged, although it did see its fair share of action. In 1944, the Germans used the port to extricate troops and refugees hemmed in by Russia's Red Army. Soviet submarines torpedoed several ships as they entered the Baltic Sea, one of which was sunk with nearly 9,500 passengers on board. It was the worst recorded sinking in naval history.

As the Germans retreated under heavy bombardment by Soviet troops, they did what German troops did best; pulverized the city, destroying 90% of all buildings and equipment and blocking the entrance to the port with the battleship *Gneisenau,* which had been undergoing repairs.

Eventually, in 1945, Polish forces fighting with the Red Army liberated Gdynia and *Gotenhafen* resumed its rightful name, Gdynia.

In December 1970, shipyard workers protesting against low pay and poor living standards opted to go on strike – with disastrous results. The police opened fire on the demonstrators, killing 18 of them.

A decade later, mindful of that atrocity, shipyard workers led by Lech Wałeşa locked themselves into the neighbouring Gdansk shipyards in order to avoid a confrontation with the communist police.

In the post-war years, Gdynia finally began to thrive. Today, the city has a population of nearly 250,000 people, who are said to have one of the highest incomes per capita in Poland.

Fortunately, Gdynia city centre and most of the city attractions are within 10-15 minutes walking distance of the cruise port.

The Emigration Museum at Polska Street No. 1 on the 'French Quay', in the northern part of the port ,looks in detail at the economic and political reasons why more than 20 million people have emigrated from Poland over hundreds of years.

After Poland became a member of the European Union, emigration became the norm for a generation of young Poles. This is the first and only museum in Poland to look at the history of the waves of emigration it has experienced. It describes its mission as being 'to recount the fates of millions of both anonymous and famous people whose names emerge in the context of great achievements in science, sports, business and the arts'.

Open: Tuesday 12 noon–8 pm, Wednesday-Sunday,10 am-6 pm. Monday: closed. Admission: 12 zlotys (£2.35, $3.10, €2,80). Seniors: 8.00 zlotys (£1.55, $2.10,€1.85). Recommended length of visit: 1½ - 2 hours.

Just over a mile (2 kilometres) south of the Emigration Museum is a cluster of attractions around ***Kościuszko Square,*** the main square and a great place to go for a walk with plenty of benches, ice cream stalls, and cafés with cakes and hot drinks. The square (more of a long oval) then extends into the Southern Pier, where the Destroyer

ORP Blyskawica Museum, and the sailing ship Dar Pomorza Museum are berthed, and from which you can take a tour round the docks on the Dragon Ship. The Gdynia Aquarium is located at the far end of the Southern Pier.

The **Destroyer ORP Blyskawica (Lightning)** is the oldest preserved destroyer in the world. She was the second of two destroyers built by the J. Samuel White shipyard at Cowes on the Isle of Wight. The first was Orp Grom (Thunder).

Launched on October 1st, 1936, the *ORP Blyskawica* served with distinction in the Polish Navy during the Second World War. The Navy commissioned the ship in 1937 but two days before the outbreak of the Second World War, she sailed for Britain with the ORB Grom and Burza. The three ships then became part of the British Royal Navy's Home Fleet.

In May 1940, *ORB Blyskawica*, joined the Norwegian Campaign, mining Norwegian waters, shooting down two German aircraft and shelling German positions almost immediately after German troops occupied Norway.

With a top speed of 39 knots (almost 45 miles an hour, almost double that of the fastest cruise ships today), the destroyer played a significant role during the Dunkirk evacuation in late May, making several trips back and forth between France and Britain's south coast. Later, she served as an escort for the Atlantic convoys and, not least, the RMS Queen Mary.

British readers will be interested to know that in May 1942, she returned to Cowes on the Isle of Wight for repairs and, whilst there, came under heavy attack during an air raid by 160 German bombers.

The crew of *ORB Blyskawica* laid down a smokescreen to hide the shipyards and manned the ship's three inch (76mm) anti-aircraft gun and its four inch (102mm) dual-purpose guns and blazed away at the aircraft with such ferocity that they had to fly much higher. This made the targets more difficult to hit and undoubtedly saved many lives. Even so, the Germans caused extensive damage to both Cowes town and the shipyard. Later, the crew told how the gun barrels became too hot to touch and had to be sprayed with water to cool them down.

ORB Blyskawica clocked up nearly 150,000 nautical miles (168,000 miles or 270,000 kilometres) during her war career. She escorted 83 convoys, shot down at least four aircraft and either damaged or helped sink several other ships. For this, the ship received the Golden Cross of the Order Virtuti Militari , one of the oldest military decorations still in use and Poland's highest military order for gallantry.

Opening times: May 1st-30th September, Tuesday-Sunday between 10am-1pm and 2pm-6pm. October 1st-31st October 31st same hours but closes at 5p.m. November 1st-November 30th, same hours but closes at 4pm. Admission: 16 zlotys (£3.20, $4.20, €3.80). Seniors 8 zlotys (£1.60, $2.10, €1.90).

A joint ticket for the Orp Blyskawica and the Naval Museum (see below) costs 24 zlotys (£4.80, $6.30, €5.65) Seniors: half price.

Lying next to the destroyer on the South Pier, is the sailing ship *Dar Pomorza (Gift of Pomerania)* a full-rigged training vessel that required a crew of 40 and which could accommodate 136 cadets.

Affectionally known as the White Frigate, she was originally built as a training ship for the German merchant maritime school in 1909 and named Prinzess Eitel Friedrich.

After the Germans lost the First World War, she passed into French hands and was taken to Saint Nazaire, where a French baron bought her. He planned to convert her into an ocean cruise ship, but the idea never came to fruition.

The committee that administered the Pomeranian National Fleet bought her in 1929 for £7,000 sterling, a sum raised by the Polish public. The ship was then renamed Dar Pomorza, (Gift of Pomorania), having twice been renamed previously, and was given to the State maritime School in Gdynia in the same year.

Used as a training ship for more than half a century, she embarked on more than 100 voyages, during which she sailed more than half a million nautical miles, with her officers training nearly 13,400 cadets. After 51 years of service, Dar Pomorza was retired and given to the National maritime Museum.

Opening times: January 13th-26th, Monday-Sunday,10am-4pm. January 27th- -30th April same hours but Tuesday-Sunday. May 1st -28th Tuesday-Sunday, 9am-5pm. June 29th-30th August, 10am-6pm. -31st August- 31st

October, Monday-Sunday, 10am-6pm. November 1-12th January closed.

Further along the South Pier, at Jana Pawla II, The ***Dragon Ship,*** imaginatively fashioned from a former military tug-boat to look like a 17th century galleon, offers 40-50minute cruises in the Bay of Gdansk.

With four masts, this 148 foot (45 metre) long vessel has four masts and can carry as many as 200 passengers. In the roomy lower deck, there is a grill restaurant and a large bar.

Tours leave at 11am. 12.30pm, 2pm, 3.30pm, 5pm and 6.30pm. Additional tours are sometimes arranged on request

8pm to see the sunset. Cost of 'cruises' is 35 zlotys (£7.05, $9.20, €8.25) Seniors: 25 zlotys (£5.00. $6.60, €5.90).

The **Gdynia Aquarium** is a useful venue to visit if it is raining, although you are likely to get wet just getting there, as it is located right at the end of the South Pier. Containing 215 species and some 2,000 fish, amphibians, reptiles and invertebrates it can be crowded, often with noisy schoolchildren. As part of the National Marine Fisheries Research Institute, it has the status of a zoological garden because all creatures there are 'bound to the aquatic environment', as the museum puts it. Some of the creatures come from illegal transports detained and confiscated by Polish customs officers.

Among the more interesting are the common snapping turtle, clownfish, giant arapaima (an endangered Amazonian air-breathing fish) clownfish , moonfish and a massive 97 pound (44 kilo Baltic cod).

Opening times vary throughout the year, but the aquarium is always open from 10am-5pm, except for public holidays and Mondays between November 2nd and the end of February.

Admission is 29 zlotys (£5.85, $7.65, €6.85). 24 zlotys (££4.85, $6.30, €5.65) for seniors.

The main building of the **Polish Navy Museum**, which is responsible for the *Orp Blyskawica* and *Dar Pomorza* ships, is located at ul. Zawiszy Czarnego 1b, just south of the South Pier and almost adjacent to Gydnia City Beach.

It opened in 2018 to commemorate the 100th anniversary of the re-creation of the Polish Navy and spans three floors replete with naval weaponry, wooden models of various famous ships, old planes, uniforms and, poignantly, some shells fired from the Schleswig-Holstein, the ship that sparked off the Second World War.

Opening times: October 1st -31st March ,Tuesday-Sunday 10am-4pm. April 1st-30th September, Tuesday-Sunday, 10am-6pm. Admission 16 zlotys (£3.20, $4.20, €3.80). Seniors 8 zlotys (£1.60, $2.10, €1.90).

Just in front of the Navy Museum, **Gdynia City Beach** is a popular, sometimes crowded but always clean, white sandy beach, located in the city centre next to the marina and seaside Promenade. Said to be the best beach in the region it is well organized and served by several cafés and five restaurants nearby. It is close to everywhere: nature, culture, good food and entertainment. It is also at the beginning of a long boulevard that leads to the wilder part of the beach and on to Orlowa pier.

Gdynia City Museum (Muzeum Miasta Gdyni) located at Zawiszy Czarneg 81-374in a modern sandstone building almost next door to the Navy Museum. The basis of the City Museum tells the story of Gdynia through tens of thousands of posters, plans, maps and photographs that document the city and, not least, the construction of the port and its destruction during the German bombing raids.

A plethora of simple items such as passports, driving licenses, marriage certificates and the like give an insight into the daily life of Gdynia. Frequent temporary exhibitions cover photography, the history of the Protestant community, Polish design, textiles, architecture and much more.

Opening times: 10am-5pm daily. Admission 10 zlotys (£2.00, $2.62, €2.35) Seniors: half price. Fridays: free.

For motorheads, the ***Motor Museum*** at ul. Swirowa 2c is a small museum fired by the passion of its founder, Witek Ciążkowski.. For him, we are told, the smell of car grease is like luxury French perfume which says less about his sense of smell than his boundless passion and love of cars and motorcycles, which as a child he felt a compulsion to draw incessantly.

The design of the main exhibition hall is of a cobbled street from the 1920s complete with the facades of tenement houses and lampposts. All the doors, windows, signs and decorations are genuine parts of interwar buildings from Gdynia and Gdańsk. Even the historic colours of the facades have been meticulously recreated.

Today, what began as a small collection in a small garage, is a museum stuffed with old motor bikes, sidecars and cars, including a classic Ford-T, the first mass-produced passenger car, a classic Mercedes-Benz, a Bentley MK6, a Buick Master Six with 'all-authentic parts down to the air in its tyres', and a Buick deluxe, the  armoured version of which was used by Al Capone.

According to the museum website, it also 'boasts a rich collection of engine diagrams, photographs from famous rallies, old road maps and a decorated vintage café.

Outside, in the overgrown garden there are also dozens of old buses, trucks, and cars – all waiting to be renovated. This is one of Gdynia's hidden gems, fascinating even for those who are not motorheads! Definitely worth a visit.

Open: Monday-Saturday 9am-5pm. Sunday closed. Admission: 10 zlotys (£2.00, $2.62, €2.35). Seniors: half price.

Gdynia has to a large extent renewed itself in the past decade from a rather dreary city into one full of attractive areas and fascinating attractions. There is no shortage of things to see and do in this city!

* * *

Warnemünde, Germany

Warnemünde is one of the busiest cruise ports in the Baltic, but most passengers take the train to Rostock, 20 minutes away, while others travel to Berlin on ship's excursions as the three hour train journey makes it impractical for passengers travelling on their own. To miss Warnemünde would be a shame because this is a delightful combination of fishing village and seaside town with a stunning white sand beach.

Its charm lies in strolling along the cobbled streets, taking time for a fish lunch in one of the many restaurants or people watching over a cocktail or a beer in one of the many open-air bars.

Located on the estuary of the River Warnow, Warnemünde began life as a small fishing village around 1200. Just over a century later, the Hanseatic city of Rostock bought it to protect its access to the Baltic Sea and it was not until the late 1800s that Warnemünde began to evolve into a popular seaside resort.

Today, the town's 8,400 people rely primarily on tourism, an economic sector greatly enhanced when the modern cruise terminal was opened in 2005. Now, about 45 cruise ships make more than 200 port calls annually, making it one of the busier ports in the Baltic.

Here, there is no need for shuttle buses. Cruise ships dock just 300 metres from the town centre and the railway station.

Alte Ström (Old Channel) is a canal lined with stylish shops, restaurants offering tasty seafood lunches, pubs and houses with attractive gardens. The other side is a canal with traditional working fishing boats, tourist boats, stalls selling seafood and a fish market. It is a fun place and you could easily spend the entire day there.

Edvard Munch House at No. 53 on Am Strom (the western side of the canal) is where the famous Norwegian painter *(The Scream)* lived for 18 months from May 1907 to October 1908. Munch spent 18 months in Warnemünde, on the Baltic Sea in northeast Germany. He settled into the harbour pilot's house and stayed there from May 1907 and October 1908, having previously spent eight years in Germany and suffered from mental stress there, notably in Berlin and Lübeck.

Warnemünde was an antidote to all that; a huge relief and a chance to relax and to get down to some serious work again. Initially, he enthused about the sea air, the peaceful atmosphere of the town, how he felt at home there and was able to work when and for as long as he wished without interruption. He wrote that he felt reborn there and, during his stay there, he did indeed produce many sketches and paintings, including the works later known as the *'Bathing Men'* and *'The Green Room'* series.

Then, in October 1908, he suddenly decided to leave the town and Germany for good. His mood had changed completely. Writing to his friend Gustav Schiefler, a Hamburg judge who was an art collector and patron, he described how he had "packed up all my work in Warnemünde and it's unlikely I'll stay there longer. It's also in the end a dreadfully bourgeois place and simply doesn't suit me..."

The sculpture of 19 bronze figures known as the ***Brunnen Warnminner Umgang*** on Alexandrinenstr. 50, depicts the tradition of Warnemünde's residents dressing up in their finest clothes each year and walking to the tax office to pay their taxes. Legend has it that they were not enamoured of the necessity of having to pay anything to the state, but recognizing that it was inevitable, decided to make it a special occasion (no doubt followed by a lunch, a glass of wine or a couple of pints by the canal).

Although 'brunnen' in German translates as 'fountain', the sculpture does not spout water. Instead, the figures walk along a channel of water - redolent, perhaps, of the Alte Ström canal nearby. According to some, the practice of making a pilgrimage to the tax office continues to this day, although you may be tempted to take that with a pinch of salt given that you can just stay at home, fill in the necessary forms online and pay by bank transfer or debit/credit card.

Heimatmuseum located at Alexandrinenstraße 31 invites visitors to discover the history of the town in a half-timbered house built in 1767. It was once the home of a former helmsman, Heinrich Jungmann, who traveled widely and brought back many souvenirs from his voyages around the world.

After his death, his daughter donated the house to the city of Rostock. It then became a small museum that offers an insight into how families in Warnemünde lived in the late 1800s and early 20th century. Although small, it is a fascinating exhibition displaying everything from pots and pans, paintings and photographs to clothing, horse drawn carts and the sledges used in winter.

Here, you can also learn about the fishermen, pilots and bathing life in the town and, not least, about the famous beach chairs said to have been invented here.

The museum is open April-October, Tuesday-Sunday 10am-5pm. Closed on Mondays. From October-March, it is open Wednesday to Sunday only. Admission is €4,00 (£3.40, €4.50). The audio guide costs an extra €2.00). No concessions.

Warnemünde Church at Kirchenplatz 1, was built on the western edge of the town in 1866 and consecrated in 1871. Said to have provided protection against flooding, the church has recently become a popular attraction, thanks to the influx of cruise passengers and tourists.

Model ships inside the church and offered in gratitude highlight the town's relationship with the Baltic Sea.

Opening times: Monday to Sunday 10 am - 6pm. Free entry.

The Lighthouse, built in 1897 is often cited as the most important attraction in Warnemünde, together with the 'Teepott (Teapot) building. In fact, they are perhaps the least interesting aspect of the town, in which the fun is just wandering around, peering in windows, popping into the shops and so on.

However, for those passengers who are sprightly enough to climb the 135 steps to the top the spiral staircase, the lighthouse, which is 121ft (37 metres) high, undeniably offers the best views of the Baltic, the town, the port of Warnemünde and the extensive beach. Best of all, it only costs €2.00 (£1.70, $2.25) for the privilege.

Open from Easter until October, 10am-7pm.

Der Teepott (The Teapot), located next to the lighthouse and instantly recognizable by its distinctive curved roof , has been described in various ways. First of all, it looks nothing like a teapot and it is a cause of some wonderment as to why it was thus named.

The original building burned down at the end of the Second World War, was rebuilt in the 1960s and renovated at the beginning of the current millennium. Designed as a hyperbolic paraboloid (i.e. a convex form on one axis and a concave one along the other), it is reminiscent of a saddle, or perhaps some kind of winged bird. In any event, it invites an imaginative response.

Inside, there are several restaurants, souvenir shops and a small maritime museum based on thousands of exhibits from Reinhold Kasten, of whom few people have heard but who was apparently one of the last great adventurers and circumnavigators of the 20th century. (According to Wikipedia, at the age of 14, he went to sea for 56 years, during which time he sailed round Cape Horn 24 times and travelled more than a million miles during 42 circumnavigations. He collected some 8,000 mementos including the King of Tonga's silver chair, Imperial chairs from China, Albert Schweitzer's pith helmet and various shrunken animal heads).

The Teapot is listed as a building worth preserving and is described as one of the major attractions in Warnemünde. Maby cruise passengers, however, seem to think it is rather boring. It is open from 11am until midnight daily.

Almost two miles (3 kilometres) long, **Warnemünde Beach** one of the widest on the German coast and with constant winds, it is a favourite place to fly kites. It is also where you will see people relaxing in basket chairs with high 'wings'. The chairs are known as *strandkörbe*. The classic *strandkorb* was specifically designed to protect people from too much sun and, more importantly, from the wind. They've been around since 1882, when a rich but rheumatic lady of a certain age asked a Warnemünde basket maker, Wilhelm Bartelmann, for help.

The result was the sturdy, hooded *strandkorb,* which, with its stripy cushions, footrest, armrest and umbrella holder, became such a spectacular success that Bartelmann's wife set up a rental business. Today, there are said to be more than 70,000 *strandkörbe* in use, although nowadays they are made of plastic.

Should you wish to try one, it will cost €8.50 (£7.20, $9.50) for the day. In summer, they tend to go quickly, so it is advisable to book online at *www.knollskoerbe.de, www.seipels-koerbe.de, www.lenas-strandkoerbe.de,* or *www.strandkorb-in-warnemuende.de.*

So, whatever you do in Warnemünde, have a relaxing day!

* * *

The Kiel Canal

It has to be said that the Kiel canal is perhaps not quite as interesting as the Panama and Suez canals – or, for that matter, the Corinth Canal, which may be why the online version of the Encyclopaedia Britannica contains only three paragraphs about it.

This may come as a surprise because the Kiel Canal authorities claim it is the busiest artificial seaway in the world! This assertion may invite a degree of skepticism. You may well ask 'What about the Panama Canal? In fact, the claim is valid; the Kiel Canal is twice as busy with an average 30,000 ships transiting it each year – twice as many as pass through the Panama Canal.

The passage between the Brunsbüttel locks at the western end of the canal and Kiel-Holtenau at the eastern end totals 61 miles (98.6 kilometres) and there are two sets of locks at each end of the canal – the old ones and the new ones. The old lock at Brunsbüttel is just 410 feet (125 metres) long and 72 ft (22 m) wide. The new locks are 1,017 ft (310 m) long, 137 ft (42 m) wide and 46 ft (14 m) deep.

Originally known as the Kaiser-Wilhelm Kanal, after the last German Emperor and King of Prussia, who was an inept war leader. Given this inadequacy, the authorities decided to rename the canal the Nord-Ostsee Canal – the Baltic Sea canal.

This short-cut through the canal saves ships sailing Northwards up the Öresund past Copenhagen and around the northern tip of the Jutland Peninsula, often through very rough seas. It also saves them steaming an extra 250 nautical miles (287 ordinary miles or 460 kilometres), so it not only saves time, it saves shipping companies a great deal of money, as well.

An average 117 merchant ships and 43 small boats use the canal each day. That translates to an average 32,000 ships a year. The largest ship the canal can accommodate is 771 ft (235 metres) or approximately 30,000 tons. A single passage through the canal will cost a ballpark figure of about €5,000 (£4,250, $5,590).

There are detailed traffic rules for the canal. Each vessel is classified in one of six traffic groups according to its length, width, tonnage and draft. Calculating the cost of the passage also considers the qualifications of the captain, and whether a pilot, specialized canal helmsman or a tug is required.

There are also strict regulations regarding the passing of oncoming ships. In some cases, a ship may be required to moor at bollards provided at intervals along the canal to allow oncoming vessels to pass. Special rules also apply to pleasure craft.

Construction of the canal began in June 1887, at Holtenau, near Kiel. It took nearly 10,000 workers eight years to build. Compared with the Suez and Panama canals, that was both painless, quick and cheap, costing only €9.17m (£7.8 m ($10.25m).

In comparison, more than 30,000 people were working on the Suez Canal at any given period, and thousands of workers died on the project, which took nearly 11 years to complete.

Similarly, the Panama Canal took a total of 19 years to complete – 80 years by French labourers and another 11 years by the Americans. In all 27,600 workers died on the project, mostly from malaria and accidents.

The Kiel Canal was officially opened on June 21st, 1895 by Kaiser Wilhelm II. It was an immediate success and in order to meet the increasing traffic and the demands of the

German Navy, engineers widened the canal and completed the installation of the new docks at Brunsbüttel and Holtenau. between 1907 and 1914, thus allowing a Dreadnought-sized battleship to transit the canal.

After World War I, the Treaty of Versailles internationalized the canal but left it under German administration. Adolf Hitler repudiated its international status in 1936 but after the end of World War II the canal was reopened to all traffic.

Even today, though, the canal is not big enough. Many of today's modern cruise ships, some more like floating apartment blocks than ships, are too big to pass through the canal due to the clearance limits under the bridges.

* * *